THE CAMBRIDGE COMPANION TO
AUGUST STRINDBERG

August Strindberg is one of the most enduring of nineteenth-century dramatists, and is also an internationally recognized novelist, autobiographer and painter. This *Companion* presents contributions by leading international scholars on different aspects of Strindberg's highly colourful life and work. The essays focus primarily on his most celebrated plays; these include the naturalist dramas, *The Father* and *Miss Julie*; the experimental dramas with which he created a true modernist theatre – *To Damascus* and *A Dream Play*; and the Chamber Plays of 1908 which, like so much of his work, exerted a powerful influence on later twentieth-century drama. His plays are contextualized for what they contribute both to the history of drama and developments in theatre practice, and other essays clarify the enormous importance to these dramas of his other work, most notably the autobiographical novel *Inferno*, and his lifelong interest in science, the occult, sexual politics and the visual arts.

MICHAEL ROBINSON is Professor Emeritus of Drama and Scandinavian Studies at the University of East Anglia, Norwich. He is the author of *Strindberg and Autobiography* (1986) and *Studies in Strindberg* (1998), and has translated a two-volume selection of Strindberg's letters (1992), a collection of his essays (1996) and five of the plays (1998). He has edited five volumes of essays on Strindberg and Ibsen, and is also the General Editor of the Cambridge Plays in Production series. His three-volume *International Annotated Bibliography of Strindberg Studies* was published by the MHRA in 2008.

THE CAMBRIDGE
COMPANION TO

AUGUST STRINDBERG

EDITED BY
MICHAEL ROBINSON
Emeritus Professor of Drama and Scandinavian Studies
University of East Anglia, Norwich

CAMBRIDGE
UNIVERSITY PRESS

CAMBRIDGE UNIVERSITY PRESS
Cambridge, New York, Melbourne, Madrid, Cape Town, Singapore, São Paulo, Delhi

Cambridge University Press
The Edinburgh Building, Cambridge CB2 8RU, UK

Published in the United States of America by Cambridge University Press, New York

www.cambridge.org
Information on this title: www.cambridge.org/9780521608527

First published 2009

Printed in the United Kingdom at the University Press, Cambridge

A catalogue record for this publication is available from the British Library

Library of Congress Cataloging in Publication data
The Cambridge companion to August Strindberg / edited by Michael Robinson.
p.   cm.
Includes bibliographical references and index.
ISBN 978-0-521-84604-2
1. Strindberg, August, 1849–1912 – Criticism and interpretation.
I. Robinson, Michael, 1944–   II. Title.
PT9816.C36 2009
839.72'6–dc22
2009011368

ISBN 978-0-521-84604-2 hardback
ISBN 978-0-521-60852-7 paperback

CONTENTS

CONTENTS

ILLUSTRATIONS

NOTES ON CONTRIBUTORS

HANS-GÖRAN EKMAN is Docent Emeritus in Literature at the University of Uppsala. His work on Strindberg includes *Klädernas magi. En Strindbergstudie* (1991) and *Villornas värld. Studier i Strindbergs kammarspel* (1997: English translation, *Strindberg and the Five Senses*, 2000). He has edited the yearbook *Strindbergiana* and served on the editorial committees for Strindberg's *Samlade Verk* and collected letters.

MARGARETHA FAHLGREN is Professor in Literature and Director of the Centre for Gender Research at the University of Uppsala, as well as Dean of the Faculty of Arts. She has published several books and articles in the field of literature and gender, including *Kvinnans ekvation. Kön, makt och rationalitet i Strindbergs författarskap* (1994) and *Spegling i en skärva. Kring Marika Stiernstedts författarliv* (1998). She is also a contributor to *Det gäckande könet. Strindberg och genusteori* (2006).

FREDERICK J. MARKER AND LISE-LONE MARKER are Professors Emeritus of English and Drama and Theatrical History at the University of Toronto; they have published extensively on many aspects of Scandinavian theatre and drama. Their books include *Ibsen's Lively Art* (1989), *Ingmar Bergman: A Life in the Theatre* (1992), *A History of Scandinavian Theatre* (1996) and *Strindberg and Modernist Theatre* (2002).

ULF OLSSON is Professor of Comparative Literature at the University of Stockholm. He has published numerous articles and two books on Strindberg, *Levande död. Studier i Strindbergs prosa* (1996) and *Jag blir galen. Strindberg, vansinnet och vetenskapen* (2002), as well as studies in modern Swedish literature. He has also written on Joseph Conrad, George Eliot, jazz and improvised music.

MICHAEL ROBINSON is Professor Emeritus of Drama and Scandinavian Studies at the University of East Anglia, Norwich. He is the author of *Strindberg and Autobiography* (1986) and *Studies in Strindberg* (1998), and has translated a two-volume selection of Strindberg's letters (1992), a collection of his essays

(1996) and five of the plays (1998). He has edited five volumes of essays on Strindberg and Ibsen, and is also the General Editor of the Cambridge Plays in Production series. His three-volume *International Annotated Bibliography of Strindberg Studies* was published by the MHRA in 2008.

FREDDIE ROKEM is Professor of Theatre Studies at Tel Aviv University. His works include *Theatrical Space in Ibsen, Chekhov and Strindberg* (1986) and *Strindberg's Secret Codes* (2004), as well as *Performing History: Theatrical Representation of the Past in Contemporary Theatre* which was awarded the ATHE prize for the best book in theatre studies for 2001.

LINDA HAVERTY RUGG is Associate Professor in the Department of Scandinavian Studies at the University of California and the author of *Picturing Ourselves: Photography and Autobiography* (1997).

ROSS SHIDELER is Professor of Comparative Literature and Scandinavian at the University of California Los Angeles. His books include *Voices under the Ground: Themes and Images in the Early Poetry of Gunnar Ekelöf* (1973), *Per Olov Enquist: a Critical Study* (1984), and *Questioning the Father: from Darwin to Zola, Ibsen, Strindberg and Hardy* (1999).

GÖRAN STOCKENSTRÖM is Professor in the Department of Scandinavian Studies at the University of Minnesota. His books include *Ismael i öknen. Strindberg som mystiker* (1972), *Strindberg's Dramaturgy* (1988) and the critical edition of *The Occult Diary* in Strindberg's *Samlade Verk* (forthcoming).

PER STOUNBJERG is Professor of Scandinavian Studies at the University of Aarhus. He is the author of some twenty essays on Strindberg, including 'A Modernist Hell: on August Strindberg's *Inferno*', *Scandinavica* (38:1 (1999)), and a post-structuralist study of Strindberg as an autobiographer, *Uro og urenhed. Studier i Strindbergs selvbiografiske prosa* (2005).

ESZTER SZALCZER is Associate Professor of Theatre at the University at Albany, State University of New York. She is the author of numerous essays on Strindberg, including 'Nature's Dream Play: Modes of Vision and Strindberg's Re-Definition of the Theatre' (*Theatre Journal*, March 2001), which was awarded the Gerald Kahan Scholar's Prize by the American Society for Theatre Research, and *Writing Daughters: August Strindberg's Other Voices* (Norvik Press, 2008). She is the co-founder of 'Strindberg New York' which organized four 'August in January' festivals in New York between 1999 and 2002.

EGIL TÖRNQVIST is Professor Emeritus in Scandinavian Studies in the University of Amsterdam. He has published widely on Eugene O'Neill, Ibsen and Ingmar Bergman as well as Strindberg, on whom his books include *Strindbergian Drama*

(1982), *Strindberg's The Ghost Sonata* (2000), *Det talade ordet. Om Strindbergs dramadialog* (2001) and *Strindberg som TV-dramatiker* (2004).

MATTHEW H. WIKANDER is Professor of English at the University of Toledo. He is the author of *The Play of State: Historical Drama from Shakespeare to Brecht* (1996), *Princes to Act: Royal Audience and Royal Performance, 1578–1792* (1993) and *Fangs of Malice: Hypocrisy, Sincerity, and Acting* (2002). He has contributed essays to the *Cambridge Companions* to Eugene O'Neill (1998) and Bernard Shaw (1998).

LYNN R. WILKINSON is Associate Professor of Scandinavian, Comparative Literature and Women's and Gender Studies at the University of Texas at Austin. She is the author of *The Dream of an Absolute Language: Emanuel Swedenborg and French Literary Culture*, as well as articles on a variety of subjects in Scandinavian and European literature and culture, including Strindberg, Ibsen and the late nineteenth-century playwrights Emma Gad and Anne Charlotte Leffler.

PREFACE

Even by the standards of his own time, Strindberg was unusually prolific. Apart from his fifty-seven plays in numerous genres, he also wrote sixteen novels (nine of them an extended sequence of autobiographical fictions covering his life from 1849 to 1905), a number of collections of short stories and three volumes of poetry, as well as several substantial works of history, numerous essays on scientific topics and some significant political tracts and works of social analysis. To these should be added a voluminous correspondence (his extant letters fill twenty-two volumes and are sometimes considered his finest uniform achievement after the plays), and his painting and photography, both of which have garnered increasing recognition and are now considered an integral part of his project.

Indeed, few major writers have been as diverse in the range of their activities as Strindberg (perhaps only Goethe juggles literature with an active interest in the natural sciences and the practice of the visual arts so extensively), but this volume is devoted primarily to those plays on which his international reputation largely rests; apart from two chapters on his novels and autobiographies, his painting and other writings are only of concern where they contribute to the understanding of his drama. In many respects, one or more of these plays have fostered much of modern drama and few later dramatists, whether expressionist, absurdist or even Brechtian, have escaped their impact while they have been central to the development of a modernist theatre from Lugné-Poe and Max Reinhardt to Ingmar Bergman, Giorgio Strehler and Robert Wilson. These developments are recognized here in three further chapters.

The editor would like to thank Sarah-Lizzie Saks at Sveriges Teatermuseum for help in obtaining several photographs, Sören Vilks for his splendid photograph of Maria Bonnevie and Mikael Persbrandt in *Miss Julie* at the Royal Dramatic Theatre, Stockholm, and Joel Persson for the picture of Keve

Hjelm and Margaretha Krook in *The Dance of Death*, at the same theatre. He is grateful to Dr Vicki Cooper for commissioning this book, Rebecca Jones for her editorial support, and Hilary Scannell for her mindful and discriminating copy-editing. He would also like to thank the contributors for their patience in the realization of this project.

Michael Robinson

NOTE ON REFERENCES

The following abbreviations denote standard editions of Strindberg's works and letters in both Swedish and English. In the interests of consistency and in order to keep the number of endnotes to a minimum, quotations are generally from these editions and are identified throughout in parentheses within the text of each essay.

ASB   *August Strindbergs brev*, 22 vols., Utgivna av Torsten Eklund and Björn Meidal, eds. (Stockholm: Albert Bonniers Förlag, 1948–2001). The masterful, annotated edition of Strindberg's some 10,000 extant letters.

Inf   *Inferno* and *From an Occult Diary*, translated with an introduction by Mary Sandbach (Harmondsworth: Penguin Books, 1979).

LIT   *Open Letters to the Intimate Theater*, translated with an introduction by Walter Johnson (Seattle: University of Washington Press, 1966).

MJoP   *Miss Julie and Other Plays*, translated with an introduction and notes by Michael Robinson (Oxford University Press, 1998); includes *Miss Julie, The Father, The Dance of Death, A Dream Play* and *The Ghost Sonata*.

SE   *Selected Essays by August Strindberg*, selected, edited and translated by Michael Robinson (Cambridge University Press, 1996).

SgNM   The standard abbreviation for any reference to the sixty-seven box files containing Strindberg's literary remains, generally known as *Gröna säcken* (the Green Bag). Initially deposited in Nordiska Museet, Stockholm, these are now in the Strindberg archive of Kungliga Biblioteket, Stockholm. An invaluable annotated *Katalog över 'Gröna Säcken'* by Barbro Ståhle Sjönell (Stockholm: Kungl. biblioteket, 1991) details the contents of files 1–9.

SL   *Strindberg's Letters*, 2 vols., selected, edited and translated by Michael Robinson (London: The Athlone Press; Chicago: University of Chicago Press, 1992).

SS   *Samlade Skrifter*, 55 vols. (Stockholm: Albert Bonniers Förlag, 1912–20). For many years the standard edition of Strindberg's Collected Works, edited by John Landquist.

SV   *Samlade Verk*, 72 vols. (Stockholm: Almqvist & Wiksell, 1981 to date). The ongoing, text-critical edition of Strindberg's Collected Works under the general editorship of Lars Dahlbäck. Each volume is accompanied by detailed notes and extensive editorial commentary concerning the genesis and reception of each work.

Translations from *Miss Julie and Other Plays* and the *Selected Letters* are sometimes lightly adapted to fit the context.

Few writers have lived such a restless life as Strindberg, with so many changes of residence from childhood onwards, and not all of these are itemized here. Moreover, the events of this often turbulent life were sometimes closely interwoven with the experiences recounted in many of his books to an unusual extent, but in a highly intricate and complex manner. While acknowledging that a change of location often entailed a shift of direction in Strindberg's writing, this chronology therefore resists the temptation to detail any such parallels or to identify in detail the frequently shifting cast of those who were caught up in a life he sometimes regarded as staged, if not scripted, for him. It is also the case that few writers have been as voracious readers in so many fields as Strindberg; but only the most significant examples of his many enthusiasms are noted here, where they particularly coloured his writing in the year, or period, in question. For brevity, 'Dramaten' stands for Stockholm's Royal Dramatic Theatre, whether or not it was always known by this popular diminutive at the time. All other theatres are located in Stockholm unless otherwise indicated.

1849   (22 January) Johan August Strindberg born at Riddarholmen in Stockholm, the third of eleven children of Carl Oscar Strindberg (1811–1883), a grocer and shipping agent, and Ulrika Eleonora Norling (1823–1862), a servant-girl and former waitress, of whom seven survive infancy. Portraying his father as 'an aristocrat by birth and upbringing', Strindberg's primary emotional identification was, as the title of his autobiographical fiction *The Son of a Servant* indicates, with his mother, but the conflict between aristocrat and plebeian was one that informed both his life and his work, in *Miss Julie* and elsewhere.

         The family moves numerous times within Stockholm during Strindberg's childhood; he emerges with an acute sense of the city's social composition.

1851–61   Attends the puritanical Klara School which seemed 'a preparation not for life but for hell', and then, for a year, the more humble Jakob School.

1853   Father goes bankrupt, but soon re-establishes himself.

1861   Transfers to the Stockholm Lyceum, a more liberal institution from which he eventually matriculates, 25 May 1967.

1862   Mother dies.

1863   Father marries his housekeeper, Emilia Petersson (1841–1887), much to Strindberg's displeasure.

1862–4   Displays an interest in the natural sciences, particularly botany and chemistry. Also experiences a period of powerful religious feeling, and is inspired by Pietism. His feelings extend to his landlord's daughter, the thirty-year-old Edla Heijkorn, with whom he discusses morality and religion.

1865   Confirmation, an experience revisited in both *Sleepwalking Nights* and 'The Rewards of Virtue' in *Getting Married* (both 1884).

1866   Twice employed as a tutor on country estates outside Stockholm. On one occasion he delivers the Sunday sermon in Ösmo church. Discovers and is captivated by the landscape of the Stockholm archipelago which becomes a prominent motif and inspiration in his literary works and paintings. Reads the American evangelical, Theodore Parker (1810–1860), with enthusiasm; likewise Byron and Dickens.

1867   Spends the autumn at Uppsala University, reading aesthetics and modern languages.

1868   Returns to Stockholm. Supports himself by supply teaching at Klara School and elsewhere, and by private tutoring in two doctors' families.

1869   Studies medicine, but fails the first examination in chemistry. Visits Copenhagen in August, then switches to acting, but fails his practical studies at Dramaten, 16 November 1869, although not before appearing in a number of walk-on parts, and 'finding little joy in the work'. Writes his first plays, the two-act comedy *A Name-Day Gift* (now lost) and *The Freethinker*, published 1870 (stage première 13 March 2003, New Intimate Theatre).

1870   Spends the spring and autumn terms in Uppsala. Reads political science, philology and astronomy, as well as Latin and aesthetics. Forms a literary society whose members take Old Norse names. Writes *Greece in Decline* (revised in five acts as *Hermione*) which receives an honourable mention in competition at the Swedish Academy, and *In Rome*, a one-act drama about the Danish sculptor, Bertel Thorvaldsen (Dramaten, 13 September 1870). Reads Kierkegaard and Georg Brandes, both of whom exert an immediate influence on his writing.

1871   Continues his studies in Uppsala. Writes an essay on 'Idealism and Realism' and a drama on Icelandic themes, *The Outlaw* (Dramaten, 16 October 1871). Receives a small grant from King Charles XV's private purse. Spends the first of several summers in the Stockholm archipelago where he commences his first major work, *Master Olof*.

1872   Finally abandons his studies in Uppsala, which he generally disliked, and settles in Stockholm. Finds desultory employment as a journalist with *Stockholms Aftonpost* and other newspapers, including *Dagens Nyheter*. (June-August) Starts painting while staying on the island of Kymmendö in the archipelago and completes the earliest version of *Master Olof*. The long delay in its staging is a potent source of Strindberg's increasing disaffection with Sweden.

        Regular member of the circle of artists and intellectuals who meet at the Red Room in Bern's Restaurant. Reads Henry Thomas Buckle's *History of Civilisation*, Georg Brandes's *Main Currents in Nineteenth-Century Literature* and Eduard von Hartmann's *Philosophy of the Unconscious*.

        (November) Another failure as an actor, this time in Gothenburg.

1873   Works as a journalist, including a spell as editor of the *Swedish Insurance Journal*. Experiences financial problems.

        (October–November) Studies telegraphy on the island of Sandhamn with a view to permanent employment.

        (December–April 1874) Engaged as a reporter on the liberal *Dagens Nyheter*.

1874   (December) Secures a position as assistant librarian at the Stockholm Royal Library, where he works intermittently until

31 August 1882, and studies sinology. Develops an interest in cartography and pursues studies in subjects that will inform many of his later literary works as well as the essays in cultural history on which he now embarks and the later historical works, *Old Stockholm* and *The Swedish People*. Produces a revised version of *Master Olof*, again rejected by Dramaten, and some occasional journalism.

1875   (Spring) Teaches in a private girls' school and meets Baron Carl Gustaf Wrangel, an officer in the Swedish Life Guards, and his wife, the Finland-Swedish aristocrat, Sigrid (Siri) von Essen (1850–1912). Events surrounding his passionate involvement with the latter, her divorce from Wrangel, career as an actress between 1876 and 1883 and subsequent life with Strindberg inform many of Strindberg's later works, including *He and Her* (the version of their correspondence from 1875–6 that he collected in 1886; first published 1919), *A Madman's Defence* (1887) and *The Bond* (1892), although to read any of these works as a straightforward account of lived experience requires an awareness of the ways in which Strindberg edited and re-edited the material for literary purposes. Nevertheless, the impact of someone he once called 'the most beautiful woman in Sweden' resonates throughout his life and colours many of his works, even after their divorce.

(October) Experiences a mental crisis during an aborted journey to Paris.

1876   (8 January) Definitive break with his father.

Revises *Master Olof* once again, rewriting it in verse, only to meet with a further rejection (première Dramaten, 15 March 1890).

(October) First visit to Paris. Sees the work of several French impressionist painters and introduces them to Sweden.

(Winter 1876–7) Writes the comedy, *Anno '48* (Baden-Baden, 1922).

1877   (January) Siri's debut at Dramaten and the death of her daughter by Wrangel.

(December) Publishes *From Town and Gown*, tales of student life in Uppsala.

(30 December) Marries Siri von Essen.

1878   (21 January) Birth of a daughter who dies 23 January, after being put out to a wet-nurse. Translates several American humorists, including Bret Harte and Mark Twain.

1879   (9 January) Files for bankruptcy.
(February–March) Writes *The Red Room*, the first modern Swedish novel and his breakthrough as an author. Published 14 November; four editions by early 1880.
Elected a member of La Société des études japonaises, chinoises, tartares et indo-chinoises in Paris and awarded the silver medal of the Imperial Geographical Society in St Petersburg for his studies in cultural history.

1880   (26 February) Birth of daughter, Karin (1880–1973, a writer). Writes *The Secret of the Guild* (Dramaten, 3 May with Siri von Essen as Margaretha), and the cultural history, *Old Stockholm*, co-authored with Claes Lundin. Conducts a correspondence with others among the loose grouping of writers of the Scandinavian Modern Breakthrough, including Edvard Brandes and Alexander Kielland, but never with Ibsen.

1881   (9 June) Birth of daughter, Greta (1881–1912, an actress). Publishes *Studies in Cultural History* and a controversial two-volume history of *The Swedish People*, with illustrations by Carl Larsson, in which he initiates an acrimonious debate by departing from the perspective adopted by previous Swedish historians and presenting the nation's history from below rather than above.
(8 October) Carl Gustaf Wrangel marries Siri von Essen's cousin, Sofia In de Betou.
Expresses an interest in Russian nihilism and an enthusiasm for Rousseau.
(30 December) Successful première of the prose version of *Master Olof*, Nya teatern.

1882   Publishes *The New Kingdom*, a sharply satirical attack on Swedish institutions and several prominent contemporary figures. Begins writing and publishing *Swedish Destinies and Adventures*, a collection of short stories on historical subjects to which he continues to add until 1891. Also writes the fairy-tale play *Lucky Peter's Journey* (Nya teatern, 22 December 1883) and *Herr Bengt's Wife* (Nya teatern, 25 November), in which he responds to Ibsen's *Doll's House* and provides a vehicle for Siri von Essen, who garners praise for her performance in the title role.

1883   Publishes his collected lyrical, personal and polemical *Poems in Verse and Prose*. Leaves Sweden for continental 'exile' and remains abroad in France, Switzerland, Bavaria and Denmark until 1889. Stays first in Paris at Passy and Neuilly, where he makes the acquaintance of the Norwegian writers Bjørnstjerne Bjørnson and Jonas Lie, and at the Scandinavian artist colony of Grez sur Loing, near Fontainebleau.

1884   Publishes a sequence of four philosophical poems, *Sleepwalking Nights in Broad Daylight* (adding a fifth in 1889), reads widely in social theory and criticism, finding more to interest him in Max Nordau's *The Conventional Lies of Civilisation*, Nils Herman Quidding's *A Settling of Accounts with the Law of Sweden* and Nikolai Chernishevskii's novel, *What is to be Done?* than in Marx. Writes a series of essays on social issues, including 'On the General Discontent' and *August Strindberg's Little Catechesis for the Underclass*.

Spends January–June in Switzerland at Ouchy, Chexbres and Geneva, visiting Italy (Pegli and Genoa) for two weeks in March.

(3 April) Birth of son, Hans (1884–1917, a bank employee).

(September) Publishes a collection of twelve short stories, *Getting Married*, one of which, 'The Rewards of Virtue', provokes a charge of blasphemy for mockery of God and the sacrament. Strindberg returns reluctantly to Stockholm and stands trial, believing that elements in the Swedish women's movement are behind the affair. Becomes the subject of bitter personal attacks, as does his Jewish publisher, Albert Bonnier.

(17 November) Acquitted, but remains for many years in a state of mutual hostility with Sweden, where he now has difficulty finding a publisher or a theatre to perform his plays. Henceforth experiences considerable penury and suffers from an increased sense of persecution. Depicts recent events in *The Sequestration Journey*.

1885   Spends January–March in Switzerland with a brief visit to Venice and Rome in February with the Swedish author, Verner von Heidenstam. Returns to Paris in April and spends July in

Normandy before residing again at Grez sur Loing. Also visits the *familistère* at Guise and interviews its founder, J. B. A. Godin. Writes the more openly anti-feminist second volume of *Getting Married*, as well as the four stories in *Utopias in Reality*. Set in Switzerland and France, like much of his writing during this period, they express a sympathy with both Rousseau and the exiled Russian anarchists with whom he was acquainted in Geneva.

1886   Partly inspired by the example of Jules Vallès's autobiographical novel, *Jacques Vingtras*, he writes the four-volume, third-person history of his life to date, comprising *The Son of a Servant*, *Time of Ferment*, *In the Red Room* (1887) and *The Author* (unpublished until 1909). Also publishes *Getting Married II* (originally written in French), and writes *Comrades*, his first drama with a contemporary setting (Lustspieltheater, Vienna, 23 October 1905; Sweden 1910). Moves back to Switzerland and stays variously at Argau, Weggis and Gersau, where he produces a sequence of photographic self-portraits designed as a visual pendant to his autobiography.

      Moves to Lindau in Bavaria.

      (30 August) Accompanied by a young sociologist, Gustaf Steffen, he embarks on a journey through the French provinces from Belfort to Dijon to gather material for his agrarian socialist account of rural life, *Among French Peasants* (journey completed 19 September, publication 1889). But he starts to turn away from social issues and now reads more widely in contemporary French and English psychological literature, with a particular interest in self-analysis as well as hypnosis and suggestion. Among the authorities he consults are Henry Maudsley, Théodule Ribot, Hippolyte Bernheim and Jean-Martin Charcot.

1887   (February) Writes *The Father* (Casino Theatre, Copenhagen, 14 November) and, during the summer, *The People of Hemsö*, a humorous novel set in the Stockholm archipelago and endowed with pungent local colour. Also becomes a contributor to the *Neue Freie Presse* in Vienna, which he visits in April, and writes *Vivisections*, a series of essays and sketches in psychological naturalism in which he explores the notions of 'the battle of the brains' and 'soul murder' that are central motivating concepts in many of his naturalistic plays.

(September) Starts writing *A Madman's Defence*, an autobiographical fiction in French related to his marriage with Siri von Essen, which disintegrates further even as he writes. Makes first moves towards obtaining a divorce from Siri and consults specialists in nervous diseases in Denmark about his health. Attacks on Strindberg in Sweden climax with the publication of *Strindbergian Literature and Immorality among Schoolchildren* by John Personne, a future bishop of Linköping.

(November) Moves to Klampenborg, near Copenhagen.

1888   (January-May) Resides at Taarbæk, north of Copenhagen, then spends May–September on a ramshackle estate at Skovlyst, where he enjoys a brief relationship with an under-age girl and a colourful rivalry with her half-brother, the bailiff and apparent lover of the estate's owner, the Countess Frankenau. Depicts these events with licence in the novella 'Tschandala' and writes *Miss Julie*, which is refused by Bonniers, and *Creditors*.

The Father published in France with a preface by Zola. Founds the Scandinavian Experimental Theatre with Siri as director and advertises for repertoire, although only his own work is ever performed. Publishes *Life in the Skerries*, a collection of short stories on contemporary themes, set in the Stockholm archipelago, and a volume of popular natural history, *Flower Paintings and Animal Sketches*, which was generally far better received in Sweden than *Miss Julie*. Corresponds briefly with Nietzsche before the latter's mental collapse, having been introduced to his works by Georg Brandes. Also displays an enthusiasm for the tales of Edgar Allan Poe.

1889   Premières of *Creditors* (9 March), *Miss Julie* (14 March), and the recently written one-act plays, *The Stronger* and *Pariah*, in Copenhagen with Danish casts plus Siri von Essen as Julie and the silent role of Mme X in *The Stronger*. To meet objections from the censor, *Miss Julie* is performed privately at the Society of Students. (It does not receive its professional première in Sweden until 1906.) Also writes the one-act play *Simoon* (Svenska teatern, 25 March 1890).

(20 April) Returns to Sweden and spends the summer in the archipelago at Sandhamn and Runmarö. Completes a dramatization of *The People of Hemsö* and 'Les relations de la

France avec la Suède'. *Among French Peasants* finally published in its entirety. Displays an increasing interest in the natural sciences as well as photography.

1890 (15 March, Dramaten) Acclaimed première of the verse *Master Olof* (Strindberg called on stage six times). Spends the spring at various locations in the archipelago and makes a fact-finding journey through mid- and southern Sweden for a work on 'Swedish nature'. Publishes his 'Nietzschean' novel *By the Open Sea*.

1891 Sued for libel and assault by Marie David, Siri von Essen's Danish friend with whom Strindberg believes Siri has a long-standing lesbian relationship. He experiences considerable penury, but makes a further exploratory journey, this time to northern Sweden, and begins to paint again and to sculpt while living mostly at Djursholm, or Runmarö and Dalarö in the archipelago.

1892 Writes the last of his short dramas with contemporary settings, *Debit and Credit*, *The First Warning*, *Facing Death*, *Motherly Love*, *Playing with Fire* and *The Bond*, as well as a fairy-tale play, *The Keys of Heaven* (Swedish première, Uppsala, 21 June 1962), in which he expresses some of his despair at losing his children, following legal separation from Siri on 21 March.

Meanwhile, other interests, both artistic and scientific, have begun to displace literature and (with his plays largely unperformed) even the theatre as his prime concerns. Increasingly, he turns away from creative writing towards science, the visual arts and alchemy, and writes no further plays for six years. He resides at Djursholm until April and Dalarö until September; experiments with colour photography; and exhibits some of his paintings in Stockholm in July, although none is sold. Observes: 'It seems Sweden will find no peace until I am dead.'

(19 July) Found guilty of libel and assault against Marie David.

(21 September) Marriage to Siri formally dissolved.

(September) Justin Huntly McCarthy publishes the first appreciation of Strindberg in Britain in the *Fortnightly Review*.

(30 September) Leaves Sweden for Germany, staying initially in Friedrichshagen with the Swedish author, Ola Hansson and his

wife, Laura Marholm. Soon alienated from them, he moves to Berlin and becomes the centre of an international bohemian circle at the tavern he christens 'The Black Piglet'. Other members include the writers Holger Drachmann, a Dane, the Pole, Stanisław Przybyszewski, the Finland-Swede, Adolf Paul, and the German poet, Richard Dehmel, as well as the Norwegian painters Edvard Munch and Christian Krohg, and Carl Ludwig Schleich, a pioneer of local anaesthesia. The circle also embraced the Norwegian pianist and writer, Dagny Juel, the subject of Munch's painting, *Madonna*, with whom Strindberg enjoyed a brief, guilt-laden relationship.

(December) Visits Weimar.

1893   (16 January) French première of *Miss Julie*, staged by Antoine at the Théâtre Libre.

(22 January) German première of *Creditors* at the Residenztheater, Berlin, in a triple bill with *Facing Death* and *The First Warning*.

(January) Meets the Austrian journalist Frida Uhl (1872–1943) and marries her on Heligoland, 2 May. Takes a turbulent and abruptly terminated honeymoon in London.

Spends July alone on Rügen and in Hamburg and visits his parents-in-law at Mondsee in August. Spends the next months in Berlin and Austria (Dornach), some of the time in landscapes he will redraw in *To Damascus*, *Inferno* and *The Cloister*. Now devotes himself almost exclusively to chemistry and botany, documenting many of his experiments in a series of essays and the scientific treatise, *Antibarbarus*. Exhibits three new paintings in Berlin.

(3 December) World première of *Playing with Fire*, Lessingtheater, Berlin.

1894   Spent principally in Austria (Dornach) and Berlin.

(26 May) Birth of daughter, Kerstin (1894–1956).

(21 June) *Creditors* staged by Aurélien-Marie Lugné-Poe and his Théâtre de l'Œuvre.

Antibarbarus, four philosophical essays in natural history on the transformation of matter and its transmutation, published in German. Corresponds with the renowned German natural scientist, Ernst Haeckel, and is charged with immorality for a pirated German edition of *A Madman's Defence* (acquitted 30 October).

Continues to paint according to the aesthetic outlined in 'Des arts nouveaux! Ou le hasard dans la production artistique', one of several new vivisections now written in French. Also experiments with celestographs (photographs of the night sky taken without a camera or lens) and corresponds with the eminent French astronomer, Camille Flammarion.

(July) Responds positively to the new scientific mysticism that he discovers in François Jollivet-Castelot's *La Vie et l'âme de la matière* and Claude Hemel's *Les Métamorphoses de la matière*, and leaves for Paris alone in August. Frida soon follows but returns to Austria on 22 October, never to see Strindberg again.

Visits Dieppe in October and spends November in the rue de l'Abbé de l'épée near the Luxembourg Gardens. But he moves frequently within the city and for the next two years has links with a network of alchemists, theosophists, Martinists and occultists of several persuasions, some of whom are connected with the journals *L'Initiation* and *L'Hyperchimie*. Gradually stops painting and is primarily concerned with a series of chemical and alchemical experiments, about which he writes in several French newspapers and journals.

(October–December) writes 'Deranged Sensations', a French exercise in the fashionable *détraqué* style, published in *Le Figaro littéraire*. Meets Frank Wedekind and fears he is in mortal danger from a conspiracy embracing the German publisher, Albert Langen, and the Danish confidence trickster, Willy Grétor (see *SE*, pp. 252–4).

13 December. French première of *The Father*, staged by Aurélien Lugné-Poe and the Théâtre de l'Œuvre.

1895   During the next two years, Strindberg undergoes a series of psychotic attacks, collectively known as his 'Inferno crisis', which may have been exacerbated by his frequent handling of toxic substances in the course of his experiments and a taste for absinthe, as well as being linked to profound feelings of guilt and persecution.

(7 January) A translation of his 1888 essay on 'The Inferiority of Women' in *La Revue Blanche* causes much controversy in the French press.

(11–31 January) Undergoes treatment for psoriasis in the Hôpital Saint Louis. Is given use of a laboratory at the Sorbonne while his experiments and pronouncements are the subject of frequent speculation in the French press.

(February) Lives at 12 rue de la Grande Chaumière. Frequents a circle that includes Paul Gauguin, for whose exhibition of Tahitian paintings at the Hôtel Drouot he writes a catalogue essay, Frederick Delius and Alphonse Mucha. Also becomes reacquainted with Edvard Munch, whom he accuses of trying to poison him. His chronic penury leads the Scandinavian community in Paris to mount a collection on his behalf, an initiative which the impecunious goldmaker finds deeply humiliating.

(12 June–14 July) Visits Ystad in southern Sweden to consult Dr Anders Eliasson about his health.

(8 August) Publishes 'Le Barbare à Paris' in *Gil Blas*.

Publishes several scientific essays in French, including 'Introduction à une chimie unitaire'.

1896   (21 February) Moves to the Hôtel Orfila, the setting for many of the most striking events in *Inferno*, where he continues his experiments in gold making. Begins the *Occult Diary* and, having expressed enthusiasms for various mentors during this period, including Francis Bacon and Linnaeus, he finally discovers Swedenborg, who becomes something of a Virgil to him during his infernal experiences. Reads Balzac's Swedenborgian novel *Séraphita*.

(19 July) Flees Paris in alarm for Ystad in Sweden. Then spends the autumn with his daughter and mother-in-law, Marie Uhl, at Klam in Austria.

(27 November) Moves via Copenhagen and Skurup to Lund.

(15 July) 'Études funèbres' appears in *Revue des Revues* and is later included in the French edition of *Inferno*. Also publishes *Sylva sylvarum*, a volume of speculations in natural history, and *Jardin des plantes* (both in Paris). An augmented collection of the same essays minus the introduction appears in Sweden, as well as two speculative studies in optics, 'On the Action of Light in Photography' and 'A Glance into Space', and several short pieces, including some reflections on Munch's paintings, 'The Synthesis of Gold', and 'The Irradiation and Extension of the Soul'. Makes a first attempt to describe his recent experiences in a sequence of letters to the Gothenburg theosophist, Torsten Hedlund. Plans *Inferno*, in which he aims to become 'the Zola of the Occult', while in Austria.

1897   Organizes his recent experiences in the autobiographical fiction *Inferno*, written in French and published in a Swedish translation by Eugène Fahlstedt. Leaves Lund for Paris in August and writes both *Legends*, also in French but set largely in Lund and published in Swedish in 1898, and *Jacob Wrestles*.

1898   (February–March) Rediscovers the 'grace' of writing for the theatre and composes part I of *To Damascus* (Dramaten, 19 November 1900, with Harriet Bosse as the Lady). Part II, completed 17 July (Munich, 9 June 1916), and in December 'a mystical fairy-tale tragedy', *Advent* (Munich, 28 December 1915; Dramaten, 22 January 1922). Also writes an account of his experiences in Berlin, first published in masked form as 'The Quarantine Master's Second Story' (1902) and in its reconstructed entirety as *The Cloister* in 1966. Nevertheless, continues his researches in the natural sciences with 'Le Télescope désiré' and 'Types and Prototypes' until, in letters dated 1 and 9 December, he takes his leave of alchemy and occultism, and returns definitively to the theatre.

    (3 April) Leaves Paris for the last time. Returns to Lund, but visits the monastery of Maredsous in Belgium during August before deciding to return to Sweden, initially to Lund. Responds with enthusiasm to the plays and novels of Maeterlinck and Joséphin Péladan.

1899   (20 June) Leaves Lund for Stockholm, where he visits his sister, Anna, at Furusund in the archipelago, and then settles in the city where he lives at a succession of addresses for the remainder of his life.

    Writes *Crimes and Crimes* (Dramaten, 26 February 1900) and the history plays *Folkungasagan* (Svenska teatern, 25 January 1901), *Gustav Vasa* (Svenska teatern, 17 October 1899) and *Erik XIV* (Svenska teatern, 30 November 1899).

1900   Writes *Gustav Adolf* (Berliner Theater, 4 December 1903; Stockholm, 4 June 1912), *Midsummer* (17 April 1901), *Kasper's Shrove Tuesday* (16 April 1901), *Easter* (Frankfurt Schauspielhaus, March 1901; Dramaten, 4 April 1901, with Harriet Bosse as Eleonora), and *The Dance of Death I–II* (Altes Stadttheater I Köln, 29 and 30 September 1905; Intimate Theatre, 8 September and 1 October 1909).

(May) Meets Harriet Bosse (1878–1961), the Norwegian actress who creates several leading roles in his plays and with whom, as she rehearses the part of the Lady for the première of *To Damascus I,* he falls in love. Writes frequently of Harriet and his 'astral' relationship with her in the *Occult Diary.*

1901   (6 May) Marries Harriet Bosse and spends a belated, and friction-filled, honeymoon in Denmark and Berlin.

Writes *The Crown Bride* (Helsinki, 24 April 1906; Stockholm, 14 September 1907), *Swanwhite* (Helsinki, 8 April 1908, with incidental music by Jean Sibelius; Intimate Theatre, 30 October 1908), *Carl XII* (Dramaten, 13 February 1902), *Engelbrekt* (Svenska teatern, 3 December 1901), *Kristina* (Intimate Theatre, 27 March 1908), *To Damascus III* and *A Dream Play* (première with additional material, Svenska teatern, 17 April 1907, with Bosse as Indra's Daughter).

1902   (25 March) Birth of daughter Anne-Marie. Writes *Gustaf III* (New Intimate Theatre, 25 January 1916), *The Flying Dutchman* (a dramatic poem, Lorensbergsteatern, Gothenburg, 5 April 1923) and *Fairhaven and Foulstrand*, a volume of prose fiction and verse.

1903   Harriet leaves with Anne-Marie though a relationship of sorts between her and Strindberg continues, as does a rich correspondence. Writes the autobiographical novel *Alone*, a volume of *Fairy Tales* and a theoretical essay on 'The Mysticism of World History', as well as the world-historical dramas *The Nightingale of Wittenberg* (Berlin, 5 December 1924; Svenska teatern, 26 January 1917), *Moses* (Hanover, 14 January 1923), *Socrates* (Mannheim, 15 October 1921) and *Christ* (Hanover, 12 April 1922).

1904   Formal dissolution of his marriage to Harriet, although they continue occasionally to meet for several years, on Strindberg's side often on a telepathic plane.

Writes the polemical novels and critiques of the age, *Gothic Rooms* and *Black Banners*, although the vituperative, Swiftian, *à clef* portrayal of several contemporary Swedish cultural personalities in the latter delays its publication until 1907.

1905   Publishes *Word Play and Minor Art*, a collection of poetry from recent years, and *Historical Miniatures*, a new volume of short stories on historical themes.

1906   Publishes *The Roofing Feast*, a stream of consciousness novella, and *New Swedish Destinies*, a further collection of historical short stories. Begins *A Blue Book*, the compendious illustrated collection of reflections on personal, religious, literary and scientific topics in four volumes on which he works throughout his last years.

1907   Publishes the short Balzacian novel, *The Scapegoat*. Founds the Intimate Theatre at Norra bantorget in Stockholm with the young actor-manager August Falck and writes four Chamber Plays for it: *Thunder in the Air*, *The Burned House*, *The Ghost Sonata* and *The Pelican*, as well as the dramatic fragment, *Toten-Insel*.
         (26 November) Opens the Intimate Theatre with *The Pelican* which, like the other Chamber Plays, is greeted with widespread critical derision. The belated publication of his personal reckoning with liberal Sweden in *Black Banners* also draws general opprobrium and vilification.

1908   Writes two rarely performed history plays, *The Last Knight* (Dramaten, 22 January 1909) and *The Regent* (Dramaten, 31 January 1911), and a last fairy-tale play, *Abu Casem's Slippers* (Gävle, 28 December 1908). Continues working on *A Blue Book*. Also writes several essays on drama, including Shakespeare and Goethe, acting, production methods, and his own plays in a series of *Open Letters to Members of the Intimate Theatre*.
         (24 May) Harriet Bosse marries the actor Gunnar Wingård; Strindberg concludes his telepathic relationship with her 27 May.
         (24 June) Suspects the pains he is experiencing are symptoms of stomach cancer.
         (11 July) Moves to his final residence at 85 Drottninggatan (called Blå tornet by Strindberg), which today houses the Strindberg Museum, and concludes the *Occult Diary*.
         Falls in love with Fanny Falkner (1890–1963), his housekeeper's daughter whom he promotes at the Intimate Theatre as Eleonora in *Easter* and the eponymous heroine of *Swanwhite*.

1909   (22 January) His sixtieth birthday is the subject of widespread public celebration, with performances of several plays in many theatres.

During his final years in Blå tornet he hosts occasional musical evenings with the 'Beethoven Boys', among them the painter Richard Bergh, composer Tor Aulin, scientist Vilhelm Carlheim Gyllenskiöld and his brother Axel.

Twice engaged briefly to Fanny Falkner.

Writes a last history play, *The Earl of Bjälbo* (Svenska teatern, 26 March), a final, more conciliatory, Chamber Play, or lyric fantasy, *The Black Glove* (New Intimate Theatre, 26 December 1911), and his dramatic epilogue in verse, *The Great Highway* (Intimate Theatre, 19 February 1910), a pilgrim drama in which he takes leave of life and declares: 'I suffered most ... from not being able to be the one I longed to be!'

1910   Instigates the Strindberg Feud, a national political and literary controversy in which he gives expression to his regained radicalism and opposes the emerging right-wing tendencies of several prominent Swedes, including Verner von Heidenstam and the explorer, Sven Hedin, and criticizes current trends in Sweden's social and military policy. Writes numerous articles in *Afton-Tidningen* and elsewhere, collected in the pamphlets *Speeches to the Swedish Nation*, *The People's State*, *Religious Renaissance* and *The Tsar's Courier* (1912). Also pursues research in linguistics. Publishes *Biblical Proper Names* and *The Origins of Our Mother Tongue*.

(11 December) The Intimate Theatre closes, having staged twenty-four of Strindberg's plays in three years.

1911   The Strindberg Feud continues, dividing the Swedish intelligentsia and much of the nation.

Signs a contract with Bonniers for the publication of his collected works and finally achieves financial security.

(April) Exhibition of Strindberg's paintings, manuscripts, letters, portraits and photographs at Hallins konsthandel, Stockholm.

Publishes *The Roots of the Languages of the World* and *China and Japan*.

(December) Falls ill with pneumonia.

1912   (22 January) Is honoured on his birthday by a torchlight procession of students and workers and by productions of his plays in Sweden, Finland, Germany, Austria and the United States (in Chicago) (*Gustav Vasa*). Although gravely ill, he acknowledges the public acclamation by appearing to the crowds below his balcony with Anne-Marie at his side.

(March) Receives an anti-Nobel prize of 45,000 kronor, collected by private national subscription.

(21 April) Siri von Essen dies in Helsinki.

(14 May) Dies, of stomach cancer. His funeral cortège on 19 May is followed to Norra Kyrkogården by an immense crowd. According to his wish, his grave bears the words: 'O crux ave spes unica' (O Cross, Our Only Hope).

Few writers have been as prolific as Strindberg, and in so many genres. Moreover many of his works, including some of the most interesting, still await English translation and there is sometimes no general agreement regarding the English title of several that have. Misunderstandings also derive from the fact that Strindberg wrote a number of major works in French: during his lifetime some of these were translated into Swedish not by Strindberg himself but by his old student friend, Eugène Fahlstedt; others were belatedly rendered into Swedish by the editor of his collected works, John Landquist, and subsequent translators. The following catalogue lists the principal works with their date of writing, which is normally that of publication, together with an English equivalent. The arrangement is chronological according to genre. Where a significant period elapsed between writing and publication or a Swedish translation, this is noted. Works included under the heading 'Autobiographical fictions' are those which Strindberg himself identified as forming a sequential account of his life, even though, in literary terms, they are frequently approached as prose fiction.

PLAYS

Fritänkaren	1869	The Freethinker
Den sjunkande Hellas	1869	Greece in Decline
Hermione	1870	Hermione (revision of *Den sjunkande Hellas*)
I Rom	1870	In Rome
Den fredlöse	1871	The Outlaw
Mäster Olof	1872	Master Olof (prose version)
Mäster Olof	1874	Master Olof (middle version)
Mäster Olof	1876	Master Olof (verse version)
Anno fyrtioåtta	1876–7	The Year of '48
Gillets hemlighet	1880	The Secret of the Guild
Lycko-Pers resa	1882	Lucky Peter's Journey
Herr Bengts hustru	1882	Sir Bengt's Wife
Marodörer	1886	Marauders

Abu Casems tofflor	1908	Abu Casem's Slippers
Riksföreståndaren	1908	The Regent
Bjälbo-Jarlen	1909	The Earl of Bjälbo
Svarta handsken	1909	The Black Glove
Stora landsvägen	1909	The Great Highway

POETRY

Dikter på vers och prosa	1883	Poems in Verse and Prose
Sömngångarnätter på vakna dagar	1884–90	Sleepwalking Nights in Broad Daylight
Ordalek och småkonst	1902	Word Play and Minor Art

NOVELS

Röda rummet	1879	The Red Room
Hemsöborna	1887	The People of Hemsö
I havsbandet	1890	By the Open Sea
Götiska rummen	1904	Gothic Rooms
Svarta fanor	1904	Black Banners (published 1907)
Taklagsöl	1907	The Roofing Feast
Syndabocken	1907	The Scapegoat

SHORTER FICTIONAL PROSE

'Början av Ån Bogsveigs saga'	1872	'The Beginning of Ån Bogsveig's Saga'
Från Fjärdingen och Svartbacken	1877	Town and Gown
Det nya riket	1882	The New Kingdom
Svenska öden och äventyr	1882–91	Swedish Destinies and Adventures
Giftas I	1884	Getting Married I
Giftas II	1885	Getting Married II (written in French)
Utopier i verkligheten	1885	Utopias in Reality
Contes et Fabliaux	1885	(written in French; published in Swedish 1891 as *Fabler* (Fables))
Vivisektioner	1887	Vivisections
'Genvägar'	1887	'Short Cuts'
Skärkarlsliv	1888	Life in the Skerries
'Tschandala'	1888	'Tschandala' (published 1889 in Danish)
'Sensations détraquées'	1894	'Deranged Sensations' (written in French)
Vivisektioner	1894	Vivisections (written in French; Swedish translation 1958)
Fagervik och Skamsund	1902	Fairhaven and Foulstrand
Sagor	1903	Fairy Tales
Historiska miniatyrer	1905	Historical Miniatures
Nya svenska öden	1906	New Swedish Destinies
'Armageddon'	1908	'Armageddon' (unfinished)

AUTOBIOGRAPHICAL FICTIONS

Tjänstekvinnans son	1886	The Son of a Servant
Jäsningstiden	1886	Time of Ferment
I Röda rummet	1886	In the Red Room (published 1887)
Författaren	1886	The Author (published 1909)
Han och hon	1886	He and She (Strindberg's correspondence with Siri von Essen from 1875–6 adapted as an epistolary novel; published 1921)
Le Plaidoyer d'un fou	1887–8	A Madman's Defence (pirated German edition published Berlin 1893; modified original French edition Paris 1895. Swedish translations John Landquist 1914 and Tage Aurell 1962 as *En dåres försvarstal*. First publication of the newly discovered original French manuscript 1978, Swedish translation by Hans Levander 1976)
Inferno	1897	Inferno (Swedish translation; French original, 1898)
Légendes	1898	Legends (Swedish translation, *Legender*)
Jakob brottas	1898	Jacob Wrestles
Klostret	1898	The Cloister (published 1966)
'Karantänmästarns andra berättelse'	1902	'The Quarantine Master's Second Story' (an adaptation of *Klostret* in the collection *Fagervik och Skamsund*)
Ensam	1903	Alone
Ockulta dagboken	1896–1908	The Occult Diary (facsimile edition 1977)

HISTORY

Gamla Stockholm	1880–02	Old Stockholm (with Claes Lundin)
Kulturhistoriska studier	1881	Studies in Cultural History
Svenska folket	1881–2	The Swedish People (2 vols.)
'Världshistoriens mystik'	1903	'The Mysticism of World History'

POLITICS AND SOCIAL ISSUES

'Om Det Allmänna Missnöjet, Dess Osaker och Botemedel'	1884	'On the General Discontent, Its Causes and Cures'
'Nationalitet och Svenskhet'	1884	'Nationality and Swedishness'
Lilla katekes för underklassen	1884	A Little Catechism for the Underclass
'Mitt Judehat'	1884	'My Anti-Semitism'
Bland franska bönder	1886	Among French Peasants
'Sista ordet i kvinnofrågan'	1886	'Final Word on the Woman Question'
'Kvinnans underlägsenhet under mannen'	1888	'Woman's Inferiority to Man'
Tal till svenska nationen	1910	Speeches to the Swedish Nation

Folkstaten	1910	The People's State
Religiös renässans	1910	Religious Renaissance
Tsarens kurir	1912	The Tsar's Courier

SCIENTIFIC AND OTHER SCHOLARLY WRITINGS, INCLUDING LINGUISTICS AND NATURAL HISTORY

Blomstermålningar och djur-stycken	1888	Flower Paintings and Animal Pieces
Antibarbarus	1893	(First published in 1894 in Berlin)
'Le soufre est-il un corps simple?'	1895	'Is Sulphur an Element?'
'L'avenir du soufre'	1895	'The Future of Sulphur'
'Om Ljusvärkan vid Foto grafering'	1896	'On the Action of Light in Photography'
'Un Regard vers le Ciel'	1896	'A Glance into Space'
'L'irradiation et l'extension de l'âme'	1896	'The Irradiation and Extension of the Soul'
'Synthèse d'or'	1896	'The Synthesis of Gold'
Sylva Sylvarum	1896	*Sylva Sylvarum* (in French)
Jardin des Plantes	1896	*Jardin des Plantes* (in Swedish, containing some of the same material as *Sylva Sylvarum*)
'Synthèse de l'Iode'	1897	'The Synthesis of Iodine'
Öppna brev till Intima teatern	1907–08	Open Letters to the Intimate Theatre
En blå bok	1907	A Blue Book
En ny blå bok	1907	A New Blue Book
En blå bok, avdelning III	1908	A Blue Book, Part III
Bibliska egennamn	1910	Biblical Proper Names
Modersmålets anor	1910	The Origins of Our Mother Tongue
Världsspråkens rötter	1911	The Roots of World Languages
En blå bok, avdelning IV	1912	A Blue Book, Part IV

PART I

Strindberg in context

I

LINDA HAVERTY RUGG

August Strindberg: the art and science of self-dramatization

Vid avenue de Neuilly	On the Avenue de Neuilly
där ligger ett slakteri,	Stands a slaughterhouse
och när jag går till staden,	that I always pass by
jag går där alltid förbi.	when I walk into town.
Det stora öppna fönstret	The big open window
det lyser av blod så rött,	Gleams with blood so red
på vita marmorskivor	On the marble counter
där ryker nyslaktat kött.	Steams fresh butchered meat.
I dag där hängde på glasdörrn	Today on the glass door
ett hjärta, jag tror av kalv,	Hung a heart, a calf's heart I think,
som svept i gauffrerat papper	Wrapped in frilly paper –
jag tyckte i kölden skalv.	I saw it shudder in the cold.
Då gingo hastiga tankar	Then my thoughts took flight
till gamla Norrbro-Bazarn,	to the old Norrbro bazaar
där lysande fönsterraden	where the gleaming rows of windows
beskådas av kvinnor och barn.	are viewed by women and children.
Där hänger på boklådsfönstret	There in a bookshop's window
en tunnklädd liten bok.	Hangs a little, calfskin book.
Det är ett urtaget hjärta	It is a torn-out heart
som dinglar där på sin krok.	dangling there on its hook.

(*SV*15, p. 165)

A calf's heart, a torn-out heart, a little book, thinly clad in calfskin; we make a leap and imagine the author's heart, dangling on its hook. It would be difficult to find a more vivid, provocative and theatrical image for an exiled author's exposure to the merciless gaze of the public. This poem forms the introduction to August Strindberg's cycle of poems *Sleepwalking Nights in Broad Daylight*, a collection composed mostly while Strindberg resided in Paris in 1884. Though poetry is not Strindberg's strongest suit (and it is unfortunate that only a little of the jarringly jolly rhythm and rhyme of the *Knittelvers* he uses comes through in translation), this particular piece offers an

3

altogether fitting emblem for Strindberg's vision of his authorship as well as a fine example of his methods. For instance, one would have to be a rather jaded or disaffected reader not to be struck, nearly offended, by the bloody violence of Strindberg's imagery; but at the same time there is a kind of perverse pathos in the way the poet represents his work (we think: himself) exposed and vulnerable to the curious gaze of idle passersby, women and children. It is as if he were confined to the stocks in a Puritan marketplace as a target for ridicule, which may in fact be his object; in one of his autobiographies he writes that he early on 'developed a liking for self-torture'.[1]

Is it a simple case of masochism that compels Strindberg almost always to adopt an aggressive stance? In one of the photographs he meant to include for publication with the first volume of his autobiography, he poses with a flexed riding whip in his hands and adds the only half-humorous caption: 'Come on you devils, let's fight!' He is not a big or physically strong man; this gesture of egging on his enemies would surely lead to a (desired?) drubbing. (He begins one series of essays, *The New Kingdom*, with an epigraph from Charles Dickens's *Pickwick Papers*: 'You, sir, are a Humbug!' You – in Strindberg's context – being the nobility and their sycophants, the *haute bourgeoisie*.) But this is more than a personal stance, more than masochism; there is a rhetorical method at play here that aims to confront the reader with an abrasive text, to challenge social and aesthetic norms through sheer provocation. It is the method Nietzsche would call 'philosophizing with a hammer', and Strindberg was to be an admiring reader and correspondent of Nietzsche's.[2] The bold language, the bravado and playacting are part of a strategy that presents the role of literature as deeply divided: on the one hand, writing is a weapon, which serves to attack established power structures and bring them down; on the other, writing exposes the writer to the wrath of the authorities and society at large. The radical writer is both a danger to the authorities and, like the people he means to champion, a victim, or at least a potential victim. In Strindberg's self-dramatization, a deep fear of the public gaze, anxiety about his many enemies (real and imagined) and not least an intense self-questioning are paired with bold aggression.

And what is the target of his aggression, the reason for this rhetoric of power? From the outset of his writing career Strindberg begins to call basic values of Western society into question: the class system, gender roles, marriage, child-rearing, sexuality, capitalism, religious institutions, education ... essentially all the foundations of the culture in which he lived. Quite pointedly he took aim at the alliance between the monarchy and the wealthy bourgeoisie that existed in Sweden at the time. He also developed and employed new forms with which to issue his challenges – the naturalist drama, a departure from stilted verse forms of the past, written in vivid, living language and featuring psychologically complex characters; the autobiographical novel,

1. Strindberg: self portrait, Gersau, 1886.

with its extreme, personal tone yet inherently ambiguous relationship to 'truth'; the Chamber Play, focused on the intense engagement of the audience with just a few figures; the 'dream play', which means to stage the workings of the dreaming consciousness; and experimental novels that approach surreal and stream-of-consciousness narration. In the later stages of his authorship, particularly, he sets the stage for modernism. In Thomas Mann's words:

> As poet, thinker, prophet, and originator of a new world of feeling, Strindberg is so far advanced that even today [a half-century later] his work does not seem in the least exhausted. Standing outside and above schools and movements, he unites them all. A Naturalist as well as a neo-Romantic, he anticipates Expressionism, making the entire generation working under that name indebted to him. At the same time, he is the first Surrealist – the first in every sense.[3]

And Strindberg produced a greater literary and artistic body of work than most English speakers would guess. It is not difficult to give an impression of the spirit of Strindberg's authorship; its sheer daring and strength make it easy to distinguish. But any attempt to give a full account of his body of texts in an essay, or even in a collection of essays, must inevitably fall short. Among European literary prodigies, Strindberg ranks nearly with his ideal, Johann Wolfgang von Goethe, in terms of the range and volume of his writing. For the world outside Sweden Strindberg is known primarily as a dramatist, and indeed his dramatic work is voluminous, varied and in many cases of enduring international importance. But he also wrote novels and novellas, (numerous) autobiographies and autobiographical fictions, serious and pseudo-scientific essays, art criticism, history, philosophical and theological meditations, botanical and geological as well as linguistic and ethnographic studies, journals and a novel that pretends to be a journal, fake interviews, histories in prose and drama, travel guides (of a sort), poetry, a thick four-volume diary/'breviary' during his last years called *A Blue Book*, and more, including a genre emblematic of the author's general world view that lacks a proper English translation: a literary *fejd* or 'feud'. In total his collected works, when edited for the third time in the Swedish national edition, will occupy seventy-two volumes. And there are twenty-two edited volumes of correspondence containing some ten thousand surviving letters, some of which Strindberg intended for publication during his lifetime, all of which he may have suspected would eventually be published.

When Strindberg is placed alongside his Scandinavian near-contemporary, Ibsen, this is largely because of the originality of their dramatic work; but while Ibsen did venture into some poetry, his *œuvre* does not begin to embrace the breadth of Strindberg's. We should not address size as an absolute standard – Strindberg was somewhat perversely preoccupied with size[4] – but Ibsen's collected works occupy eleven volumes to Strindberg's seventy-two. A painter, a photographer, a scenographer, an occasional inventor and (al)chemist, Strindberg produced innovative scientific and visual art as well, and he would no doubt have felt a strong sense of vindication had he known that his paintings would be displayed at the Musée d'Orsay in Paris in a special exhibition in 2001–2 and at the Tate Modern Museum in London in 2005.[5] When Strindberg's international reputation is placed on the scales alongside the immense volume and force of his *œuvre*, he easily takes his place as Sweden's primary canonical writer – Sweden's Goethe, Sweden's Shakespeare. And Strindberg, like Shakespeare, takes up the mantle of national poet by writing a series of historical plays that, in Strindberg's case, chart the course of the Swedish nation, a series Strindberg begins in his early twenties, and which are discussed elsewhere in this *Companion*. Clearly Strindberg put himself on the path to becoming the national poet, although in his later years, after he had returned from exile, he realized that that kind of official recognition from the establishment would never be his. He was, for instance, never granted a Nobel Prize, though both his country-woman Selma Lagerlöf and his fellow naturalist writer Gerhard Hauptmann were deemed worthy before Strindberg died in 1912.

So Strindberg, unfortunately for the Swedes, is an uncomfortable and unruly national icon, not as invariably awe-inspiring as Shakespeare or as solidly respectable as Goethe or as avuncular as America's Mark Twain. Even most English speakers, who remain unfamiliar with much of Strindberg's *œuvre*, know that Strindberg was a difficult character. So what do we know of Strindberg, or what do we think we know? Near the conclusion of Ingmar Bergman's family epic, *Fanny and Alexander*, one of the characters proposes that the theatre she directs should stage a new play by August Strindberg: *A Dream Play*. The reaction her suggestion elicits is 'Ugh, not that nasty old misogynist!' And the audience laughs in recognition. Ah, yes, the nasty old misogynist. This is an image we can recognize and deride. And certainly Strindberg provides us with plenty of ammunition in plays like *The Father*, in which a wife intentionally drives her husband insane in order to gain control of their daughter's upbringing. Strindberg's preface to the short-story collection *Getting Married II* (1886) catalogues the evils of Woman: she is a cheater, she is lazy, she is a liar, she is cowardly, she is incapable of unselfish love, she is power-hungry, she is better paid than men and on and on.[6] The question of whether Strindberg actually reviled women as much as he seemed to in his writing can be debated; certainly there is strong evidence that he opposed the feminist revolution of his time on the (supposedly Darwinian) grounds that it espoused an 'unnatural' view of woman freed from her biological destiny as Mother. Yet in *Getting Married I*, published just two years before the second volume, Strindberg had argued in revolutionary terms for a radical equality between the sexes in a treatise entitled 'The Rights of Women, to which Nature entitles her, but which through the perverse [*förvända*] order of society (and not through masculine tyranny) have been stolen from her'. Among these rights he lists the right to equal education, the right to sexual freedom, the right to divorce without establishing wrongdoing by either party, and the right to vote (pp. 24–6). One could of course argue that Strindberg radically changed his mind in the two years between volumes I and II of *Getting Married*, an argument that would seem to be supported by the events of his personal life in the interim (i.e. extreme marital distress). And there is often a temptation, excited by Strindberg's own self-dramatization, to assume that the events of his life tally perfectly with his textual representations. But if one pays close attention to his writing on women and feminism one sees that his more immediate concern is that gender roles for both women and men are perverted by the power structures of society as it exists. This can account for the near simultaneity of apparently radical arguments and apparently outrageous reactionary ones. Thus the received image of Strindberg as woman-hater may be more complex than a quick quip can convey, and it is important to attend to the way in which we can be lured into an all too easy identification between the author and the texts.

Another thing we may think we know: Strindberg was insane. Throughout his life he was accused of insanity and feared possible commitment to an institution. An overall image of paranoia and psychosis does indeed emerge from a reading of his various autobiographical texts and letters. He suspects his first wife of having a lesbian affair with an alcoholic artist. He imagines that someone is trying to electrocute him through his hotel wall. In despair over his love affair with his first wife (who was married at the time), he throws himself from a ferry into the freezing water and has to be rescued. He believes that he has inadvertently caused his child to fall ill by sending telepathic messages to her via a photograph. He also rages against his many enemies, a good number of them former friends. He drinks a significant amount of absinthe at a time when he also claims to find art produced by nature, such as a miniature Byzantine figure of the Madonna and child in a piece of burnt coal plucked from his stove (*Inf*, p. 136). It has thus become an absorbing task for scholars and lay readers over the past century to attempt to diagnose Strindberg's mental illness, and readers can also derive some amusement from Strindberg's extreme language, which seems at times to certify that he is indeed unhinged. In writing in a letter to a friend, for example, Strindberg claims that his arch-rival Ibsen has plagiarized him, and he pronounces in triumph, 'Do you see that my seed has fallen into Ibsen's brain pan and fertilized! Now he carries my seed and is my uterus!' (*SL*, p. 438). Strindberg's writing sometimes springs so far outside the bounds of what seems normal or acceptable or rational that a reader can be tempted to resort to the verdict of insanity. Yet a close reading of either *A Madman's Defence* or *Inferno* (the sources for several of the admissions made by Strindberg cited above) precludes the idea that their author was anything but fully in control of his texts and his thoughts. This madness of Strindberg's, whether expressed in fictional or autobiographical texts or in letters, is a textual performance, as Ulf Olsson argues in his study of Strindberg's insanity.[7] A reader is well advised to think of Polonius' line from *Hamlet*: 'Though this be madness, yet there is method in't' (II: ii). Strindberg developed a highly sophisticated mode in which to respond to the claims that he was mentally ill. Insanity is a figure in Strindberg's texts that performs as an extension of the rhetorical method mentioned above, philosophizing with a hammer. By pressing against the boundaries of the sane and normal, Strindberg explores new forms and challenges cultural assumptions of normality – and at the same time, places himself at risk, offers himself up as a dangerous element in need of confinement.

In both of the examples cited above, misogyny and madness, one of the central modes of Strindberg's authorship comes to light: his self-dramatization. In using this term I do not mean to flip back into the trap of analysing the author through his works; I do not mean to say 'Strindberg was a theatrical, exhibitionist personality', and leave it at that. On the contrary, Strindberg's focus on elements of his own life and mind in his writing were part of an experiment in which he interrogated the meaning of language and truth, and of selfhood as a textual and societal construction. It is indeed the case that much of Strindberg's writing deals closely with representations of his life events and his own fears, desires and dreams. He writes that he uses himself, his life and his experience as his primary focus in writing because he is the only person he can truly know – and he uses himself clinically, scientifically, as the object for observation and analysis. For instance, he wanted the fifth volume of his autobiography (entitled *He and She*) to consist of the actual, lightly edited correspondence he conducted with his first wife during their (extramarital) love affair, courtship and elopement, but his long-suffering publisher Albert Bonnier refused to take it on. One can understand Bonnier, who had nearly been taken to court in Strindberg's stead for blasphemy in *Getting Married 1* when the accused author initially refused to return to Sweden to stand trial. Bonnier judged that it would be too risky to publish the intimate letters, since in the little world of Swedish cultural life everyone would guess who the writers were, and his firm would indubitably be in for another lawsuit. But Strindberg's argument to Bonnier is revealing:

> The question is really whether the private interests of some individuals should not be set aside for the vital purpose of bringing to light for the first time a human being's entire and true life's account … As you can see, my book is not meant as a rescue of my marriage or a purification ritual, but a self-analysis, an anatomical psychology. (*SL*, p. 204)

The book is not, in other words, personal (despite its inflammatory revelations), but a kind of scientific case study (anatomical psychology) which can be used to advantage in analysing (and challenging) the existing institution of marriage. And in fact, Strindberg keeps pace with the development of the field of psychology throughout his lifetime. In Strindberg's view readers who jump immediately to an association between the published letters and the (scandalous) persons who were the original actors are simply bad readers.

The figure that stands at the centre of his writing, this subject that resembles himself, is a matter for intense interrogation in Strindberg's work. His texts ask, sometimes explicitly, sometimes implicitly: how is subjectivity, that is, agency, constructed through language? One arena in which Strindberg engaged the question of the subject's construction was autobiography. Here he takes inspiration from Rousseau, who begins his *Confessions* by saying 'I have unveiled my inner self ... opened my heart', but while Rousseau confines himself to an abstractly metaphorical evocation of 'heart', Strindberg goes straight to the butcher's shop, its windows gleaming with blood, and the autopsy table for his metaphors as when, in a letter to his publisher, Albert Bonnier, he envisages reading and writing the history of the person he knows best, i.e. himself, by close scrutiny of his 'cadaver' (*ASB*5, p. 344). In the language he also employs with reference to scientific methodology, Strindberg proclaims his adherence to the naturalist literary project begun in France by Hippolyte Taine, the Goncourts and Émile Zola. He also answers the call of Danish critic Georg Brandes, who issued a demand for a literature that would turn away from Romantic nostalgia and fantasy in order to treat the issues of the day and serve as a locus for debate, for social change. So when Strindberg insists on his own life and experience and perceptive apparatus (i.e. body) as the central focus for his work, it is not primarily out of personal interest.

Following the lead of Goethe, who at the outset of his autobiography *Dichtung und Wahrheit* (*Poetry and Truth*) describes in fateful terms the astrological configuration of the planets at the moment of his birth, Strindberg opens the first volume of his autobiography with an account of a constellation of historical events in conjunction with his birth in January 1849, focusing in particular on the revolutionary fervour of 1848. In a word, Strindberg wishes to underscore that he was born under a revolutionary star, on the cusp of modernity. The first of his works to attract significant critical attention was a richly Dickensian comic novel, a political and aesthetic satire entitled *The Red Room* (1879), which served up a darkly humorous and critical portrait of Stockholm's political, Bohemian, bluestocking, publishing and journalist circles at a historic moment of transition in the Swedish class system and government. The deadly accurate blow aimed at overgrown bureaucracy and corrupt business practices ensured the novel's lasting popularity. With this critical debut Strindberg distinguished himself as an anti-establishment force to be reckoned with, and throughout his life (despite some occasional rather contrary reactionary strains in his thinking and political sentiments) he was held to be a poet of the people, a radical voice. He formed a long-standing relationship with the Swedish Workers' Movement; at his funeral, thousands marched with the red flags of the radical left.

Indeed, the first volume of his autobiography, *The Son of a Servant*, from the title onwards, carefully crafts an image of the nascent author as aligned with the working classes through the child's identification with his mother, who was a waitress when Strindberg's father, the son of a successful mercantile family, met her. Strindberg exaggerates and overdramatizes the tension that erupts when his 'servant' mother (she was the daughter of a tailor) marries into what he calls his aristocratic paternal family (they were solidly bourgeois). He also pushes the boundaries of empirical fact when he describes himself as an illegitimate child; his parents married after their second child, his older brother, was born, which was not as much of a scandal at the time as the autobiography would have it. Such lapses in accuracy move a biographer of Strindberg like Olof Lagercrantz to remark that the autobiography is not dependable, not, as the Rousseauian gesture of unveiling the heart would claim, strictly truthful. But the object of the autobiography is precisely dramatization. The book is not intended to be an accurate portrait or to win pity from the reader for the author; instead the story of 'Johan', as Strindberg calls his childhood self, writing of himself in the third person, stands in as a model for a sensitive Swedish child caught between social classes. His plight offers the opportunity to examine the psychology of childhood in general, and to launch attacks against the authoritarian structure of the family and its injustices, the class structure of Swedish society, the failure of the educational system, the idiocy of gender role construction and so on, often in a biting, satiric moral tone: 'Glorious moral institution, the sacred family, irreproachable divine institution meant to raise citizens to a life of truth and virtue!' (p. 17). Johan is not simply 'August Strindberg', in other words. Per Stounbjerg will deal with *The Son of a Servant* and Strindberg's autobiographical impulse in his essay in this *Companion*.

The narrative style of *The Son of a Servant* parallels Strindberg's dominant literary form, the drama, in terms of its dialogic structure. At times fully situated in the consciousness and cognitive space of a young child, immersed in the child's fears, ignorance and desires, and at other times leaping into a position of moral authority (as in the passage quoted above), the narration poses an evolving consciousness against a hotly engaged critical sensibility. This is true in a slightly different way of Strindberg's debut novel, *The Red*

Room, in which the young protagonist serves as the evolving consciousness at the mercy of both the satiric omniscient narrative voice and other perspectives represented within the novel, producing a rich heteroglossia. In Strindberg's early prose the point of narrative dramatization is a call for social change.

Drama, of course, involves dialogic tension in a social setting, and the creation of dramatic characters who are meant to represent real, psychologically complex humans is one project that seeks to perform the construction of subjectivity. In his preface to *Miss Julie*, for instance, Strindberg exhibits an overt awareness of the problems of creating humans in language; he discusses in depth his desire to produce truly realistic figures, 'characterless characters', that is, characters who do not perform in a stereotypical or predictable way, but who vacillate, act on unconscious impulses, are products of genetics and environment (according to Darwinian precepts), etc. How do existing societal structures determine who we are (the son of a servant?), and how might we write our way out of these structures? Despite Strindberg's professed desire to produce complex psychologies in *Miss Julie*, he ends up with a rather abstract structure: the power struggle takes place between decadent nobility (represented as female in the person of Miss Julie) and the rising underclass (represented as male in the servant Jean). But he does attend to the forces of nurture and nature in the formation of his characters, drawing on Darwinian models of evolution on a psychological scale, and moving toward a modern psychological vision of the power of the unconscious, when, for instance, he engages the use of hypnotism both at the conclusion of *Miss Julie* (1888) and in his earlier play, *The Father* (1887): 'You could hypnotize me when I was wide awake, so that I neither saw nor heard, only obeyed' (*MJoP*, p. 37).

Strindberg's commitment to science was related to his experiments in drama and literature as well, in the sense that science was a means to get at the essence of things, their structures, their origins, as literature provided the tools to come to grips with 'the evolution of a soul' (this was the subtitle to his first autobiography) and the structures of society. He studied botany (following in the footsteps of Carl Linnaeus), geology, psychology, optics and other disciplines, especially chemistry, or with time more accurately, alchemy. In solitude in his hotel room in Paris he mounted chemical experiments in pursuit of the chimerical universal element, a theoretical position harking back to that of alchemists in search of gold, though Strindberg's concern was not gold in the sense of wealth, but an understanding of the basic material nature of the world. He had developed a similar preoccupation in his earlier study of philology; he taught himself some Hebrew and Chinese with the idea that he would be able to establish the ties between these languages and modern European languages, and thus begin to reconstruct the original world language, pre-Babel, so to speak. Another interest spurred by his Naturalist bent was ethnographic; in his book *Among French Peasants* he turns to a study of the work, tools and customs of rural France, studying European peasants using the same strategies employed by anthropologists in researching 'primitive' peoples. Initially he meant to include photographs as well as interviews and observations, but photographic technology had not yet achieved the level required for such a field project, and the images were lost. Still, within the text he recalls one of the lost images, calling it an 'impressionist photograph', drawing on a painterly vocabulary in order to say that the single photograph with its isolation of a moment experienced in the country landscape captured the entire essence of the project.

For a time, while in self-imposed exile during the 1890s, Strindberg called into question the usefulness of attempting a representation of human consciousness or social struggles in prose or drama. His explorations of other representative modes led him to experimentation in photography and take an interest in painting, both his own works – often wild, nearly abstract renderings of the landscape of the Stockholm archipelago, almost as thick with paint daubs as a Jackson Pollock canvas – and the work of painters from the artistic vanguard, such as Paul Gauguin and Edvard Munch, with whom he had personal relationships. Photography was of particular interest because of its status as a medium situated between art and representation on the one hand and scientific documentation (dependent on chemical processes) on the other. His photographic experiments included double and triple exposures; he was fascinated by the effect of visually stacking different views of the same place that were taken at different moments, thus playing with time and space coordinates in a way that calls to mind the author's foreword to *A Dream Play* which maintains that 'time and space do not exist'. Although his conviction in the power of scientific observation led him to abandon literary production for a time in favour of journalism and alchemical experimentation, the discoveries he makes during his scientific period find their fullest expression in the literature he produces subsequently.

The crisis in Strindberg's personal and professional life marked by the years in which he turned his back on literary production is generally known as his 'Inferno' period, named for the autobiographical novel he wrote about that time in his life. Indeed, *Inferno* (1897) ranks as perhaps the most compelling act of self-dramatization in Strindberg's *œuvre*. Drawing on Dante's *Inferno* and Emanuel Swedenborg's mystical theology, Strindberg's protagonist wanders the streets of Paris with a growing awareness that he is being guided, punished, inspired, threatened and chosen – by unseen Powers that speak to him through street signs, cloud formations, the words and actions of strangers, snatches of music overheard, a chance piece of paper dropped on the sidewalk. Ultimately he is led to madness and then religious conversion. The novel's protagonist, who has often been understood as simply paranoid, might have had some reason to suspect surveillance; conducting his dangerous experiments in a hotel room, he might well have excited the attention of the police on the look-out for the anarchists active in France during this period. But the reader of *Inferno* will recognize the novel's protagonist again in the central figure of Strindberg's 'first dream play', *To Damascus* (1898) as the Stranger (or Unknown, *den Okände*). It is already clear from the title that the play deals with the same theme – a conversion. And it is commonly held that Strindberg's authorship also undergoes a conversion in this process, moving from naturalism to expressionism. Instead of close observation of the empirical world, the texts strive to represent an interior landscape. Rather than grappling with the laws of nature, they move toward supernaturalism, the irrational, the occult.

But it is important to keep in mind the ways in which the authorship does not veer off course or experience a deep break in the Inferno crisis. For one thing, the divide between naturalism and supernaturalism, while it may seem clear from the vantage point of the twenty-first century, was not at all so well defined at the beginning of the last century. Hypnosis, which ultimately found acceptance as a therapeutic method, played a significant role in attempts to communicate with people who had died, for instance. If there could be X-ray images of the physical body, why should it not be possible for photographs to be made of other things the naked eye could not see: the soul, the aura? Strindberg was not the only person of his time to ponder such questions. His experiments in various types of science resided on either side of what we would today consider the line separating hard and pseudo-science. But, perhaps more importantly, his commitment to close observation and challenge to existing social structures continue through this period in which he has, according to many literary accounts, turned inward.

In this incarnation of Strindberg's self-dramatization, the subject stands at a nexus of powers beyond his control. This is not, in fact, far from the experience of the fragile child in *The Son of a Servant*, or any of Strindberg's naturalist figures. They, too, are at the mercy of the forces of society, genetics, the environment. They, too, consist not of a single identity or will but of confused and chaotic and unconscious desires, fears and misapprehensions. The protagonist in *Inferno* and the Unknown in *To Damascus* stand at the centre of a universe in which they are addressed directly, but in mysterious signs that must be interpreted, not unlike the position of the child's evolving consciousness in the autobiography. Further, the people in the world around them are not perceived as autonomous beings – rather, they act as agents of the Powers. A group of people who annoy the *Inferno* protagonist at a café are demons sent to punish him. The Great Dane blocking his path is a sign that a particular enemy is hovering nearby. In *To Damascus*, the people encountered by the Stranger are mysteriously related to the Stranger, have led parallel lives, share a past with him or share his appearance so that they can be confused with him. The Lady of the play (tellingly, the characters are named as archetypes rather than individuals) is his supernatural and fated partner.

The frequent explanation for these uncanny correspondences and relationships is that we are not dealing with multiple figures at all in these works, but with a single consciousness. Peter Szondi characterizes the innovative and modernist aspect of Strindberg's theatre as 'Ich-Drama' – 'I-Drama' – theatre that does not mean only to produce mimesis of the speech and actions of the objectively experienced world, but instead stages a dramatization of an individual's mind, the literary equivalent of expressionism in painting, which renders subjective interior experience in external signs.[8] Strindberg's sometime drinking companion Edvard Munch produced the same type of proto-expressionism in his painting at around the same time, in the 1890s. In *To Damascus* we have an example of this practice when a funeral procession enters with the mourners dressed in brown. When the Stranger asks the mourners why they are wearing brown, they respond that they are not – that they are in fact wearing black. Since the audience shares the Stranger's perception that the men are wearing brown, the whole issue of objective reality is called into question. Yet this does not overturn Strindberg's interest in science. Instead he wonders, in an essay on optics and eyesight reminiscent of Goethe's *Theory of Colours*, whether our vision is not a product of our individual cognitive faculties. Could not each of us have a vision that is not fully reconcilable with another's? As he writes in a letter to a friend:

> Why does the bee construct a hexagonal cell? Because he is a subjective little devil and sees everything as six-sided with his hexagonal eye. Why do people see the planets as round? Because the subjective beggars have round eyes ... Suppose the world isn't round, but hexagonal? (*SL*, p. 212)

Certainly in his naturalist plays it is the case that the figures who stand opposed to one another – women and men, in most cases – live in entirely different moral, cognitive and expressive worlds.

With Strindberg's expressionist turn he simply continues the project of anatomical psychology and enters into an investigation of the cognitive faculties of the individual person. In his preface to *A Dream Play* Strindberg describes a model that could account for the authorial figure in all of his writing: 'The characters divide, double, evaporate, condense, float away, coalesce. But one consciousness stands above them all, the dreamer's; for him there are no secrets, no inconsequential events, no scruples, no law'

(*SV*46, p. 7; *MJoP*, p. 176). The many figures of his dream play, then, are indeed meant to be understood as emanations of a single consciousness, and Strindberg called *To Damascus* his earlier dream play, indicating that we can understand the Stranger as a representative of the dreamer, with the other characters in the drama acting as subfigures to the protagonist. In *Inferno* as well, the odd instrumentalization of the other figures in the novel does not convey simple narcissism (a diagnosis not infrequently assigned to Strindberg), but an attempt to get at the problem of subjective perception, the inability to know the Other.

A *Dream Play* was written in 1901, just a year after Freud's *Interpretation of Dreams*. *To Damascus* I and II, the first 'dream plays', were written before Freud's study, in 1898. Thus Strindberg anticipates Freud in imagining an associative logic in a dreaming consciousness, a logic that disregards ordinary constructs of space and time, a logic that disregards distinctions between persons, a logic that argues for a vast unknown territory of mind beneath the light of consciousness. Here the subject, the person, has been refracted into dozens of prismatic facets – but certainly Strindberg always doubted the idea of a fully integrated and autonomous subject, as we see when we revisit his notion of the 'characterless character'. He struggles in general with the concept of selfhood, as seen in this snippet from his unpublished manuscripts: 'I! The Others! Many I's make up one object = objective'.[9] It is not that Strindberg moves away from science, in other words; instead, he moves forward with science from Darwin to Freud, anticipates science. In his proclamation on dream logic, issued in his prologue to *A Dream Play*, that 'time and space do not exist', we have an intimation of the theory of relativity, which Einstein worked out and wrote down five years later, in Switzerland.

The theatre is an odd place in which to represent the erasure of time and space. Its heavy materiality and absolute presence resist the kind of fluid quality that Strindberg envisioned for his dream plays. When he demanded in the Preface to *Miss Julie* that real objects appear on stage (when you slam the door, the door ought to slam, not swing limply as a painted stage door does), real smells, real faces (no painted facial expressions that remain the same no matter what the mood), he engaged the theatre's abilities and possibilities to create a present reality. But when he asks in *A Dream Play* that a castle start to grow or that roses wither in a lover's hands or that a door to one building become a filing cabinet in another (without the benefit of a black-out), he seems to work against the theatre's natural proclivities. It would require a rethinking of the institution of theatre, the development of both new approaches and new technology in order to mount a production of *A Dream Play* that did not require frequent, awkward, undesired black-outs between scenes during which the audience would hear the sound of heavy props dragged across the stage. Strindberg began to develop some innovations towards the end of his life that had been on his mind for decades: the creation of a small space, his Intimate Theatre in which the audience and actors would confront and engage with one another more naturally and more intensely. The employment of real objects as props, yes, but objects that transcended their use and meaning in ordinary life, objects as symbols, but often mysterious, unreadable symbols. In *The Ghost Sonata*, one of the Chamber Plays composed for performance in the Intimate Theatre, the audience is confronted by a woman called 'the Mummy', who has lived in a closet for many years. How is this staged? What does she wear? The only clues we get as to her appearance come from characters' lines; we hear that she looks like a mummy, and when one of the characters gets his first glimpse of her, he exclaims, 'Oh, Jesus ...' When she speaks, she speaks as a parrot: 'Pretty Polly! Is Jacob there? Awwk!' Why is she a parrot? Neither her appearance nor her behaviour receives direct commentary in the stage directions or the plot. In the opening scene we see a woman who appears as real as any actor on the stage, but we learn subsequently that she is a ghost, and only the protagonist can see her. Using the logic of his dream plays, Strindberg has both re-used some of his older strategies and developed new ones for staging subjective reality. The audience does not occupy a privileged position; we do not stand outside the dream, but are lost with the characters in the confusion of symbols and inexplicable behaviour. This 'unreal' theatre, however, brings across terrifying realities: the stripping away of illusion, confrontation with the past, unveiling of desire and repulsion – the themes that preoccupy Strindberg's authorship from the beginning.

Strindberg's later prose work also anticipates modernist literature. In particular his novella *The Roofing Feast* calls to mind at moments the stream-of-consciousness narrative style that James Joyce will perfect in *Ulysses* and the topos Faulkner will use in *As I Lay Dying*. Strindberg's protagonist, like Faulkner's, is on his deathbed throughout the narrative, and when he is administered morphine he drifts into a state of associative memory, unveiling his past in long monologues that confront his guilt, longing, jealousy, hatred and love. The form is not yet fully divorced from realistic prose narrative in that the protagonist's language is coherent, the associations often a bit too neat, the structure of his memories too chronological and complete. But the seeds of modernism are certainly there, and we can see how the methods developed in writing *Inferno* – Strindberg's notion of *l'art par hasard*, for instance, a forerunner of the surrealist *objets trouvés* – take root and find further extension in *The Roofing Feast*.

But if we are to think of Strindberg as a modernist, we must also think of him as something more than a Swedish national icon. His modernism begins, perhaps, in his rootlessness, his suspension between places. It is not that he is not thoroughly Swedish. His works include *Svenska folket*, a (revolutionary, of course) history of Sweden, as well as an account of great Swedish heroes, the historical plays already mentioned, a guide to *Old Stockholm*, many stories and a novel and paintings devoted to Stockholm's archipelago (his favourite landscape), and a wonderful long essay entitled 'Swedish Nature', in which he describes meticulously the plant and animal life and the geological history of Sweden from south to north based on a field trip by rail. His muscular and voluminous employment of Swedish in his writing, particularly in the 'natural' speech of his dramas, contributed enormously to the development of the language. But he also lived in Paris, Berlin, Switzerland, Austria and other points on the European continent, and he wrote several of his major works in French.

The leap that takes place in his little poem between a Parisian butcher's shop and a Stockholm bookshop illustrates the transnational aspect of Strindberg's work, his thinking, his writing, his life, his reputation. Born at the periphery of Europe, and mindful of his status as the most important Swedish writer, Strindberg aspired nevertheless to be more than a Swedish writer. At a time when his incendiary rhetoric (and his elopement with his first wife) made a pariah of him in Sweden, he went into exile on the Continent. He worked to establish himself as a European writer, to become part of a tradition he considered his own, a tradition that included Kierkegaard, Rousseau, Goethe, Darwin and Nietzsche. During the 1880s and 1890s he wrote two autobiographical novels (*Le plaidoyer d'un fou/A Madman's Defence* and *Inferno*) and a good number of essays in French, with the thought of entering the heady cultural arena of the capital of the nineteenth century. Strindberg's close relationship with his German translator, Emil Schering, ensured that thoughtful German translations of his work reached a reading public simultaneously or even before the Swedish versions were published. Some of Strindberg's plays, including *The Dance of Death*, enjoyed either premières or significant productions during his lifetime, in part thanks to Schering. Support from Edvard Brandes, Georg Brandes's brother and an important literary and cultural critic in *fin-de-siècle* Copenhagen, brought *Miss Julie* to the stage in Denmark before it was produced in Sweden. And with Ibsen preceding him at the vanguard of what the French termed the 'Nordic wave', three of Strindberg's plays were staged in Paris during the 1890s: *Miss Julie, The Father* and *The Creditors*. While one cannot claim that Strindberg gained the recognition and reception he desired – in France, particularly – it is important to note the international and modernist bent of his writing and his world view. His wanderings through the streets of Paris, eyes open to the messages framed in butcher's shop windows and elsewhere, run parallel to his wanderings through the streets of Stockholm, where he becomes captivated by the scenes he observes through apartment windows, recorded (among other places) in his late novella, *Alone*. Walking through European capitals with his gaze attuned to the same kind of street-scapes as those captured by Parisian photographer Eugène Atget, Strindberg performs as the prototypical *flâneur*, succeeding Charles Baudelaire, whom he read, and preceding Walter Benjamin, who read Strindberg. From the butcher's shop in the Avenue de Neuilly to the bookshop in Stockholm is no distance at all – for a modernist mind like Strindberg's.

NOTES

1. August Strindberg, *The Son of a Servant: the Story of the Evolution of a Human Being (1849–1867)*, ed. and trans. Evert Sprinchorn (Gloucester, Mass.: Peter Smith, 1975), p. 21.
2. Strindberg's brief correspondence with Friedrich Nietzsche lasted from the end of 1888 to the beginning of 1889; the English translation of Strindberg's letters and postcards to Nietzsche can be found in *SL 1*.
3. 'August Strindberg', in *Altes und Neues. Kleine Prosa aus fünf Jahrzehnten* (Frankfurt am Main: Fischer Verlag, 1961), pp. 219–20. Translation by the author.
4. Here I refer, perhaps a bit too coyly, to the infamous episode in Strindberg's life when he had his penis measured by a doctor in order to affirm its normal size.
5. See the exhibit catalogue from the Tate: Olle Granath, *August Strindberg: Painter, Photographer, Writer* (London: Tate Publications, 2005). Also Michael Robinson, 'New Arts, New Worlds: Strindberg's Painting', in his *Studies in Strindberg* (Norwich: Norvik Press, 1998), pp. 145–67.
6. August Strindberg, *Getting Married*, ed. and trans. Mary Sandbach (New York: Viking Press, 1973). The cited points are taken from pp. 197–207.
7. Olsson presents this argument in his book *Jag blir galen. Strindberg, vansinnet och vetenskapen* [I'm going crazy: Strindberg, insanity, and science] (Stockholm/Stehag: Brutus Östlings Bokförlag Symposion, 2002). A shorter version exists in English in 'Going Crazy: Strindberg and the Construction of Literary Madness', in Poul Houe, Sven Hakon Rossel and Göran Stockenström, eds., *August Strindberg and the Other: New Critical Approaches* (Amsterdam/New York: Rodopi, 2002).
8. Peter Szondi, *Theory of the Modern Drama: a Critical Edition*, ed. and trans. Michael Hays (Minneapolis: University of Minnesota Press, 1987). First published in German, *Theorie des modernen Dramas* (Frankfurt am Main: Suhrkamp, 1956).
9. Magnus Florin and Ulf Olsson, eds., *Köra och vända. Strindbergs efterlämnade papper i urval* (Stockholm: Albert Bonniers Förlag, 1999), p. 12. Translation by the author.

2

MARGARETHA FAHLGREN

Strindberg and the woman question

In 1913 the prominent Swedish poet and novelist, Verner von Heidenstam (1859–1940), was quoted by the Stockholm daily, *Aftonbladet*, on dying gloriously. He observed that he had always dreamt of dying in battle, to fall among the crowd on a dusty road.[1] The rhetoric of male bravery in this remark accorded with that of a generation for whom, in 1914, 'the full and hideous flowering of the politics of masculine dominance finally become more candidly proclaimed than ever before in history',[2] and, for a period during the 1880s, Strindberg too had looked with envy at Germany, Bismarck and militarism. In a frequently cited letter to Heidenstam from January 1887, he wrote that in Germany one could still find men who were real males (*SL*, pp. 221–2), in contrast to Sweden where, as a result of the movement for the emancipation of women, society had become weak and female. According to Strindberg, Sweden was no longer a place for strong men who longed for traditional gender roles and masculine authority and, like the Captain in *The Father*, he passionately mourned the past. To understand why he wrote so much about the troubled relations between men and women, one therefore has to take into account his sense of loss. He held up the past as a mirror to modern, changing times where middle-class women no longer accepted male dominance. The problem of how to deal with women concerned him throughout his life, and it is striking how, although in different ways, Strindberg continually returned to this issue in his writings.

During Strindberg's lifetime Stockholm, where he grew up, changed radically. Among the changes listed by Allan Hagsten in his study of Strindberg's early years were paved streets, gas lighting, increased commerce and the appearance of daily newspapers[3] while, according to Per Stounbjerg, as Strindberg matured his writings became a veritable catalogue of modernity. He is almost the first Swedish writer to describe these changes in society in a language that takes account of new technologies such as the telephone, electricity and X-rays.[4] For Strindberg was undoubtedly a writer of the modern era. Living abroad in Berlin and Paris, he acquired an international outlook and rarely felt comfortable in the small Swedish cultural establishment. As one of the first Swedish writers with the potential to live reasonably well from his pen, he was highly receptive to changes in the literary climate, and aware of what kind of books would sell well. Notwithstanding his innovatory dramaturgy, therefore, both his novel, *The People of Hemsö*, and the fairy tales which he wrote at the turn of the century show his awareness of genres which would attract readers.

In many respects Strindberg was thus engaged in the process of modernity. But where gender issues were concerned he preferred to look back and mourn the order of the past. The movement for women's emancipation both scared and angered him. It was an affront for women to question male authority. Men were bound to support their families while their wives should stick to their duties as mothers and wives. Strindberg strongly opposed the idea that a woman should have the right to dispose of her own money after marriage. The husband should be responsible for economic matters simply because, as a man, he was better fitted to handle money. During the 1880s he wrote several essays, including 'Woman's Inferiority to Man, and the Reasons for Her Subordinate Position' (published 1890, and in French in *La Revue Blanche*, 7 January 1895), in which he sought to demonstrate the inferiority of women. Among other arguments, he deployed so-called biological facts to prove that women were intellectually inferior to men, not least on account of their smaller brains. And at the same time, as a writer, he chose to pose as a scientist who was merely collecting evidence, not taking sides. However, while writing these articles, Strindberg was obsessed by the woman question, an obsession that does not equate with the scientific approach that he sought to apply in his articles. It is evident that the enormous interest which he invested in issues of gender was deeply rooted in his own anxiety, aware as he was of how middle-class women chafed against the obstacles to their education and professional work.

Strindberg was not the only man to be worried on this account. Marc Angenot's study of attitudes to women in French literature and the press during 1889 highlights the fear expressed by several men, who felt that love and poetry would soon be at an end when 'the new woman' craved her place in society.[5] Such men longed for the traditional 'angel in the house', and attacked the feminists who had supplanted her. Nevertheless, they mixed their attacks with some sort of gallantry, as Strindberg did in 'The Hatred and Worship of Women' where he observes: 'I have always worshipped women, these enchanting, criminal idiots whose worst crime isn't registered in the criminal code ... Many thanks, my delightful enemies!' Strindberg is able to forgive women because they are so adorable and thus cannot be held responsible for their actions. Behind this indulgent attitude one can, however, detect a man who feels threatened by women, and who therefore chooses to reduce them to whimsical geese.

For many of Strindberg's contemporaries being a man meant being a soldier or a scientist. Unlike the Captain in *The Father*, who was both, Strindberg was neither, although he strove hard to become a scientist. His third wife, Harriet Bosse, recalls of their early meetings that he was prouder of his experiments in chemistry than of being a writer.[6] He showed her an article in *Le Figaro* about his goldmaking and explained that he enjoyed greater renown as a scientist than as a writer. This quite absurd remark reveals his ambiguous relation to his profession. Unlike the practice of science, Strindberg never felt that writing fiction was a truly masculine occupation. As a writer, he always had to strive for recognition and, quite rightly, never felt that the Swedish cultural establishment gave him full credit for what he wrote. Thus he envied Selma Lagerlöf's Nobel Prize for literature in 1909 and thought that he should have received it instead. He also felt that the recognition he did not receive as a writer should have been accorded him as a scientist. Had he been able to make gold no one could have denied his greatness, and he would have fulfilled all the expectations one could have of a real man!

The traditional male ideals which Strindberg maintained represent the hegemonic masculinity of the late nineteenth century.[7] However, other masculinities were also present, especially among writers and artists. The dandy of the 1890s, who dressed in a feminine manner, challenged the norms of traditional masculinity. The arraignment of Oscar Wilde in 1895 made it impossible to ignore homosexuality. But men who adopted feminine features and did not seek women as sexual partners were, of course, also a threat to those who defended traditional masculine values, which depended on heterosexuality and a hierarchical gender order. The existence of various forms of masculinity during this period indicates that patriarchal power structures were being challenged, something which can be seen in a stronger gender polarization, as well as in a broadening of masculinities. Strindberg was all for retaining a hierarchical gender system, although he also sensed that this was not possible. Hence his characteristic melancholia and nostalgia for the past.

Comparing Strindberg with Ibsen, one finds in the Norwegian writer a different way of dealing with gender issues. In *A Doll's House* Ibsen portrayed the consequences for traditional marriage when the wife finally rebelled against her role as the ignorant doll in 1879. His play prompted an intense debate throughout Scandinavia, and several Swedish women writers commented on the play, one of whom, Alfhild Agrell, wrote a drama depicting the difficulties that would befall a woman who divorced her husband.[8] Nor was

Strindberg slow in responding. *Getting Married* includes a short story with the same title as Ibsen's play, where the blame for matrimonial discord is attributed to an ugly and aggressive feminist. Her feminism is credited to the fact that she cannot attract the love of men. So, when the husband begins to flirt with her, she forgets her feminist ideas and is driven out of the home by the jealous wife. When the threat to married life is removed, order is re-established and conjugal happiness reigns. It is interesting to note that, as late as the 1950s, Strindberg's story was made into a film, a romantic comedy which presented the story without a trace of irony.

Ibsen continued to portray women who strove to break gender boundaries, as in *Hedda Gabler*. In this respect he seems much more in line with the modern emancipation movement than Strindberg, which may explain why his dramas continue to be performed to a greater extent than Strindberg's. For Ibsen, however, the conflict between the sexes was never as important a part of his works as it was for Strindberg. For Strindberg, gender issues were primarily about masculinity and male power. Contemporary women who fought for women's rights were a threat to him as a man, whereas Ibsen appears not to have shared this anxiety and could therefore write with greater understanding about the situation of women. Because Strindberg desperately defended the privileges of men and cherished traditional masculine ideals, he had to fight so hard a battle and sensed that it was a lost cause since the past could not be recaptured. Thus, during the 1880s, he wrote about women's threat to male power but when his world view changed in the 1890s, and he focused less on society and more on spiritual matters, it became obvious that to him the 'woman question' was really about men and masculinity. In his later writings, 'woman' becomes a kind of phantom whose main role is to be moulded to man's needs, as is apparent from Strindberg's relationship with Harriet Bosse, which he sometimes believed was conducted on what he called the 'astral plane'. Here, however, it helps to concentrate on certain crucial themes in Strindberg's writings from the 1880s, namely rationality, economy and sexuality, and how they reflect the way in which traditional masculinity is put under pressure, before briefly discussing how the notion of masculinity changes in Strindberg's later writings, and women are both marginalized and elevated in his search for spiritual fulfilment.

Masculine rationality: *A Madman's Defence*

At the start of the novel, Axel, the narrator, states his aims. He wants to find the truth and is prepared to use all necessary means to obtain it: 'But I need to know the truth absolutely! And for that, I'm going to undertake a profound, discrete and ... scientific enquiry; I shall employ all the resources of the new science of psychology' (SV25, p. 23). The truth Axel wants to reveal concerns his marriage to Maria, which is falling apart. Who is to blame for this, who is sane and who is mad? The insecurity regarding his own status is already indicated in the title of the novel: Axel must defend himself since he might appear a madman whereas, according to him, it is really Maria who is mad, and this is what he attempts to prove to the reader. But does he succeed? At the end of the novel, Axel is far from being in total control of his emotions, and sure of victory; in fact, his project has failed. But what has brought Axel from his early confidence to the breakdown he experiences at the end? His task, which seemed so simple at the outset, has proved far more complicated than he could have predicted.

Throughout the novel the male narrator is in charge. Maria is never allowed to speak except through Axel. As Arne Melberg has remarked, it is as if the male narrator invents woman himself and then, by looking at her and describing her, tries to adapt her to his world view.[9] The order into which the woman must fit is based upon male supremacy and heterosexual love; she is supposed to have no sexual drives of her own. This becomes apparent in Axel's use of whore/madonna images when describing Maria. He first describes her as the mother/madonna:

> She lay stretched out on her unmade bed with her beautiful little head buried in the white pillows as her wheat-blond hair coiled over the covers; her lace nightdress had slipped down from her shoulders and suggested her virginal breast; her slim and elegant body was discernible beneath the soft, red and white stripped cover ... a complete work of art, moulded in human flesh in the manner of an antique marble; carefree, smiling, with an expression of chaste motherhood, she watched her three, chubby little ones climbing and diving in the florid down cushion, as in a pile of newly-mown flowers. (SV25, pp. 21–2)

This idyllic scenario can be compared to an image of Maria later in the novel: 'Unfortunately, there's a mirror in front of us, and I glance quickly at it, enough to catch sight of a terrible, pale ghost whose wildly staring eyes fasten on my face so that our searching glances meet' (SV25, p. 250). Maria is no longer a living image of the Virgin Mary but some kind of insane, perverted ghost. This transformation is caused by her refusal to become part of the male order. She is situated by Axel as the virginal mother and is supposed to remain as such, because only then is Axel able to control her. When Maria proves to be a woman with sexual desires, he is scared and proclaims that their love should be elevated and pure. He portrays himself as the victim of a woman with an unnatural sexual appetite.

In the late nineteenth century, female sexuality was gaining scientific recognition and had become the subject of an intense debate as to how it should be defined. Nor was Strindberg alone in fearing that women, like men, might also enjoy their sexuality. Contemporary painting abounds in images of women who express an insatiable desire. Edvard Munch's canvases in which the loving woman is presented as a vampire appear to summarize the enormous fear which lustful women could evoke. Hitherto the only women related to sexuality were prostitutes. In their relations with prostitutes middle-class men were never challenged, since they controlled the sexual encounter by paying for the prostitute's services. The recognition that women in general, including those from their own social group, had sexual feelings threatened this order. This prompts Axel's anxiety. He needs to be in control and is finally able to achieve this by raping Maria: 'And then, the shame of appearing shy, beside myself with humiliation, perhaps even suspected of being impotent, I rape her, if indeed rape exists, and stand up noble, happy, swollen with pride, pleased with myself as if I had paid a debt to woman' (SV25, pp. 128–9).

However, this blissful moment of male power soon passes and Axel is brought back to the struggle with his ambivalent feelings towards Maria, who refuses to adapt to his images of femininity. She, who wanted to be an actress and to live with a writer, is supposed to stay at home with the children and Axel is only truly happy during her pregnancies, whereas he cannot bear to look at a picture of her as an actress. According to Axel, the picture indicates that she is available to all men; in short, she is a prostitute.

In the novel the narrator's view becomes increasingly narrow, focusing only on Maria. Axel nurtures a suspicion that she is having a lesbian relationship with a Danish friend, and becomes totally obsessed by the thought. Thus, Maria becomes the abnormal which Axel must reject. But his obsession shows that he cannot achieve this since he is really writing about his own confused feelings. When the narrator looks at Maria, he is therefore also looking at himself: the ghost in the mirror is his own image as Axel projects his own feelings on to Maria in an attempt to live up to his masculine ideals of emotional control and supremacy. Maria thus becomes everything that Axel needs to distance himself from but which he cannot escape. This was already apparent to a contemporary reviewer, Henri Albert, who declared that such inconsequential women portrayed here as perverse, dominating monsters would easily have been put in their place had Axel been a real man, and not this weeping, feminine misfit![10]

At the end of the novel, Axel considers suicide the only solution. His grand project has failed and he, the rational man, faces madness. Throughout the novel femininity is defined as irrational, but it transpires that the same applies to the male protagonist. In this sense, the novel is tragic since it demonstrates how devastating the struggle between the sexes turns out to be for the man. Axel is lonely and unhappy and, like Maria, he becomes the victim of the gender hierarchy that he has so ardently defended.

Male breakdown: *The Father*

Even more so than Axel, the Captain in *The Father* seems to incarnate all that Strindberg regards as desirable masculine qualities. He is both a high-ranking officer and a scientist, and seems to be in complete control of the women in his family. However, there are signs of his weakness even as the drama begins: the Captain is nervous and his home is said to be a cage full of tigers in which he has continually to maintain his power.

The road to his nervous breakdown is neatly paved in a play which ranges over a very short period of time. However, the rapid change in the Captain's mental condition does not seem entirely convincing. I therefore see the drama as a fantasy about what would happen should woman gain control over man, both mentally and financially. *The Father* can thus be seen as Strindberg's worst nightmare at a time when he was obsessed by the question of women's emancipation and wrote the many articles in which he sought to prove their inferiority. He was evidently fearful about what would happen if women's demands were met, and *The Father*, in which he shows what will happen to man if the worst comes to the worst, dramatizes the threat that Strindberg dealt with in these articles.

The main issue in the drama is fatherhood, which was a topic of current concern; Ibsen had already explored it in *The Wild Duck* (1884). If a man could not be sure about the origin of his children, what then remained of patriarchal power? The fight over Bertha's future is therefore a fight about power, about the right to define the laws of society and control financial matters. If man is destroyed, a primitive matriarchy will replace the present order. In *The Father*, Strindberg presents Laura, whom he called 'the woman from hell', as someone governed entirely by her evil instincts. Her primitive will triumphs over the male intellect when she succeeds in making the Captain believe that he is not Bertha's father. Strindberg even makes her say that her actions were unplanned and that she never considered the consequences for her husband. In a sense, she is therefore innocent in so far as Strindberg saw women as innocent because they could not be held responsible for their actions. It is, nevertheless, striking how many critics accept Strindberg's view of Laura and simply ask whether the Captain's breakdown is caused by her evil actions, or whether it could be explained by his personal shortcomings.

2. Keve Hjelm and Lena Granhagen in *The Father* at Stockholm Stadsteater, 1981.

One can, of course, see Laura as the evil woman of Strindberg's imagination. However, if one looks more closely at the drama it is obvious that she acts much as a man would have done. Living with the Captain, Laura has studied how he exercises power in the household. In her struggle against him, she therefore uses exactly the same tools as he would have done. She is determined to reach her goal: to replace the Captain as head of the family. In her determination she resembles a traditional male protagonist. Nor can the end of the play, when the audience sees Laura seated at the writing-desk administering the family finances just as her husband used to do, be regarded as a scene of primitive matriarchy, as Strindberg suggested. In the meantime, the Captain loses his senses and regresses to childhood where the only person who can control his outbursts is his former nurse, who lures him into the straitjacket. But how can this seemingly superior man come to this? At the première in Copenhagen in 1887, Strindberg did not want the Captain to appear weak but as a man who could not escape his fate in the fight with his evil, monstrous wife. However, when the play was performed at the Intimate Theatre in 1908, he changed his mind since the drama lost its dramatic tension if the Captain was played as a man who retained his sanity. Thus, the Captain really became the loser in the play, a victim who evoked pity, something that Strindberg felt did not befit a man.

It is, however, important to relate the Captain's fate to historic and social reality, and not to regard him as a suffering man, fighting a demon in a woman's shape. Thus one can view him as a man who is marked by the hegemonic masculinity of his time. The drama makes the limits of this masculinity very clear. Although conventionally the Captain is the ruler and his authority is secured by society and its laws, the doubt that Laura arouses in him about being Bertha's father is something which cannot be regulated by law. This is the crucial point where the Captain is vulnerable and open to attack, and the question of fatherhood becomes indistinguishable from the Captain's power to rule over the family. As Laura declares: 'Power, yes. What has this whole life-and-death struggle been about if not power?' (*MJoP*, p. 34). The Captain's breakdown can therefore be seen not only as a personal catastrophe but as the breakdown of patriarchal power.

Originally Strindberg thought that the Captain should be considered superior to Laura, although he breaks down. However, when Strindberg portrayed the struggle for power between the Captain and Laura, he could not maintain the pretence of objectivity which he applied in his articles. The play did not work in performance when the Captain was presented as if he were still in control, in spite of his nervous breakdown. Gender relations become far more complex in Strindberg's drama. There is a strong sense of loss which the Captain expresses when he asks: 'Whatever happened to love, healthy sensual love?' (*MJoP*, p. 51). As Strindberg himself experienced, love is impossible when women are no longer satisfied with subordinate roles as wives. Then love turns into a power struggle and since woman, in Strindberg's view, is totally governed by her instinct and will, she manages to break down even the sharpest male intellect. But in so doing, Laura deploys the same tools to obtain power as the Captain, and hence replaces him as head of the family. This is the ultimate threat to man. Through the fate of one man, the Captain, the drama shows the fate of every man were woman ever to take command.

Female sexuality and death: *Miss Julie*

In the final scene of *Miss Julie*, the manservant, Jean, sees no other end for Julie than suicide. According to Jean, this is awful but inevitable. But was it really necessary for a woman of the nobility like Julie to commit suicide after having slept with a servant? In fact, no, and this drama, like *The Father*, goes well beyond the naturalistic struggle between the sexes that Strindberg wanted to portray. One can, of course, view the drama as a conflict between a new order, represented by the male servant with high ambitions, and the past, incarnated in a degenerate noblewoman with no future. The problem, however, is that it is she who moves the audience and gains its sympathy, not the rational servant with the European train timetable in his pocket.

Harry Järv has observed of Julie that, in the first part of the drama, she displays 'a primitive and thoughtless, but on the whole sound sensuality'.[11] By this Järv seems to mean that there is something which could be called a normal female sexuality, from which Julie deviates later in the drama. This was probably Strindberg's intention: he wished to demonstrate her degenerate state and did this in her sexual encounter with Jean, a man with a rational and sound view of sexuality. However, Strindberg could not predict that the drama he wrote would turn out to be more complicated than the argument he wished to demonstrate. The verbal battle between Jean and Julie about the consequences of their sexual encounter reveals how sexuality pervades language itself, and cannot be avoided.

How to control sexuality is really the main issue in the drama. For Jean this is not a problem since he regards sexuality as an uncomplicated physical need. He uses the language he has learnt from the upper classes to seduce Miss Julie. Jean knows the power of language and warns Julie when she wants to tell him about herself: 'Wait a moment. Forgive me, but you might come to regret telling me all your intimate secrets' (*MJoP*, p. 93). Jean is a practical man who wishes to rise in society. He simply does not understand Julie's talk about love:

> For the last time – what do you want me to do? ... what am I supposed to do? What do you want? This is getting tiresome! But that's what happens when you get involved with women. Miss Julie! I can see you're miserable, I know you're suffering, but I simply can't understand you. We don't carry on like this. We don't hate each other. For us love's a game, when work allows; but we don't have all day and all night for it, like you do. I believe you're sick, and your mother was certainly mad. We've whole parishes gone mad with pietism, of course, but this is a kind of pietism run wild. (p. 97)

Jean emphasizes the contrast between the rational man with future prospects and the degenerate noblewoman. The 'pietism run wild' he refers to can, however, be interpreted as the threat posed by women in the liberation movement, whom Strindberg found perverted, claiming rights that were against their nature. Jean becomes a representative for Strindberg and other contemporary men who wished to define and control sexuality, and who were deeply disturbed by female sexuality. Thus Jean cannot understand why Julie suffers. However, her behaviour is a threat to his plans for social advancement. This becomes evident when Julie's father commands Jean's attendance, which leads him finally to use his mastery of language to make Julie commit suicide.

Jean convinces both Julie and Kristin through his rhetorical skills. Julie, on the other hand, fails to communicate her dreams about a future with Jean, prompting Kristin to ask: 'Listen, Miss Julie, do you really believe all this?' (p. 105). This is said following Julie's monologue about a future life in Switzerland near Lake Como, where she begins by talking about Kristin's new position in the household. Gradually, however, her speech grows incoherent:

> And you – you'll sit like a queen in the kitchen. – You won't have to stand over the stove yourself, of course – and you'll be nicely and neatly dressed when you appear before the guests – and with your looks – I'm not flattering you, Kristin – one day you'll get hold of a husband, a rich Englishman, you'll see – they're so easy to (*slowing down*) – catch and then we'll get rich and build ourselves a villa on Lake Como – it rains a little there now and then, of course, but (*subsiding*) the sun must shine there too, sometimes … though it looks dark … and then – otherwise, we can always go home again – back (*pause*) … here – or somewhere else   (p. 105)

Julie can no longer express her feelings in coherent language. She seems lost in her feelings. From a psychoanalytical standpoint, this loss of words reveals how language and sexual drives connect. Julie's incoherent speech demonstrates that language, like sexuality, is not as rational as Jean seems to think. Her speech conveys the complexity of human drives. Therefore Julie becomes the character who captivates the audience, something which makes the struggle between her and Jean more complicated than Strindberg probably intended. He wanted Jean to be the winner, not Julie. However, when he wrote about sexuality and made Julie the central figure, he also projected on to her his own insecurity and vulnerability.

Julie has to die, but is Jean really a winner? It is obvious that he can only carry out his final act of verbal power over Julie with help from the Count, the patriarchal symbol. When the Count repeatedly calls for Jean, he sees no other way out than to persuade Julie to commit suicide: 'It's horrible! But there is no other way!' (p. 110). But this was not really inevitable; as a noblewoman, Julie could get away with a sexual fling on midsummer night. If one looks at her character as a projection of Strindberg's fantasies about a threatening female sexuality which cannot be controlled, however, she has to die. And since her character turns out to be far more complicated than Strindberg was aware of, the struggle between her and Jean becomes ambiguous. As in *A Madman's Defence* and *The Father*, no one really emerges the winner; Strindberg's literary works from the 1880s thus seem to contradict his articles on gender issues, which is what makes them so interesting today.

Masculinity re-established

'Why couldn't you be the woman I created?' Strindberg addressed this question to his third wife, Harriet Bosse, just before she was to remarry. When he met the young actress, whom he married in 1901 and divorced in 1904, his outlook on life had changed considerably, as had his view of the opposite sex. He no longer perceived woman as a threat; his focus had moved from daily life and social struggle to the spiritual realm, and she now seemed man's helper in his search for the meaning of life.

Bosse was allotted this role by Strindberg in both his life and the plays he wrote. During their engagement she played the part of Eleonora in *Easter* and he seems to have seen her and Eleonora as one and the same. Strindberg was not really interested in finding out who Harriet was. Instead, he wanted to create an image of her that suited him. Thus she was not allowed to take any personal belongings with her to their new home, which Strindberg had furnished, and later observed that, for their marriage to have worked, she would have had to have adapted completely to him and his needs; but this was, of course, not possible.[12] Thus, in 1901, when she went to Denmark against his will, he was desperate. Not just because she rebelled against him but because she did not fulfil her mission: 'If you go, if you've gone, I don't know. Going, gone, without having reconciled me with mankind – and woman!'[13]

In the correspondence he conducted with her after their divorce, Strindberg was free to create Harriet as he wished her to be. In real life he could not handle their relationship but in his letters he could imagine her as an ideal woman, who fulfilled his needs. Thus he wrote to her in 1908: 'You see, my child, you live in your letters and reveal yourself as "The Great Woman" I divined you to be' (*SL*, p. 774). When he wrote about her and experienced her presence without having to meet her, even sexuality could become elevated. Strindberg both told Harriet how he sensed her presence at night, and how they united sexually, and regarded her as a female redeemer. But when she was to remarry he could not ignore the fact that she was no longer there for him, and therefore posed the crucial question: why couldn't she be the woman he had created, why, in short, was she no longer Agnes in *A Dream Play* but prepared to marry an ordinary man?

The role which Strindberg created for Harriet was one that she was not willing to play other than on stage as Eleonora or Swanwhite. In reality she could not meet Strindberg's need to be redeemed with life through her or, rather, through his image of how woman could be of use in his search for the meaning of his own life. From the start of their relationship, he could not differentiate between Harriet and the young women he created in his plays, and therefore she also became a fictional figure, much like Maria in *A Madman's Defence*. The crucial difference was that Strindberg created Harriet during their relationship whereas the picture of Maria was drawn in retrospect, after his first marriage had failed.

What then does this merging of fictitious images of women and real life mean unless that woman is only a projection of the male imagination? She is significant in so far as she may have a role in man's search for existential meaning. Woman thus becomes not a separate being but a part of man; an extension of himself. She seems to become some kind of supernatural creature and the ideal marriage really comes about when the wife dies and the man may bear her memory in his heart. He can talk to her; that is, he can both pose questions and answer them himself. Woman has thus become a memory buried within the man.

It is hardly surprising therefore that, in *Black Banners*, Strindberg portrayed monastic life as an ideal form of existence. His monastery is a haven where men can live with dignity in beautiful surroundings and engage in elevated discussions about ideas and life. Gluttony and other physical vices are banished from the monastery where masculinity can finally be established on a sound basis. However, the ideal man cannot exist in relation to women in contemporary society: in that respect, Strindberg never really overcame the 1880s. But in the monastery, in male seclusion, it is possible for man to find the peace he has been seeking. Perhaps this was the only solution to his troublesome relationship with woman that Strindberg could imagine: a purely masculine world.

NOTES

1. Anna-Maria Roos, 'Ett besök på Naddö', *Aftonbladet*, 13 August 1913.
2. Betty Roszak and Theodore Roszak, eds., *Masculine/Feminine: Readings in Sexual Mythology and the Liberation of Women* (New York: Harper and Row, 1969), pp. 91–2.
3. Allan Hagsten, *Den unge Strindberg* (Stockholm: Albert Bonniers Förlag, 1951), p. 82.
4. Per Stounbjerg, 'Det ustadiges aestetik. Modernitet og modernisme hos August Strindberg', *Litteratur, Aestetik, Sprog*, 14 (1989), pp. 7–46.
5. Marc Angenot, 'La fin d'un sexe. Le discours sur les femmes en 1889', *Romantisme: revue du dix-neuvième siècle*, 63 (1989), pp. 5–22.
6. *Strindbergs brev till Harriet Bosse* (Stockholm: Natur och Kultur, 1932), p. 82.
7. R. W. Connell, *Gender and Power: Society, the Person, and Sexual Politics* (Cambridge: Polity Press, 1987), pp. 183–90.
8. See Ingeborg Nordin-Hennel, *Dömd och glömd. En studie i Alfhild Agrells liv och dikt* (Stockholm: Almqvist & Wiksell, 1981).

9. Arne Melberg, 'Sexualpolitiken, *Fru Marianne* och *En dåres försvarstal*', *Ord och Bild*, 2–3 (1980), pp. 50–65.
10. Henri Albert, 'Auguste Strindberg', *La Revue Blanche*, 1 December 1894, pp. 481–98.
11. Harry Järv, 'Den "karaktärslösa" Fröken Julie', *Svensk Tidskrift*, 38 (1951), pp. 163–74.
12. *Strindbergs brev till Harriet Bosse*, p. 75.
13. *Ibid.*, p. 58.

PART II

The works

3

ULF OLSSON

Learning to speak: Strindberg and the novel

It was as a novelist that Strindberg made his definitive, and scandalous, entry into Swedish literature: *The Red Room* (1879) was only the first in a line of prose works that were to outrage a conservative readership but also, and increasingly, to puzzle a more progressive or radical audience. Hailed as something alarmingly new, *The Red Room* signalled the somewhat belated entry of Swedish literature into modernity. But the novel was not without precursors and its effectiveness owed much to tradition. One might regard Strindberg's novels and prose fiction as born out of Balzac and Dickens but ending just this side of Kafka. Bearing an epigraph from what Roland Barthes called 'the last happy writer', Voltaire, *The Red Room* is one of Strindberg's happy works: happy to fight a society that is hypocritical, corrupt and conservative.[1]

Strindberg's novels are restless and versatile, but sometimes also confusing and even tedious. They can be charged with ideological prejudice but are also sharp-eyed anatomies of the modern subject under construction. Sometimes Strindberg uses prose fiction as a means of disseminating ideology; at other times he seems to be learning to speak in these texts, reaching for new literary forms and modes of literary language.

Starting as a traditionalist who learnt to write in such established forms as classical drama and the Icelandic saga, Strindberg was forced to become a modern writer when tradition could neither support him nor allow him to speak out. Journalism became Strindberg's schooling in modernity, teaching him to sharpen both his gaze and his pen, and to confront different aspects of contemporary society. To say this is to concede that as a writer Strindberg represents the effect of a growing liberalism, both economic and ideological, but in his writing we also encounter what Leo Löwenthal called 'the breakdown of liberal confidence'.[2]

Contemporary conservative opinion in Sweden always denied Strindberg the title of *Dichter*, or author, and portrayed him instead as a 'scribbler', a purveyor of filth. He was himself aware that he was a new kind of writer, exemplifying, for instance, what Roland Barthes saw as a decisive difference: 'The author performs a function, the writer an activity'. And this activity, this practice, consists, according to Barthes, in a constant and subjective form of writing: *'the writer's function is to say at once and on every occasion what he thinks'.*[3] Perhaps no writer better exemplifies this aspect of modernity than Strindberg: always ready to act, prepared to comment on anything. But also, as a writer, conscious of his function.

The Red Room is the first example of how Strindberg writes the discursive conditions under which he works.[4] But his most concentrated account of the struggle between tradition and modernity is perhaps a short prose text from 1894, originally written in French, 'Sensations détraquées' ('Deranged Sensations').[5] This autobiographical text describes Strindberg's journey from Austria and his second wife, the journalist Frida Uhl, to Paris, the capital of modernity. But in so doing he also allegorizes the condition of literature under capitalist modernity. Travelling, Strindberg leaves behind him not only 'mountains and valleys' but also 'the good old days when people had oil lamps, stagecoaches, boatwomen, and six-volume novels' (*SE*, p. 218), all of which contrasts sharply with the new urban world he describes in 'Sensations détraquées' where the experience of modernity is given allegorical form as *katabasis*, a descent into the kingdom of the dead. Surrounded by an 'immense sea of light', the self finds itself transformed: 'Am I changing skin? Am I about to become a man of today?', the narrator asks (*SE*, p. 128). The metamorphosis of the self that Strindberg writes is an allegory of writing: the writing of the self results in a transformation of the self as it, by writing, is resituated, bereft of tradition and propelled into modernity.

This modern subject that Strindberg construes is also nourished by colonialism and the fantasies it produced. Strindberg depicts himself as a 'savage', a 'redskin' sneaking up on the heart of civilization. He also uses the idea of the 'barbarian' nature of the Scandinavian writer in the self-marketing with which he promotes himself in Paris,[6] which comprises 'the dirty little houses of the buyers and the sellers' (*SE*, p. 134). This is what it all comes down to: buying and selling. Selling and buying. And the commodity for sale is ultimately the writer whose naked heart hangs for sale in the bookstore windows.[7] Thus capitalism, as the contemporary form of buying and selling, becomes, together with such integral aspects of modernity as electricity, a nucleus of Strindberg's metaphors, which reflect 'a larger social process, a new social reality: urbanization and the beginnings of industrialism'.[8]

With 'Sensations détraquées' Strindberg bids farewell to the realistic and naturalistic tradition on which he had relied up to *By the Open Sea* (1890), a novel which concludes with its hero sailing into madness, but also into symbolism. From this point onwards, Strindberg's works steer towards a modernist aesthetic. But he never denies the importance of his earlier works. *The Red Room* includes features of his prose writing to which he would return, for example in seeking to repeat the scandalous success of his first novel in *Gothic Rooms* (1904). More importantly, the dialogism and parodic realism of *The Red Room* remains central in *Black Banners* (1907), a satire on contemporary Swedish liberal intellectuals with which he more than repeated the scandal of *The Red Room*.

The central target in *The Red Room* is capitalism and its reliance on the newly emerged division of labour. A key scene depicts a curious gathering of the Workers' Association Northern Star: 'On the front bench below the platform sat the most eminent members of the Union: officers, civil servants, merchants, who strongly supported all constitutional proposals and with superior parliamentary skill opposed every measure of reform'.[9] These workers, who speak of themselves as 'all workers in the sight of the Eternal' (p. 219), employ a language that is charged with rhetorical, bureaucratic figures, at once correct, ornamental and totally impenetrable. This gathering has been assembled to repudiate a wave of strikes throughout Europe, but among these gentlemen a few genuine workers have sneaked in, one of whom, the carpenter Eriksson, requests the floor and twice uses the formulation, 'om jag hade ordet i min makt' (if I had the power of words, p. 220). And it is the relationship between language and power that is at the heart of *The Red Room* and permeates all Strindberg's writing.

The Red Room thus stages a fight over the word, its meanings and the right to speak. It seeks to unmask society by unmasking its language, particularly those governing words which circulate in the economy of language:

> Tim. Ch. X., 27. 28. 29
> 1st. Corinth. Ch. VI, 3.4.5.
> Dear Brother,
> With the Grace of Our Lord J. C., the love of God, the fellowship
> of the H. G., etc. Amen.   (p. 72)

This is how the Reverend Skåre begins his letter to the novel's hero, Arvid Falk. The letter concerns a business transaction and Strindberg, of course, exaggerates the religious vocabulary, but does not immediately reveal its meaning. Each reader has to decipher it for himself, and the mechanical form of the (false) allusions to the Bible do not accord with its alleged piety. Moreover, the fact that the novel was so effective in its unmasking of social hypocrisy (or rather, in writing society as a semblance), was grounded in the fact that Strindberg was writing within a tradition: as a genre, the novel was constructed precisely in order to perform this kind of fight.

Like the scene in which Eriksson maintains his right to speak, Falk's attempt to interpret Skåre's letter makes clear that the language of power is masked, ornamented and rhetorically charged, while its opposite is simple and inquiring. Rhetoric is the driving force in the language of power; with its help, speech can be prolonged endlessly. Its opposite, a personal manner of speaking – which to the agents of power only seems 'reckless and shameless' (p. 219) – is concise, serious and investigative. And these scenes make clear that, where power resides, only a chosen few are allowed to speak, something from which Eriksson is debarred by his working-class identity.

Parody is Strindberg's privileged weapon in this *agon* over the right to speak, a battle that he himself would have to fight throughout his life.[10] Thus *The Red Room* parodies different sociolects, all socially hegemonic. The language of Christianity is depicted as sales jargon, parliamentary speech-making as empty rhetoric, and the language of welfare work as paternalism by distorting each sociolect until they are turned against themselves. And it is this demand extended by the merciless but self-critical parodist for the right to speak (and to speak differently) that accounts for the novel's impact on publication and its pivotal place in the history of Swedish literature. Moreover, as a novel, it proceeds by critical negation, playing upon and testing other people's words only to find them unsatisfactory, unreliable or false. The novel's hero is a feeble idealist, and in demonstrating the gulf between his idealism and the reality that confronts him, the novel seeks to break free from the imprisoning power of illusions. For Strindberg, as for his precursor, Balzac, the *Bildungsroman* becomes a novel of disillusion. Here the *agon* is fought out between a masked word, a word that conceals its real significance, and a personal word, of which the sincerity and truthfulness is guaranteed or legitimized by the speaker's presence, his body and way of life.

The critique that this novel delivers in the form of parody and satire is directed upwards, towards a word that is hegemonic and impregnated with power. Its success was due to Strindberg's finding an adequate form for the battle of the word. To be able to speak, he had to break through the aesthetic norms of his time, which in Sweden were usually generalized as 'ideal-realism', what Strindberg considered a combination of antiquated ideals and trivial realism. The norms of a rigid, highly conservative idealistic realism regulated what literature should be written and published, and how it was to be read. Hence *The Red Room* is formed as a critique of power.

Above all, Strindberg's novel directs its critique towards the language it is itself forced to speak. It portrays society as a kind of conspiracy, a network of hidden relations that is governed by the language of power, subjugating its interlocutors as it is articulated in everyday practice. Since it is impossible to speak another language, parody and the inverted world it produces becomes the only way of subverting this subjection. The delicate and relatively honest Arvid Falk pays a visit to his brother, Carl Nicholas, a capitalist entrepreneur and hypocritical parvenu. But it is he who criticizes Arvid by pretending to say what their father would have said: 'You are not straight, Arvid. You are not straight' (p. 18). Arvid falls silent because, 'since childhood he had heard those terribly impressive words: upright, honest, true, daily and hourly repeated, until they stood before him like a judge for ever pronouncing him "Guilty!"' (p. 18). Words exercise power; spoken frequently they become true and we subject ourselves to them. Arvid is not capable of uncovering and making public the double nature of his brother, but the novel is happy to do so. There is nothing redemptive in its representation of a small-time capitalist seeking legitimacy and social status by promising to donate 20,000 crowns (at the time a stupendous sum of money) to his wife's charity for needy children, money which actually consists of worthless stock in his bogus insurance company, Triton.

On his journey through the language of Oscarian (the Swedish equivalent of Victorian) class society, the novel requires more experienced observers than Arvid, who still dreams of, and values, poetry and literature. Two other characters, both artists, are introduced to enable the reader to penetrate power masked in language: the sculptor, Olle Montanus, and the actor, Falander. They represent different aspects of truth-telling, and compared to them, Arvid is, in the jargon of our time, nothing but a 'wannabe' in the tough school of truth-telling.

In Falander we encounter the ancient rhetorical technique of *anakrisis*,[11] the art of enticing, or forcing, the other's speech. Likewise, Olle Montanus's presence in the novel may be understood by reference to antiquity: he is a carnivalesque *parrhesiastes*, someone who, though risking his life, always told the truth to his sovereign.[12] When Eriksson is not permitted to speak at the meeting of the Workers' Association, the unstoppable Montanus delivers his celebrated speech on Sweden, a speech that actually implies dismantling everything known as 'Swedish'. His speech is scandalous and interfoliated by protests from the audience: 'Is he crazy?', 'Now what the hell is all this?', 'Down with the traitor! He's making fools of us!' – invective that soon dissolves into violence: 'Kick him out! Beat him up!' (pp. 220–4). Thus, by explicitly expressing the truth in public in the presence of power, Montanus puts himself and his life at stake, so demonstrating that he has the moral qualities which a truth-teller must possess (a truth reserved for a closed room is without value).

Montanus is not killed directly because he tells the truth. But the letter he leaves on committing suicide is characterized by the ethos that truth-telling calls for. He declares suicide to be his 'right', and that he is not acting 'out of despair, for an intelligent person never despairs' (p. 260). The letter contains an analysis of the circumstances of his life; he explains that what brought a worker like himself to become an artist was revulsion at the curse of manual labour (p. 262). His suicide is therefore a rational act, and in itself a question of truth: 'In order to free myself from this intolerable condition and find clarity and peace, I go to seek the unknown' (p. 263).

A decisive difference between Montanus and Falander is the extent to which they speak in public or in private. Montanus practises the art of truth-telling openly, in the *agora*, while Falander's speech favours intimacy: it is alone with one other that he performs his truly demoniacal art, the art of talking so that the other will react as if Falander is saying what he himself wishes to say, but could not: 'you are expressing my very thoughts' (p. 134), the aspirant actor Rehnhjelm exclaims, but the conversation ends with the latter feeling that Falander has deprived him of all his supports. Asked how, since he seems entirely lacking in morals, he can claim to be considered trustworthy, Falander replies: 'That word again. What a remarkable word it is; it answers all questions, stops all discussion, excuses all errors – one's own, not other people's – strikes down all adversaries, pleads both for and against – just like a lawyer' (p. 149). Thus Agnes pronounces him 'a fiend!' (p. 151), and society is certainly correct in accusing him, as a demoniacal character, of lacking morals. But at the same time he is in fact a true moralist since, having seen through the specious manner in which the words 'morals' and 'morality' are used in society, he practises a form of ethics that entails provoking the other's word and attitude towards the world. He is thus the opposite of Eugenie Falk who has learnt from her husband, Carl Nicholas, 'how to frame her questions so that the answer must defeat the answerer. It was her husband's own method she employed. If he were not to be defeated, he must keep on changing the subject' (p. 34). Where Falander delivers his demoniacal speech as a means of enticing, or provoking, the other to step forward, the speech of both Carl Nicholas and Eugenie aims at depriving the interlocutor of his status as a speaking subject. Moreover, Eugenie succeeds in making her husband obey her without him noticing.

Meanwhile, to Arvid is left a positive but, in comparison with the approaches adopted by Falander and Montanus, more ambiguous role of truth-teller. In his conversation with the philosopher, Ygberg, he, too, practises the art of enticing another to speak, but more in the form of translation, as he transposes Ygberg's jargon into plain speech. However, in keeping with the element of *Bildung* in this Strindbergian *Bildungsroman*, Arvid learns the art of truth-telling for himself. His childhood experience of big but empty words is here extended to society as a whole. He develops into someone who can see through at least the words which others use. But the price he pays is his lost illusions and the bitterness that replaces them:

> He had been present at parliamentary assemblies, church councils, company meetings, philanthropic gatherings, police court enquiries, festivals, funerals, and mass meetings. Everywhere big words, many words, words that are never used in common parlance, words that don't express anything, or at least not what they are meant to express ... therefore he was very bitter.   (p. 153)

The Red Room unmasks these big words, demonstrating how they act as masks covering power relations. And if they permeate every aspect of the novel, this is only to encourage us to seek for what they are masking. For Arvid comes to understand that the words through which power is exerted do not stand in any expressive relation to the person currently employing them, or to the thoughts of the speaker.

Strindberg has Arvid expressing a longing for an alternative to such dictatorial words: a personal word. This is demonstrated by his criticism of the torrent of words which issue from his fellow journalist, Struve. Arvid maintains that Struve's view of the law as written by 'the people and the universal sense of right', and by God (p. 169), conceals the fact that words are articulated by people, and that they are always inscribed within power relations. But Arvid's notion that words must be a manifestation of their speaker is also something of an illusion, nourished by his dream of becoming a writer. Therefore he is written out of the novel while still growing in insight: 'He is going to return to the Civil Service ... re-enter society, register with the herd, become respectable, win a social position, and hold his tongue until what he says has some authority' (p. 253).

In the more private company of the Red Room of Berns Salon, Falk is 'high-spirited and wild', and to Borg 'a regular sap' whose behaviour is gratifying to him. So much for the personal, expressive word: perhaps Borg is someone who, by rhetorical manipulation, educates Arvid to function as a truth-teller, while Arvid sees himself as the honest poet? The latter has still to conquer the (a)moral qualities that the truth-teller, like Montanus, must possess, and that is why Strindberg despatches Arvid back to society until he has become fit for the fight. But if so, *The Red Room* warns its readers that these are not August Strindberg's final words. As a work of art it stages the fight for words, and as a work of art it also knows that the fight can never be settled: language does not acknowledge any such peace treaties between high and low, true and false or power and the powerless.

Strindberg would return to this *agon*, and in fact never really ever abandoned it. *The Red Room* acknowledges language as a shared medium: parody depends on the possibility that the reader will recognize what is being parodied or, at least, experience the mode of parody and therefore also the agonistic character of language. But the novel also tends toward an increasingly important feature of Strindberg's writing, its self-reflexiveness. Strindberg allegorizes the writing process. *A Madman's Defence* starts with two forewords, both of them signed 'The Author', in which he says that he has just met the hero of his novel in the street. But in an autobiographical text such as this, that hero is supposed to be the writer. Moreover, the narrative proper begins with the hero at his writing-desk, ready to commence his work, when he is suddenly struck down by fever, as by a thunderbolt. Subsequently, another of Strindberg's autobiographical novels, *Inferno*, employs every traditional allegorical trick in the book, yet leaves the reader unsure as to precisely what this allegorical machinery means. The novel is filled with signs in the form of crumpled pieces of paper, letters in a shop window, or a sprig lying in the street, and on to this detritus, Strindberg imposes allegorical meaning, thus illustrating the capriciousness of the allegorical writer that Walter Benjamin would explore in his studies of Baudelaire.[13] For, having read *Inferno* and *To Damascus i–iii*, it is easy to understand why Benjamin would point to Strindberg as the modern inheritor of the allegorical baroque drama.[14]

These autobiographical works, as well as *By the Open Sea*, *Legends* and *The Roofing Feast*, are formed as studies in consciousness, explorations of modern subjectivity, be it in the self or a third person. But the dialogism in Strindberg's writing, which cannot be reduced merely to the idea that he was also a dramatist when he occasionally wrote in prose, makes him parodic and satirical, but also self-reflective. He splits the subject into two, using the agonism between two speakers as a narrative vehicle. *Inferno* has a paranoid structure, with the narrator calling upon the Almighty, though without ever receiving the answer Strindberg expected. In *Jacob Wrestles*, which serves as an addendum to *Legends* and is named after the monumental painting by Delacroix in the church of Saint Sulpice in Paris as well as the biblical text that Delacroix portrays, he constructs a *Doppelgänger*, a Christlike figure who silently interrogates the hero and makes of the novel a judicial establishment of guilt, in which the hero is forced to speak and confess.[15] On the surface monologic, these texts are agonistic dialogues with powers that remain silent, withdrawn and reclusive.

By the Open Sea, however, may be read as a study in monologism. It relates how an inspector of fisheries, Axel Borg, confronts both the nature and the natives of the Stockholm archipelago. Regarding himself as a superman, in a novel that is fuelled by a very partial reading of Nietzsche, Borg turns out to be nothing but a colonialist. He tries to discipline the local population through illusions, including the construction of a small island which, under specific weather conditions, appears to the natives as a mirage in the sky, in the form of an Italian Renaissance garden. But it turns out to represent 'a colossal moon, deathly white, rising over a churchyard of cypresses'.[16] In this novel, Strindberg demonstrates how a monologic attitude, however 'civilized', brings death by killing its object. Once again, *By the Open Sea* allegorizes the act of writing since Borg is an Orpheus-like figure who tries to inscribe his script on nature.

With *By the Open Sea*, Strindberg became a modernist writer. As it concludes, Borg sails out into the unknown after having gone mad, and the novel transports its author into new territories. And Strindberg will, in a masterpiece like *Inferno*, become a writer of precisely the sort that Adorno discusses as characteristic of modernity in *Ästhetische Theorie*, with Strindberg's descriptions of a fractured world in *Inferno* and *To Damascus* as one of his prime examples. Indeed, his final work of narrative prose, *The Scapegoat* (1907), is perhaps his most Kafkaesque. After reading *By the Open Sea*, Kafka wrote in a diary entry for 23 March 1915 that he felt 'hollow as a mussel on the shore, ready to be pulverised by the tread of a foot'. *The Scapegoat* appears to explore a state of mind and a bereft world that is reminiscent of Kafka's. Its hero is such an empty shell who moves through the world wearing an expression that is reminiscent of Buster Keaton, 'desperately empty'. That is the point at which Strindberg's prose fiction ends: in desolation and despair. We have entered the twentieth century.

NOTES

1. The epigraph reads 'Rien n'est si désagréable que d'être pendu obscurément'. For Barthes on Voltaire, see 'The Last Happy Writer', in Susan Sontag, ed., *A Barthes Reader* (London: Vintage, 2000), pp. 150–7.
2. 'Exkurs über Strindberg', in Leo Löwenthal, *Das Bürgerliche Bewusstsein in der Literatur, Schriften*, vol. II (Frankfurt am Main: Suhrkamp, 1981), p. 238.
3. 'Authors and Writers', in *A Barthes Reader*, pp. 186, 191.
4. I am referring here to Michel Foucault's concept of discourse and discursive order. See, for example, 'The Order of Discourse', in Robert Young, ed., *Untying the Text: a Post-Structuralist Reader* (London: Routledge & Kegan Paul, 1981).
5. See *SE*, pp. 122–4.
6. See the essay 'Le Barbare à Paris' in *Gil Blas*, 8 August 1895.
7. Cf. Strindberg's poem 'Vid avenue de Neuilly', *SV*15, p. 165.
8. Karl-Åke Kärnell, *Strindbergs bildspråk. En studie i prosastil* (Stockholm: Almqvist & Wicksell, 1962), p. 81.
9. *The Red Room: Scenes of Artistic and Literary Life*, trans. Elizabeth Sprigge (London: Dent; New York: Dutton, 1967), p. 217. All future references to *The Red Room* are to this edition with page numbers in parenthesis following a quotation.

10. His prosecution for blasphemy in *Getting Married* in 1884 is the most obvious example of Strindberg's fight for the right to speak. But it cannot be reduced to this single, symbolic incident. The problem of speaking out is a constant throughout his work as well as the history of its reception. See here my *Jag blir galen. Strindberg vansinnet och vetenskapen* (Stockholm/Stehag: Brutus Östlings Bokförlag Symposion, 2002). Some aspects of this problematic can be found in my essay 'Going Crazy: Strindberg and the Construction of Literary Madness' in Poul Houe, Sven Hakon Rossel and Göran Stockenström, eds., *August Strindberg and the Other: New Critical Approaches* (Amsterdam, New York: Rodopi, 2002), pp. 115–31.

11. On *anacrisis*, see Mikhail Bakhtin, *Problems of Dostoevsky's Poetics*, trans. Caryl Emerson (Manchester: Manchester University Press, 1984), ch. 4.

12. The ethics of *parrhesia* is discussed by Michel Foucault in *Fearless Speech* (Los Angeles: Semiotext(e), 2001).

13. See *Das Passagenwerke* (Frankfurt am Main: Suhrkamp, 1983), J 80, 2/J 80 a, 1.

14. *Ursprung des deutschen Trauerspiels* (Frankfurt am Main: Suhrkamp, 1978), p. 114.

15. See *Jacob Wrestles* in *Inferno, Alone and Other Writings*, new translations ed. and intr. Evert Sprinchorn (Garden City, New York: Doubleday & Company, 1968), pp. 291–346.

16. *By the Open Sea*, trans. Mary Sandbach (Harmondsworth: Penguin Classics, 1984), p. 114.

4

PER STOUNBJERG

Between realism and modernism: the modernity of Strindberg's autobiographical writings

In writing *The Son of a Servant* in 1886 August Strindberg ventured upon an autobiographical project that would occupy him for more than twenty years. The first three volumes were published in rapid succession. The fourth did not come out until 1909, now accompanied by a preface in which Strindberg reviewed his writings to date, including several volumes with himself as the main subject. In the meantime he had written about two marriages (*He and She* and *A Madman's Defence*, which relate to his marriage with Siri von Essen, and the 'The Quarantine Master's Second Story' (ultimately *The Cloister*) depicting his relationship with Frida Uhl), about his religious conversion (*Inferno* and *Legends*) and about the single life that he was anticipating at the end of his third marriage (*Alone*). Together with his letters and his *Occult Diary* this sequence of works constitutes the body of writings which he identified on several occasions as forming his autobiographical *œuvre*.[1]

For more than a quarter of a century Strindberg was engaged with questions concerning self-representation. He published several versions of his own story seen from different points of view (matrimonial, theological, political, etc.), rather than one singular and authoritative version. The many revaluations and supplements prevent the single text from being a closed and complete work of art. And by claiming in his 1909 preface that 'the author was not finished in 1886; maybe he did not even begin until then and thus, being but a fragment, the present book is only of secondary interest', Strindberg reduced the earliest works in the series to mere drafts. At the same time, he contested the self-identity of the subject by stressing his discontinuity with his former ego:

> The person of the author is just as strange to me as he is to the Reader – and just as disagreeable. As he no longer exists, I feel no complicity, and since I took part in killing him off (1898), I think I am right to consider this bygone time atoned for and deleted from The Great Book.
>
> October 1909. The Author (of *Gustav Vasa*, *The Dreamplay*, *The Last Knight*, and others) (*SV*21, p. 267)

Strindberg's autobiographical project is an early manifestation of what Anthony Giddens has depicted as a late modern condition: that identity is maintained by permanently revised life (hi)stories.[2] The delegitimation of the authority of tradition made autobiography useful for a subject forced to define its own identity and negotiate its place in social communities.

Modernity is the horizon of Strindberg's written self-representation. On the first pages of *The Son of a Servant*, the still anonymous central character is inscribed in a dynamic cultural history, where everything is in transition:

> The 1840s had come to an end. Having won in the revolution of 1792 some of the rights of man, the third estate had been reminded that fourth and fifth estates were also wanting to get ahead ... After forty-eight years of convulsions, the enlightened despot Oscar I took charge of the movement. Recognising that evolution was irresistible, he decided that he might as well receive credit for carrying out the reforms ... Society is still based on classes ... which hold each other in check ... Consequently, the house that stood near Clara Churchyard was in the early 1850s still a rather democratic familistery ... Three flights up ... the son of the wholesale dealer and a housemaid awoke and grew conscious of himself. (*SV*20, pp. 9–10)

At the beginning of the new century, in *Alone*, Strindberg generalized this impermanence into an ontological condition: 'But there has to be movement and travelling, uprooting, shaking, renewal, turning inside out, it seems. I, who have never done anything but move on and travel, regained a sense of my roving life, which I condensed in a poem called "Ahasverus"' (*SV*52, p. 43). Uprooting is the emblem of modernity: a loss of place and local community, the destabilization of existential certainty as well as traditional schemes of understanding.

The experience of modernity affects the way this roving subject is conceived. Strindberg makes it obvious that autobiography is based on a modern subject, but not necessarily on early modern notions of solid character and autonomy. In *The Son of a Servant* he dissolves the 'I' into a 'multiplicity of reflections, a complex of instincts, desires, some of them repressed, others unrestrained' (*SV*20, p. 167) and concludes that the self is 'a motley confusion without body, which ... has no more reality than the rainbow' (*SV*21, p. 214). In Strindberg's autobiographies forms of subjectivity, which have in late modernity become generalized, were still precarious.

The speaking subjects are labile and driven by uncontrollable desires. In *A Madman's Defence* Axel's discourse has more in common with the hystericized women he is up against than with the patriarch he wishes to be. Equally, the panic insistence on the principle of individuation ('To strive for the preservation of my Ego in the teeth of all the influences that a domineering sect or party may impose upon me, that is my duty', *SV*37, p. 126; *Inf*, p. 169) demonstrates above all a lack of self-sufficient sovereignty. The problem is precisely that Strindberg's characters cannot maintain a distance from their surroundings. They are never closed and complete. Strong bodily metaphors describe their mental permeability. They fear influence as a sort of infection, but they also see separation, like the impending divorce in *A Madman's Defence*, as an amputation. Often they experience mental boundary states such as fury, jealousy or paranoia. The subject, around which autobiography revolves, could no longer be taken for granted.

Autobiography as existential and artistic revival

Strindberg's reason for telling the story of his life was not, of course, to update concepts of character. He launched his autobiographical project because he was stuck. In 1886 he was living in exile, having just been tried for blasphemy following publication of the collection of short stories, *Getting Married*. He won the case, but his literary room for manoeuvre was severely reduced. His left-wing friends criticized his views on feminism; his marriage was unhappy; and he had reached an artistic dead-end. His sarcastic remarks about the 'literature of construction' throughout the mid-1880s indicate that he was tired of fiction, particularly the kind of satirical or utopian criticism of society he had made his hallmark in *The New Kingdom*, *Getting Married* and *Utopias in Reality*.

His response to this crisis was a pause in the writing of fiction. Instead he ventured into two complementary genres: an ethnological travel book (*Among French Peasants*) and autobiography. *Among French Peasants* is subtitled 'Subjective Travelogues' while *The Son of a Servant* is narrated in an emphatically objectifying form. In a clinical third-person discourse, Johan, the main character, is portrayed as if he were just as foreign as a French peasant. An ordinary Swedish childhood is defamiliarized into a piece of ethnographica: a collection of strange rites from a remote culture, as when the church is called 'the pagoda' (*SV*21, p. 100).

This distance allows Strindberg to write off his past. By a remarkable sort of conversion, *The Son of a Servant* performs a change of existential course. Johan learns to abandon his faith in God and woman, and he also comes to mistrust such modern great narratives as the idea of historical progress. What makes life narratable is exactly its detachment from communities and shared beliefs. And subsequently, new crises lead to new autobiographical revisions of the past. *A Madman's Defence* is provoked by matrimonial complications, while *Inferno* is written not about Strindberg's most famous self-transformation, but is that transformation itself.

Together with the new subject a new text is created. The autobiographical endeavour was also an attempt to break ground by exploring new literary forms. Strindberg called *The Son of a Servant* an 'attempt at the literature of the future' (*SV*20, p. 373), one written in 'an extraordinary novelistic form' (*ASB*5, p. 306). By the use of the third person, he fictionalized the autobiographical subject and thus contested the identity between author, narrator and protagonist which Philippe Lejeune made the distinctive feature of autobiography.[3] The protagonist is called neither 'I' nor 'August' but 'Johan': a Christian name that Strindberg did not use. Throughout his autobiographical prose, from the novelistic anti-hero Axel who, in *A Madman's Defence*, repeats intimate details of Strindberg's life, to the anonymous 'I' of *Alone* who bears only a vague resemblance to the author, he played with names and identities. In 1909 he suggested that he might have 'experimented with points of view or, embodied in different personalities, polymerised himself' (*SV*20, p. 377).

Strindberg's experiments with two kinds of naturalism (*Among French Peasants* is descriptive and full of empirical facts while *The Son of a Servant* is based on advanced psychology) made an artistic breakthrough possible. During the next years he created several major works such as *The Father* and *Miss Julie*, and even achieved some popular success with a combination of naturalist illusion, psychology and the depiction of rural life in *The People of Hemsö*.

In the 1890s this pattern was repeated. *Inferno* once again fused conversion and literary reversal: it introduced a mystical world view, and simultaneously it departed from naturalism so demonstratively that scholarship still identifies Strindberg's 'post-Inferno' works as a specific grouping. Acts of self-portraiture, in short, opened the two most important phases of Strindberg's writings. The autobiographical texts are, however, more than mere catalysts for his literary process of change. They are major works in their own right. In their own textual movement, they enact a movement from realism to modernism. It can be traced as an escalating destabilization of realist forms of representation.

An aesthetics of destabilization

One of the qualities of Strindberg's autobiographical prose is an unpredictable versatility, by which it not only undermines its own ideological petrifactions (for example, the recurrent misogyny), but also avoids what Adorno called 'false reconciliation'. The connection between the singular and the universal, part and whole, is always precarious. A central theme in nineteenth-century autobiography is the relationship between the individual and society. Johan's social contexts appear as inhuman power systems: 'Religion had corrupted him, for it had educated him for heaven instead of earth, family had ruined him ... and school had prepared him for university instead of for life' (*SV*20, p. 164). Crushed between institutions, Johan is unfit for society, but the opposite is also the case. Instead of integrating with Swedish class society, he becomes its judge: a rebel and a reformer. A decade later the pattern is repeated. Now the individual relates to a religious rather than a social order. The 'I' of *Inferno* has to go through infernal sufferings before he confesses his sins (atheism, an alchemist rivalry with God and pride) and gains new faith. This development does not, however, remain uncontested. The book hovers between repentance, doubt and regular heresy. The metaphysical powers are no more trustworthy authorities than were the leaders of the established Sweden. In a gnostic myth, God is portrayed as the demiurge, who created the world as a bad joke. Instead of an omniscient divine unity, the 'I' in *Legends* meets multiples of politicizing and corrupt powers: 'Sometimes it seems as if Providence has been badly informed by its satraps ... and that its prefects and under-prefects are guilty of embezzlement, of forgery and false informing' (*SV*38, p. 256).

The reluctance towards larger wholes does not only include social or religious communities, authorities and ideologies. It also manifests itself textually as a resistance to closure. In a self-critical movement the autobiographical works subvert the conventions that they use to transform life into an intelligible whole. Strindberg surely worked hard to establish stable patterns of meaning. The repetitive writing of autobiography is in itself indicative of his efforts to construct readability and coherence. But simultaneously he disavowed the means of representation, which he could not avoid using if his experiences were not to remain incommunicable.

To avoid being trapped in a genre, Strindberg oscillated between putting forward and withdrawing invitations to autobiographical readings. He explicitly insisted that the public should not know whether the letters published in *He and She* were 'documents or mystification' (*ASB*6, p. 74).[4] This infidelity to genre is part of a centrifugal, self-negating turn in Strindberg's texts. Like Rousseau, he displays an aggressive 'anxiety over being "fixed" in a narrative as well as existential sense'.[5] In parallel with the fear of absorption in social or religious groups, he stresses his own singularity against other people's definitions and against the shared means of understanding.

A good example is narrative, which in *The Son of a Servant* functions not only as a compositional device but also as a way of thinking. The paradigm of understanding is, as so often in the nineteenth century, historical.[6] The subtitle 'The History of the Evolution of a Human Soul' regards Johan as the product of his own history, which is specified as a series of determinations arising from 'heredity, upbringing, temperament ... influenced by the external events and intellectual currents of the historical epoch' (SV21, p. 214). The unity of this frame of reference is, however, challenged by the introduction of another master plot resting on idealist ideas of entelechy. An immanent finality is assumed when Johan's poetical talents are finally recognized and explained: 'He had finally found his destination, his role in life' (SV20, p. 261).

The wavering between naturalist determinism and idealist finality may undermine the singular plot, but not plot as such. More aggravating is the text's own denunciation of the philosophy of history. History, it is proposed, is nothing but a 'capricious hotchpotch'. Instead of an 'evolution towards reason and human happiness', Johan finds a jumble of change, repetition and unorganized randomness (SV21, pp. 138, 188). In short, history is without a plot. It lacks narrative coherence. As Paul Jay has pointed out, the crises and methodological choices of history writing also affect autobiography.[7] If life is a random series of circular movements, an evolutionary history of the soul would be impossible. Even though Strindberg does not draw these consequences, his historiographical objections affect his own narrative, especially because they support its reluctance to conclude.

The Son of a Servant thus rejects a final summary of the life story told. It is worth noting that the desire for a synthesis is invoked by Strindberg's own narrative. Its first part concludes with a chapter entitled 'Character and Destiny', and later on it tries to define 'the key to his personality and to his writings' (SV21, p. 111). But before it ends with an open reference to a future sequel, it has emphatically turned down our expectations of a conclusion:

> But the result, the summing up, they ask? Where is the truth that he was looking for? It lies here and there in the thousand printed pages, seek them, collect them, and see if they can be summarised ... And do not forget that truth cannot be found, since, like everything else, it is in constant evolution.   (SV21, p. 215)

Meaning lies disseminated across the book, or is postponed to a future supplement. In the 1909 preface, the whole work is reduced to mere 'raw material. If you want to see the result, take up and read *A Blue Book*, which is the Synthesis of my life' (SV20, p. 377). In the sequence of autobiographical works, this resistance to closure is repeated. *A Madman's Defence* questions beginnings, endings and even the empirical reality of central events. When the book is finished, Axel still lacks proof of Maria's adultery. And lacking a conclusion, he is placed in 'an endless hell' (SV25, p. 605). In *Inferno* the protagonist condenses his experience into 'a single word' (SV37, p. 284; *Inf*, p. 256), but soon the unity found is dissolved into objections so manifold that his conversion becomes dubious. In the epilogue new supplements reverse the attempts to conclude.

The allergy to closure is paralleled by a decentring of narrative. Strindberg's prose is organized around scenes charged with strong affective energy. Depictions of Johan as a victim (of institutions, family, unreliable relations, etc.) abound. Traumatic points are repeated, and so are the words describing them, allowing pleonastic aggregations of synonyms to break narrative balance and progression. When Johan draws back 'hurt, humiliated, cast down, passed by, and overlooked', he is not the only one who has been 'cut loose from his surroundings' (*SV*20, p. 45). Textual elements are also detached from their context and foregrounded to the detriment of the unity of the story. Similarly, in *Inferno* epic coherence is punctured by questions and exclamations and fragmented by stand-alone paragraphs of merely a few lines, culminating in the use of the discontinuous diary form.

The tribulations of narrative here serve as just one example of the destabilization caused by a revisionist treatment of the frames of reference used. In *A Madman's Defence* similar effects are achieved by the reversibility of central notions. Defence turns into accusation, which, however, turns back on Axel, who seems just as gossipy and inconsistent as his wife Maria. By mixing science, magic and madness he emasculates his own authoritarian discourse.

Such self-negating movements are pervasive in the major autobiographical works. With *A Madman's Defence* instability becomes so dominant that it challenges the readability of the text and releases a crisis in representation which is a motor in Strindberg's shift from realism to modernism.

Beyond the boundaries of realist representation

The Son of a Servant, He and She and *A Madman's Defence* all sought to expand the boundaries of realist representation. Strindberg's realism is not a perfect illusion, but rather a perforation of pure fiction. In a mongrel prose which combines fiction, essayist polemics, satire, self-representation and science, he opened literature to other discourses. Here it is worth noting that Strindberg was familiar with the results, methods and terminology of several scientific fields, including history, psychology, biology and chemistry. Autobiography not only told a story; its loose form also allowed for an integration of conceptual discourses that would ruin the balance of the classical novel (and almost did so in Strindberg's late novel, *Black Banners*).

Referentiality characterizes most realism, but in Strindberg it is so excessive that it transgresses the accepted limits of literary representation. One instance is the presence of identifiable models. Living models are, of course, used in every autobiography that claims to tell the story of a real person. But even here the reader is confronted with facts of which he would rather remain ignorant. In *A Madman's Defence* Maria is drunk and vomits in the children's room. The book claims to be a novel, but Maria's resemblance to Strindberg's wife, Siri, is so conspicuous that referential readings of even controversial details such as the description of her defective genitals are inevitably disturbing. Just as disturbing as this intimacy is the demonstrative presence of the writing subject. One of the first reviews of *A Madman's Defence* concluded that Strindberg was 'no true realist' because he was always polemical and the 'least impartial, the most passionate, and the most subjective of all the Scandinavians'. Instead he was a master of 'cruel literature'.[8] Strindberg's narrators impose their opinions on their readers with such know-all vehemence that disinterested aesthetic distance and realist illusion cannot be maintained.

The impurity of Strindberg's prose contested illusion, but not realism as such. Decisive for the movement beyond realism is an acceleration of instability into an epistemological crisis. The crisis manifests itself in escalating difficulties with the interpretation of experience. By and large *The Son of a Servant* succeeded in revising an image of life that had become uncertain. While it neither doubted the authority nor the mental health of the narrator, *A Madman's Defence* does so by its very title. Axel's discourse is invaded by jealousy, revengefulness and paranoia. Emblematic of his disorientation is the trouble he has in understanding woman. Traditional oppositions collapse, women dress in men's clothes, play billiards and piss in gateways (*SV*25, p. 486). They are made the incarnation of deviant forces disturbing the social, sexual and discursive orders. Such calamities continue in *Inferno* where the protagonist drifts in fields of forces which dissolve solid substance and penetrate bodies and walls. The confrontation with undefined opponents and with a series of paranormal events releases sheer horror. It also generates a desire for understanding. Eventually the incidents are interpreted as the intervention of an invisible hand belonging to 'the Powers' (even the metaphysical centre is multiplied and indeterminate). The problem is, however, that the handwriting is unreadable, just as its origin remains invisible and thus beyond realist representation. When the narrator proclaims 'the unanswered question, the doubt, the uncertainty, the mystery' his hell (*SV*37, p. 244; *Inf*, p. 233), we are inclined to agree. For the reader is not granted any more stable knowledge than the protagonist.

The conditions of knowledge are eagerly discussed in *A Madman's Defence*, *Inferno* and *Legends*. Questions, hypotheses and objections put forward at a breathless pace all bear witness to an epistemological insecurity. The distrust in the available means of representation even includes the author's own medium: language.[9] To a remarkable degree, words are often described as inaccurate, unreliable or uncontrollable. The hero of *Inferno* is not only exposed to strange kinds of irradiation; he also moves through a shower of opaque signs. In *A Madman's Defence*, jealousy makes Axel focus on the promiscuity of language. In vain he tries to control the proliferation of rumours concerning his marriage. In a significant passage he links his loss of property rights to his books, his children, and his biography:

> I see my children in the hands of a stepfather or the clutches of a 'stepmother' who would grow fat on the proceeds of my 'complete works', someone who would write the story of my life, seen through the eyes of a hermaphrodite ...
>
> (SV25, p. 514)

The entire book thus becomes a kind of linguistic hygiene: an attempt to cleanse and control Axel's (and August's) public image. In *Alone*, finally, the problem is formalized. The first chapter describes how language creates incongruence, distance, and difference: 'we uttered clichés ... but eyes did not accompany the word, and the smiles did not correspond to the eyes'. Words are detached from feelings and referents. Their meaning is constantly displaced: 'each of us had added new meanings to the words, given new values to old ideas'. The result is 'a Babylonian confusion', pauses and finally, silence (SV52, pp. 10–13). A central endeavour in literary modernism is exactly to rethink the relations between world, perception, language and literature in the light of what is conceived as a crisis in representation.[10]

Strindberg stresses the inadequacy of the given means of representation, not the impossibility of representation as such. He moves beyond realism by experiments with new forms of representation. Narrative, for example, is rivalled by other compositional devices. Johan was often treated as an *exemplum* demonstrating a general sociological, political or psychological state of affairs. Narrative thus became an anecdotal illustration of a didactic discourse conveying the opinions of the author. *Inferno* similarly suggests that the protagonist is meant to serve as 'a sign and an example for the betterment of others' (SV37, p. 12; *Inf*, p. 272). He is, at least momentarily, an everyman demonstrating the metaphysical order of the world. To this end Strindberg's post-*Inferno* prose introduces non-narrative allegorical or thematic structures. The first chapters of *Legends* provide a quasi-systematic description of mystical signs of the times, and *Alone* is a meditation on iterative aspects of a contemplative solitary life. Temporal progression and linearity are now, as in the Chamber Plays, replaced by simultaneity and spatial divisions, as in interior experience or street life.

The experimental character of Strindberg's undertaking makes him a participant in the process of modernization, not its victim. The crisis of language and representation was real and shared by many turn-of-the-century intellectuals and artists. But it was also a component in a calculated reorientation. Strindberg actively tried to invalidate tradition by disturbing the order of representation and describing the world as strange. To this purpose he sought out cultural, mental and literary borders. Broken in body and mind, and living down and out in Paris, the narrator of *Inferno* nevertheless tries to revolutionize literature and science and revise the world order. He makes major (al)chemical discoveries, and like Jacob he wrestles with unknown powers, maybe even with God. His solitude is self-inflicted; he is an avant-gardist cut loose from his surroundings exploring 'another world where no one could follow me' (*SV*37, p. 32; *Inf*, p. 115).

Inferno is a literary version of this new world. And so are *To Damascus, A Dream Play* and *The Ghost Sonata*, the visionary dramas that follow. Strindberg often dreamt of a restoration of the Christian middle ages, as in *Legends*, but he ended up in modernism. 'It is not a reactionary phase that awaits us, nor is it a return to what has already run its course; it is an advance towards something new' (*SV*37, p. 282; *Inf*, p. 254). Strindberg's experiments with literary self-representation constitute a decisive part of this advance towards something new.

NOTES

1. See for example the letters to Gustaf af Geijerstam, 2 November 1898, Emil Schering, 13 June 1904, and Karl Otto Bonnier, 1 July 1904. But Strindberg's autobigraphical enterprise is by no means restricted to these works. He experimented with photographic self-portraits (see Linda Haverty Rugg, *Picturing Ourselves: Photography and Autobiography* (Chicago: University of Chicago Press, 1997)), and in many of his writings he drew no clear distinction between fiction and life history. The textual qualities of Strindberg's autobiographical writings are discussed by Michael Robinson, *Strindberg and Autobiography: Writing and Reading a Life* (Norwich: Norvik Press, 1986), Wolfgang Behschnitt, *Die Autorfigur. Autobiographischer Aspekt und Konstruktion des Autors im Werk August Strindbergs* (Basel: Schwabe & Co., 1999) and Per Stounbjerg, *Uro og urenhed. Studier i Strindbergs selvbiografiske prosa* (Århus: Aarhus Universitetsforlag, 2005).
2. Anthony Giddens, *Modernity and Self-Identity: Self and Society in the Late Modern Age* (Cambridge: Polity Press 1991).
3. Philippe Lejeune, *Le pacte autobiographique* (Paris: Éditions du Seuil, 1975).
4. The first text in *He and She*, a letter instructing its addressees how to read, reinforces the doubt: 'Read it anyway as an ordinary story or as the idea for a novel, or as an apology, or as a will, or as anything' (*SV*22, p. 8). The keyword is 'as': the texts are meant to permit several readings, and they do not inhabit genre as a stable property.
5. Louis A. Renza, 'The Veto of the Imagination: a Theory of Autobiography', in James Olney, ed., *Autobiography: Essays Theoretical and Critical* (Princeton: Princeton University Press, 1980), pp. 268–95 (289).
6. Cf. Michel Foucault, *The Order of Things: an Archaeology of the Human Sciences* (New York: Vintage Books, 1973), pp. 217f.

7. Paul Jay, *Being in the Text: Self-Representation from Wordsworth to Roland Barthes* (Ithaca: Cornell University Press, 1984), pp. 108–10.

8. G. Valbert, 'M. Auguste Strindberg et la Confession d'un fou', *Revue des deux mondes*, 1 November 1893, pp. 213–24 (217).

9. See in particular the discussion of Strindberg's linguistic scepticism in Robinson, *Strindberg and Autobiography*, pp. 47–83.

10. Strindberg only overcomes the crisis by displacing epistemological problems to ontological conditions. In *The Cloister* and especially *Alone* an acquiescence to contingency and variability moves the focus from the difficulties of the subject of knowledge to the order of the world. In 1907 the old sage of *A Blue Book* found 'one constant among all the variables ...: the instability of life, the transitoriness and changeability of everything' (*SV65*, p. 175). This 'solution' to the crisis certainly does not save realism; it rather ontologizes a modernist aesthetics of instability.

5

Miss Julie: naturalism, 'The Battle of the Brains' and sexual desire

> My hair ought really have turned white after these most recent experiences, but it hasn't done so yet. To be continually tormented by uncertainty has made me insensible to the reality of life, however horrible it is! An interest in the psychological aspects also sustains me – most remarkable of all, the hypnotic state in which sexual desire places a man, so that he neither hears nor sees – and woman's vast talent for simulation, an incredible talent. An unaroused male would spot her gigantic effrontery, stupid plotting, and foolish attempts at concealing things right away!
>
> (*SL*, p. 244)

Though authors often use their lives as a source for their fiction, few writers have blended fact, research and fiction as effectively as August Strindberg. *Miss Julie* typifies Strindberg's creative energy and the close relation between what he wrote and what he lived. The play has been one of his most widely read and performed works, translated into numerous languages and performed on stage, radio, television and film. Touching on some of the most complex and controversial topics in Western literature, the play's influence can be seen in the works of authors ranging from Ibsen to Chekhov, O'Neill and Genet.

Public responses to *Miss Julie* have always been complicated; its shocking subject matter and dialogue made it difficult to stage in its own time, though these elements surprise the modern reader less. Yet the play confronts issues that are as current now as they were when the play was written: class conflict, gender stereotypes and a degree of sexuality that ranges from the seductive to the sadomasochistic. A lower-class servant and a nobleman's daughter entice each other into an isolated sexual encounter; afterwards their conversation and emotions range from almost affectionate recrimination to bitter hostility and finally despair. Facing the consequences of their act, and the possibility that they will be tempted again, they realize what they have done affects not only the other servants but the father and the family name. The resolution is almost as controversial as the play itself, and the entire work derives from Strindberg's life and times with exceptional immediacy.

While Strindberg's writing always reflects the cultural and social environment around him, in 1887 he was in the throes of a painful and complicated divorce, one that only he could have orchestrated as he did. He regularly accused his wife, Siri von Essen, of having affairs with men and with women, and he wrote to various colleagues and friends to try to discover who her lovers actually were (*SL*, pp. 238, 271). When the couple finally began divorce proceedings, however, they apparently continued occasional sexual interaction and, indeed, even when he was proclaiming her guilt in public Strindberg was concerned about the well-being of Siri and their two children should he die (*SL*, p. 254).

During the painful and emotionally disturbed years of 1887–9, Strindberg wrote frenetically, producing essays, plays, novels and short stories, all the while reading an extraordinary range of contemporary writing. He had long admired the Dane, Jens Peder Jacobsen (1847–1885), who, besides translating two of Darwin's major works and introducing his ideas into Scandinavia, wrote two powerful if pessimistic novels in the tradition of Zola's naturalism. More important to Strindberg than Jacobsen, however, was Georg Brandes (1842–1927). Brandes led the so-called modern breakthrough in Scandinavian literature with his five-volume *Main Currents in 19th Century Literature* (1872–5). He emphasized 'optimistic individualism' and called for Scandinavian authors to become involved in current public debates. In 1888 Brandes's lectures, titled 'Friedrich Nietzsche: a Treatise on Aristocratic Individualism', presented Nietzsche's work to the European public; at the same time, Brandes introduced Nietzsche to Strindberg and the two men corresponded until Nietzsche's lapse into madness.[1]

Within this complex intellectual environment, Strindberg chose to identify himself as a 'naturalist'. When he mailed the manuscript of *Miss Julie* to his publisher he called it 'the first Naturalistic Tragedy in Swedish Drama', and he subtitled the play a 'Naturalistic Tragedy' (*SL*, p. 280). But, as Törnqvist and Jacobs point out: 'Strindberg's conception of naturalism floats somewhere between the poles represented by Brandes and Zola, and his assertive use of the term [naturalistic] here was doubtless prompted by Zola's criticisms of *The Father*' (*SMJ*, p. 17). Zola had admired Strindberg's *The Father* though he thought the characters needed more detail, but his comments were based on Strindberg's French translation which, as Gunnar Ollen points out, was less precise than the original Swedish (*SV27*, p. 290). Evert Sprinchorn argues that Zola was one of the two people that Strindberg most wanted to please.[2] For Zola naturalism in literature meant an attempt at a scientific or objective representation requiring meticulous detail of description and based on the assumption that man was a product of environment and heredity. Zola's theories involved what we would think of now as naïve mixtures of behaviouralism and evolutionism derived from thinkers such as Hippolyte Taine (1828–1893) and Claude Bernard (1813–1878) with Auguste Comte (1798–1857) figuring in the background.

Strindberg was also studying a range of psychologically oriented authors, such as Jean-Martin Charcot (1825–1893), Théodule Ribot (1839–1916), Henry Maudsley (1835–1918) and Cesare Lombroso (1836–1909). Strindberg had written his naturalistic autobiography *The Son of a Servant* (1885–6) in the spirit of Taine and Brandes as well as Ribot. *The Father*, written just before *Miss Julie*, reflects Strindberg's marital conflicts, his fear of the loss of male authority in the family, as well as the Darwinian and naturalist intellectual and cultural influences around him. Another crucial aspect of this influence is his misogyny and growing sense of Nietzschean individualism. Misogyny was a common characteristic in this era, but Strindberg's became even more vitriolic after he faced a trial for heresy in 1884 after the publication of *Getting Married* (1884), a collection of short stories. Though he was acquitted, he blamed the conservative women's movement in Sweden, perhaps with some legitimacy, for the attack. If his marriage and public reputation were already in trouble, the trial made his difficulties even worse. Although Swedish liberals supported him strongly during the trial, Strindberg fled Sweden afterwards; he also left behind his earlier support of the working classes and, within two years, he was more aligned with Nietzsche's aristocratic individualism than socialism.

In a collection of works which are as much short stories as essays, called *Vivisections* (1887), Strindberg presented part of the intellectual framework that underlies *Miss Julie*. The notion of vivisection itself reflects Zola's famous image from the introduction to the novel *Thérèse Raquin*, in which he says: 'I simply apply to two living bodies the analytical method that surgeons apply to corpses'.[3] Though Strindberg had attempted this kind of self-autopsy analysis in his autobiography, he now applies it to others. The first three essays/stories reflect the transition he is making away from his earlier identification with the working classes, which had once constituted a central part of his creative and intellectual vision, to a new Nietzschean elitism. The third of these essays is 'The Battle of the Brains', a moderately fictionalized version of his trip to the French provinces with a young Swedish sociologist Gustaf Steffen (1864–1929). In it, the narrator and his young companion end up in an undeclared war of nerves and will. As Törnqvist and Jacobs describe it, '"The battle of the brains" is Strindberg's name for hypnosis in the waking state, and it generally results in what he called "psychic murder", which is the subtitle of his essay on Ibsen's *Rosmersholm*' (*SMJ*, p. 19).[4] 'The Battle of the Brains' opens with the following lines: 'Doctor Charcot accepts the possibility of suggestion only where hypnotised hysterics are concerned: Doctor Bernheim goes somewhat further and grants that anyone who can be hypnotised is susceptible to ideas from without' (*SE*, p. 25). This quotation not only reveals Strindberg's reading of some of the most popular if controversial scientists of his age, it establishes his belief in the potential effect of hypnosis on an individual, and it identifies one of the intellectual premises behind *Miss Julie*.

But the play has more than just a literary and biographical foundation in Strindberg's own life; it also reflects the suicide in July 1888 of the Swedish author Victoria Benedictsson (*SV*27, p. 297), as well as the story of a Miss Emma Rudbeck, a general's daughter, who supposedly seduced her servant (*SV*27, p. 299). I have argued elsewhere that the play continues Strindberg's obsession with the family and the role of the father.[5] All of these intellectual, psychological and financial circumstances combined with Strindberg's sexual insecurity and the frustrated sexual desire that he was particularly aware of during this period of his divorce.[6] This intricate interweaving of his life and his works was highly productive for him as an author, as Michael Robinson has persuasively argued, giving him the energy to experiment with several literary genres at once.[7]

Miss Julie is one of the most powerful works to be churned up in this intense fermentation of Strindberg's conscious and unconscious life. Törnqvist and Jacobs have given a variety of more detailed biographical sources for the origins of the play. These sources range from Strindberg's own childhood as the son of an upper-middle-class merchant and a serving woman to the circumstances in which he was living just prior to writing the play. Strindberg's own love affair with the upper-class Siri von Essen, who was married when their affair began, may well constitute another psychological part of the play's background. Indeed, in his autobiographical novel, *A Madman's Defence* (1888), written in French as a kind of testament, Strindberg describes the characters of his alter ego and wife in terms similar to those he uses for Jean and Julie (*MJoP*, p. xvi).

But in 1888 Strindberg and Siri, from whom he was soon to be divorced, had moved to a town on the outskirts of Copenhagen, and the house they rented and its neighbourhood provided two additional sources for the play. First, there was a bailiff living with a countess in her rundown estate; the neighbours assumed that they were lovers though they were in fact half-siblings, the young man a product of the father's relationship with a servant (*SMJ*, p. 20). Another source was Strindberg's own brief and casual affair with the bailiff's seventeen-year-old sister. This affair led to an accusation of child molestation, a trial and a good deal of bad publicity and embarrassment for Strindberg, before the girl, who was not legally under age, admitted that she had willingly participated (*SMJ*, pp. 22–3). Strindberg turned all these events into several different literary works, but for *Miss Julie* the combination of these various class conflicts based on sexual relationships provided him with more than enough material for his drama. Perhaps the suicide of Victoria

Benedictsson was one of the most crucial background events, since it concerned writers closely connected with Strindberg's intellectual and cultural life. The essence of the play, however, derives from an entire psychological creative structure unfolding in Strindberg's writing at the time. Yet its emotional impact may well come from Strindberg's identification with his main character: 'But Miss Julie is much more than just a "conglomerate .... snatches from books and newspapers, bits of other people". In many ways she is really one of Strindberg's most revealing self-portraits' (*SMJ*, p. 25). It is important to note, however, that Strindberg identified with both of his main characters; thus, their battle offers an insight into the struggle within himself between his own sense of a lower- and upper-class split identity.

Equally important to the character and the plot is the play's structure. Strindberg wanted to revolutionize theatre. The polemical 'Preface' makes it clear that Strindberg is taking up the assumptions made by Zola and others regarding the modern drama in Europe. It is dying and needs to be changed. The preface was written after the play and it offers a fascinating, if often offensive and irritating, piece for academic reading and research. However, it must be read as a counterpoint to the actual play, an author's attempt to impose a reading on the play as well as to explain the changes that he hoped to accomplish in theatre itself. Strindberg's combative intentions are clear from the opening paragraph in which he begins by arguing that the theatre has served as a Bible for the poor as well as a kind of forum for mass hypnosis:

> That is why the theatre has always been an elementary school for the young, the semi-educated, and women, who still retain the primitive capacity for deceiving themselves or for letting themselves be deceived, that is, for succumbing to illusions and to the hypnotic suggestions of the authors.   (*MJoP*, p. 56)

Strindberg claims to have taken the play's plot from a real incident and then continues, always in polemical prose, to argue for the complexity of his play and the multiplicity of motives that shape the characters' actions. To demonstrate how new and original his work is, he explains how he has motivated his protagonist, and, indeed, emphasizes the hereditary, biological and environmental circumstances that shape her behaviour. But he adds not only what one might call the Darwinian context, but even more modern psychological conditions:

> I have motivated Miss Julie's tragic fate with an abundance of circumstances: her mother's 'bad' basic instincts; her father's improper bringing up of the girl; her own nature and the influence her fiancé's suggestions had on her weak, degenerate brain; also, and more immediately: the festive atmosphere of Midsummer Night; her father's absence; her period, her preoccupation

with animals; the intoxicating effect of the dance; the light summer night; the powerful aphrodisiac influence of the flowers; and finally chance that drives these two people together in a room apart, plus the boldness of the aroused man. (*MJoP*, p. 58)

This paragraph is a revolutionary statement in the history of drama. However irritating it is in terms of its obvious sexism and its dubious biological assumptions, it is more explicit and challenging than most nineteenth-century theatre. And one of its primary themes is the hypnotic ambiance of desire that drives Jean and Julie into a bedroom. Almost surprisingly, Strindberg then argues for the 'characterlessness' of his characters, but by this he means they are not limited to a narrow identity; they are more modern, more complex products of evolution and environment.[8] In his attempt to explain both his use of hypnotic suggestion and his evolutionary perspective, Strindberg's misogyny, which, it should be remembered, reflects not only Nietzsche but much of European patriarchal society, comes to the fore. 'Miss Julie is a modern character which does not mean that the man-hating half-woman has not existed in every age, just that she has now been discovered, has come out into the open and made herself heard' (*MJoP*, p. 60).

Though Strindberg makes such pejorative claims, the viewer of the actual play experiences little of this vitriolic perspective. A seduction and a battle take place between Jean and Julie, but as they themselves finally realize, they are more the victims of society, and of a hypnotic state of desire, than they are exemplars of social ills. The opening citation from his letters, with which I began this essay, describes this hypnotic state which Strindberg attributes to the male, but the play itself dramatizes how both male and female are in a heightened state of arousal which leads them into Jean's bedroom. Strindberg makes his argument against Miss Julie in the Preface more to establish his 'naturalist' credentials, and to express his occasional fury at women, than to describe the play.

Likewise, his description of Jean may define the character's early appearance, but not his final actions, and one assumes that, in this passage, Strindberg sees himself in this description of Jean:

He has been quick to learn, has finely developed senses (smell, taste, sight) and an eye for beauty. He has already come up in the world, and is strong enough not to be concerned about exploiting other people. He is already a stranger in his environment, which he despises as stages in a past he has put behind him, and which he fears and flees, because people there know his secrets, spy out his intentions, regard his rise with envy, and look forward to his fall with pleasure. Hence his divided, indecisive character, wavering between sympathy for those in high positions and hatred for those who occupy them. He calls himself an aristocrat and has learnt the secrets of good society, is polished on the surface but coarse underneath, and already wears a frock coat with style, although there is no guarantee that the body beneath it is clean.   (*MJoP*, p. 62)[9]

As Strindberg describes his characters for his audience, he defines them in terms of his own idealistic and persecuted perceptions at the time. However, the play itself succeeds in transcending these limits and it does so partially because of the success of his technical modifications. As a result of his experience of trying to create a little theatre and reading other contemporary dramas, the play is a long single act.[10] The dialogue is consciously broken and fragmented: 'I have avoided the symmetrical, mathematical artificiality of French dialogue and allowed my characters' brains to work irregularly as they do in real life' (*MJoP*, p. 63). Strindberg's goal then is to revolutionize drama both in terms of its subject matter and the technical details of presentation, including lighting, acting style and set.

The sexual subject matter is thrust upon the audience in the play's opening scene. First, the 'craziness' of Miss Julie implies a state of sexual aggressiveness attributed to her 'period' – a remarkable comment in a country still in the sway of its own version of Victorian morality. Second, the forced miscarriage of the thoroughbred dog Diana which was impregnated by the 'gatekeeper's mutt' (*MJoP*, p. 73) continues to develop the theme of a misplaced or animal sexuality. At the same time, the 'battle of the brains', the struggle for dominance, appears in Julie's failed effort to dominate her fiancé, who jumped over her phallically extended riding crop twice, but 'the third time, he snatched the whip out of her hand, broke it' and left (*MJoP*, p. 72). The themes of class conflict and the struggle for dominance in a surprisingly sexualized battle of the sexes is thus powerfully established; the play proceeds to enact and intertwine the themes, just as the two main characters gradually move towards their feared and desired interlocking in Jean's bedroom.

In 1972 Lennart Josephson pointed out the complexity in Strindberg's representation of the class conflict in *Miss Julie*; for Josephson, both Jean and Julie fall between standard upper-/lower-class divisions. Only the absent Count is a true aristocrat; Julie's heritage is mixed, but her sense of shame and doubt connect her more to her aristocratic heritage than her attempt at an elitist disdain and snobbery. Similarly, her suicide, assisted but not forced by Jean, makes her more the genteel if shattered woman that is far from the stereotype of a half-man, half-woman referred to in the Preface.[11]

Törnqvist and Jacobs identify three major themes in the play: class struggle, the battle of the sexes, and finally 'the question of guilt (or responsibility)' (*SMJ*, p. 83). The first two dominate the first half of the play, but they are permeated with the issue of sexuality itself. The appeal and clash of gender

3. Maria Bonnevie as Julie and Mikael Persbrandt as Jean in Thommy Berggren's staging of *Miss Julie*, Royal Dramatic Theatre, Stockholm, 2005.

and class are prominent from the opening dialogue between Jean and Julie. Julie appears on stage to entice Jean to dance with her. The reluctant but titillated Jean reveals his sophistication by speaking French and drinking wine rather than beer, but he also makes it known that he has slept with Kristin. This establishes not only flirtation but sexual intercourse itself as the underlying tension beneath their conversation, a tension already present in the opening scene between Kristin and Jean. Julie's entrance simply adds to the sexual ambiance when Julie orders Jean to kiss her foot. He responds, 'This can't go on, Miss Julie; someone might come in and see us' (*MJoP*, p. 78).

All of this takes place as the two characters seem both to enact and to question their own roles (*SMJ*, pp. 87–91). As Jean demonstrates his various talents, in different costumes, he is both aware of them and aware of their effect on others. Julie consciously and at first fearlessly moves back and forth between her self-proclaimed role of socializing with the servants and her role as mistress of the house. But their role-playing leads directly and inevitably to the action of intercourse which lies at the centre of the play and which was on Strindberg's mind. Robinson comments on the close connection between sex and creativity for Strindberg, and he identifies how the absence of sex affected Strindberg during the writing of *Miss Julie*:

> Sometimes casually, in the coarse vein of Flaubert or the Goncourts, at others drawing the kind of parallel between sexual and verbal ejaculation that Balzac espoused, writing is in any case frequently related to sexuality by Strindberg. 'I acknowledge that a woman's embrace resembles the joys of birth when a new thought is hatched [or] a beautiful image wells up', he concedes to Littmansson, 'but the unsatisfied sexual instinct and half-hunger transforms itself into mental power. (I have written my strongest pieces – *Miss Julie* and *Creditors* – in 30 days during enforced celibacy', *ASB*10, p. 130). As Asta Ekenvall has pointed out: 'For him sexual and mental production were closely related'.[12]

Ironically, there may even be a link between the sexual preoccupation of this play and Strindberg's hostility to women. The misogyny in his letters and in the preface that so embarrasses the modern reader can be related to his own statement written shortly after *Miss Julie*. 'Can you understand my misogyny? Which is only the reverse of a terrible desire for the other sex' (*SL*, p. 289).[13] Desire and frustration, then, serve as motivating factors in both the actual writing of *Miss Julie* and in its structure. Following in Zola's tracks, Strindberg in letters to Edvard Brandes and Hans Österling refers to the idea that depictions of the sexual act are just as legitimate as those of giving birth or dying. In this sense, *Miss Julie* was a conscious effort to challenge the public's conservative morality (*SV*27, p. 295). Strindberg's affair with the Hansen girl, and the publicity attached to it by the brother's accusations, may also have played a role in his willingness or need to give the topic a central place in the drama.

The play itself is loaded with symbolism that can be read in terms of sexual imagery that is consistently mixed with guilt and shame.[14] Julie dreams of being on top of a pillar that she cannot get down from; Jean wishes he could climb up a tree but cannot; he also tells her a story, supposedly of himself as a boy, when he excitedly explored an elegant outhouse on the estate and, to escape being discovered, had to exit through the toilet. The young Jean's plunge into the outhouse's sewage to escape being detected becomes a powerful image of how desire and humiliation are intimately connected.[15] This hints at the play's resolution: shameful desires result in being immersed in excrement or death.

Another example of Strindberg's symbolism is the mention of Julie's period at the beginning of the play; this develops a theme of blood that may be implicit in the dog's miscarriage and Julie's loss of virginity, and which becomes explicit when Jean chops off the head of Julie's siskin and, finally, when she takes the razor off stage to kill herself.

Julie's death, however, is closely linked to the ruptured family and the mixture of aristocratic and common blood from which she comes. While class and gender are obvious linchpins of this drama, the structure of the family is equally central, and that history is tied to sex. As Julie and Jean talk, the audience learns that Julie's mother, a commoner, tried to rebel against the gender and family norms of her era by taking over the man's role in the household. When the father resisted and tried to resume the paternal role, the mother took a lover who loaned them the money (really the mother's money) to rebuild after a mysterious fire. Julie's family, then, had been tainted long before Julie fell from her own perch, and the father's name that she is trying to save from dishonour was disgraced long ago. Yet even as the characters understand their own histories, they cannot escape their own sexual impulses, and these impulses, as in the mother's and the father's case, have always led to shame.

In 1985 Ingmar Bergman staged a celebrated production of this play which emphasized its eroticism (*SMJ*, pp. 175–9). Among other changes, Bergman inserted a second serving couple whose vulgar sexuality parallels Jean's and Julie's, and the dance scene reflects a 'cruel eroticism that runs beneath the surface of the play' (*SMJ*, p. 177). Mike Figgis in his 1999 film of the play combines the class conflict, sexuality and authority in a probing cinematic production. He dramatizes the constant preoccupation with repressed desire and its dangerous awakening that permeates both Jean and Julie. Jean warns Julie of the dangers of her flirtation with him, yet he keeps involving her in their mutual attraction. When he tells her the story of his youthful fantasy of love with the young Miss Julie he seems honest, but it is part of his seduction of her, just as her asking him to kiss her foot is a simultaneous demonstration of authority and arousal.

In the original play, the two characters go off stage when the servants invade the kitchen, but in the film they hide in the background and watch as the servants sing obscene songs and dance provocatively. Jean and Julie hide, pressed together in fear and desire. When the servants leave, Figgis has Jean remain standing caressing Julie as he slips between her legs. He is hypnotised by his own sexual desire and Julie accepts his action.

Once the intercourse is completed Strindberg's play moves quickly towards its conclusion. Critics have debated the legitimacy of Julie's suicide; for Sprinchorn, it is Julie's complexity that explains her suicide; she 'kills herself not because she is an aristocrat but because she is Julie'.[16] The shame that Julie would face, the fear of pregnancy, of later repetitions of intercourse, all drive her towards her death. Sexual desire and shame have served as the driving forces and structural momentum of the play, and they make the conclusion, Julie's suicide, logical and inevitable. Though covered in what might be called the filth of his lust, Jean can and will recover. He returns to his servant identity by answering the Count's call and fetching his boots. Figgis's film nicely dramatizes Jean's own hypnotic response to the Count's call on the speaking tube. Julie has nowhere to go. She asks for Jean's help, using the metaphor of the hypnotist, but at this point it is not so much a battle of the brains between Jean and Julie but rather a self-hypnosis using Jean's command as the trigger.

Hilton Als, in a recent review of a New York production of *Miss Julie*, says that Strindberg was 'among the first modern playwrights to examine the Gordian knot of family, class differences, and sexual desire' (*The New Yorker*, 30 May 2005). What is apparent, as Strindberg's play continues to be performed, is that by using his own life and desires he has plumbed the often dark depths of human relationships.

NOTES

1. Egil Törnqvist and Barry Jacobs, *Strindberg's Miss Julie: a Play and its Transpositions* (Norwich: Norvik Press, 1988), pp. 15–16. Further references to this valuable and extensive study of the play are henceforth included in parenthesis in the text as *SMJ*, followed by the page number.
2. In *Strindberg as Dramatist* (New Haven: Yale University Press, 1982), p. 26, Evert Sprinchorn suggests that Zola and Antoine, the great French theoretician and producer, were important influences on Strindberg. Sprinchorn has an insightful discussion of Strindberg's relation to Zola and others connected to naturalism.
3. *Thérèse Raquin*, trans. L. W. Tancock (Harmondsworth: Penguin Classics, 1962), pp. 22–3.

4. Sprinchorn describes 'Battle of the Brains' as 'an essay in experimental psychology in which the Darwinian idea of the struggle for existence and the Spencerian idea of the survival of the fittest were applied to the life of the mind': *Strindberg as Dramatist*, p. 26.

5. See Ross Shideler, *Questioning the Father: from Darwin to Zola, Ibsen, Strindberg, and Hardy* (Stanford, Calif.: Stanford University Press, 1999), pp. 114–18.

6. Strindberg's correspondence offers a surprising number of explicit references to his own desire for sex and the fact that he seems to have turned to masturbation regularly as a substitute when a woman was not available. See *SL*, pp. 238, 244 'reduced to masturbation'; p. 247 'can't live on masturbation'; p. 253 'We sometimes have to pretend to be chaste, naïve, ignorant, simply in order to copulate as we desire!'

7. See Michael Robinson, *Strindberg and Autobiography: Writing and Reading a Life* (Norwich: Norvik Press, 1986), pp. 72–3.

8. Törnqvist and Jacobs also discuss this notion of characterlessness and relate it to the modern concept of 'role psychology', p. 85.

9. Törnqvist and Jacobs suggest the character is a combination of Ludvig Hansen and Strindberg, p. 47.

10. Sprinchorn discusses the development of the play's original structure, *Strindberg as Dramatist*, pp. 36–7.

11. Josephson notes that Strindberg viewed Jean and Julie differently after he had written the play in Ulla-Britta Lagerroth and Göran Lindström, eds., *Perspektiv på Fröken Julie* (Stockholm: Raben och Sjögren, 1972), pp. 73, 81.

12. See *Strindberg and Autobiography*, p. 72.

13. One of Strindberg's most surprising letters written during this time is a remarkably detailed description of his decision to prove his virility by a visit to a brothel. Few things document more clearly his preoccupation with sex during this tumultuous period of his life: *SL*, p. 239.

14. Sprinchorn comments on Strindberg's effort 'to preserve the integrity of the symbolic prop or set against a growing tendency to obscure it': *Strindberg as Dramatist*, p. 29.

15. Sprinchorn draws a parallel between Jean's childhood entrapment in the outhouse and Julie's lack of escape from the servants' quarters: *Strindberg as Dramatist*, p. 39.

16. *Strindberg as Dramatist*, p. 40.

6

HANS-GÖRAN EKMAN

Strindberg and comedy

Introduction

If we are to believe Strindberg himself, the first play he ever wrote was a comedy. The circumstances were somewhat remarkable. After a failed spell as an actor in 1869, he tried to take his life via a dose of opium, but failed at that as well. Upon emerging from his opium dream (or so he claims in *The Son of a Servant*), he wrote this now-lost play. Only the title remains: *A Name-Day Gift*. Next (and considering only the dramas) we find several relatively unimportant historical plays, followed by the drama which should have been his breakthrough, *Master Olof* (1872–6) about a passionate idealist which, despite its author's ambition to follow in Shakespeare's footsteps by mixing high with low, is at a considerable remove from comedy. Nor was it as a writer of comedies that Strindberg wished to become known. He was on the whole somewhat sceptical of the genre. But it was easier to gain acceptance on the contemporary Swedish stage with comedies and, in addition, Strindberg thought that his first wife, Siri von Essen, would find them more congenial to her abilities as an actress. Hence, throughout his career, Strindberg wrote a number of plays that he designated 'comedies', including *The Secret of the Guild* (1880), *Playing with Fire* (1892) and *Crimes and Crimes* (1899).[1] The two last are among Strindberg's most frequently produced plays, and for that reason alone merit consideration here.

Taken together, these three comedies stem from different periods of Strindberg's life. The first represents the beginning of his career, the second is one of the last plays he wrote towards the end of his naturalist period, following his first divorce and shortly before the Inferno crisis, and *Crimes and Crimes* is one of the 'penitential plays' that he wrote after regaining his ability to write for the theatre in 1898. Hence collectively they enable us to see how Strindberg deals with one and the same genre at different stages of his life.

The Secret of the Guild

The Secret of the Guild represents Strindberg's first preserved attempt as a writer of comedies.[2] Certainly it is a play that he does not hesitate to designate a 'comedy'. Unlike in the case of *A Name-Day Gift*, the circumstances surrounding this play were more auspicious since Strindberg had just achieved his breakthrough as an author with the novel *The Red Room* (1879), and furthermore his wife was pregnant. *The Secret of the Guild* was thus the work of an unusually harmonious and triumphant author, a state of mind that might be thought an appropriate starting point for a comedy. But this need not be the case. In general, success did not sit well with Strindberg; he was far too quick to see the seeds of disaster in others' praise and, in his comedies, as in many of his other plays, the motif of hubris is a powerful presence. Indeed, the dominant position of this motif in Strindberg's plays helps elide the border between tragedy and comedy.

The Secret of the Guild is a history play which, given his concern for authenticity and period detail, was based on considerable research on Strindberg's part.[3] Its plot unfolds at the beginning of the fifteenth century when the construction of Uppsala Cathedral had long been underway yet had made little noticeable progress. Indeed, work on the cathedral appears to be cursed, and life at the construction site is steeped in frustration, despair and intrigue. In themselves, these matters are by no means an impossible starting point for a comedy (on the contrary, perhaps), but when Strindberg calls the play a comedy, it is hardly these aspects to which he is referring.

If what may be demanded of a comedy are, as a minimum, first, a happy ending and second, entertaining dialogue, then Strindberg, who had only recently produced brilliant satire and verbal wit in *The Red Room*, had little success in writing such dialogue in *The Secret of the Guild*. And where on occasion a comic note is heard, its tone anticipates both Chekhov and the theatre of the absurd as, for example, when the Cathedral Builder and Martin comment on life's lack of meaning.[4] In fact the Master Carver is characterized as having become 'feeble-minded and weak-eyed', and difficult to communicate with. This could be comic, an example of black comedy based on physical handicap perhaps, but in that case it is counterbalanced by the reply: 'Well, let's let him live in the peace of his ignorance and not disturb his final days' (*SV*11, p. 52). It has been pointed out that *The Secret of the Guild* in many ways adumbrates ideas that we encounter in Strindberg's dramas from after the Inferno crisis,[5] and such a reply foreshadows the frequently raised issue there about how far our senses serve as organs of knowledge, as in the Chamber Plays of 1907, not least in *Storm*.[6]

Strindberg has not created, or has not wished to create, witty dialogue of the kind associated with comedy, although twelve years later, in *Playing with Fire*, he excels in this respect. Instead, he has provided *The Secret of the Guild* with two aspects that justify the designation: (1) a court jester, or fool, who sets in motion something that is described as 'a prank'; (2) various authentic, archaic-sounding proverbs that are used as weapons in the verbal duels in which the play abounds. In the prank, the Jester gets to play various roles and in a dialogue with himself comment on the disastrous building project, thus provoking laughter among his listeners. Here he invokes the jester's privilege of speaking out where others do not dare. But the prank ends, and the comic gambit concludes, when he removes his fool's cap, saying 'let us speak seriously' (p. 73).

This is the first time Strindberg employs a jester, a figure of whom he was ultimately sceptical, describing him in the vivisection 'Soul Murder' (1887) as 'someone who made himself irresponsible by pretended folly' (*SE*, p. 71), and remarking of his role here in 1909: 'The sketch for my jester is one I made 30 years ago in *The Secret of the Guild*, where the Jester was given a personal history and is no mere Clown' (*SV*64, pp. 241–2). In fact the Jester in *The Secret of the Guild* wearies of his jokes and prefers 'serious' speech. He thus comes to speak on behalf of the author himself, who not infrequently allows a stage character to comment on, or request, a closer definition of the degree of seriousness in the dialogue in progress. This occurs even in tragedies such as *Miss Julie*, for example in the exchange:

JULIE:	Cheek!
JEAN:	Are you joking or serious?
JULIE:	Serious!
JEAN:	Then you were serious just now too. (*MJoP*, p. 81)[7]

The response to this request serves as clarification for both the figures on stage and the audience in the theatre. To ensure that emotions or jokes do not lead the listeners where the playwright does not wish them to go, certain occasions are used to take the temperature of the dialogue and adjust the degree of seriousness, if necessary.

The person who uses language in jest is dangerous, someone not easily pinned down. The ideal is to speak 'seriously', but then the witty comic dialogue will be lost. If we are to speak in jest, we should preferably wear the costume of the clown, Strindberg appears to be saying. This is naturally a precarious position for a writer of comedies. In Act 2, scene 9 of *The Secret of the Guild*, the players comment, yet again on a 'metadramatical' level, on the flighty tone of the dialogue, and then censure it. Thus the Judge: 'But I have no time to listen to jokes, these are serious matters' (p. 76). Next he declines an offer of a tankard of ale with the words: 'No thank you, Alderman, I don't drink, but I'll say something, promptly and sincerely'. This honesty and sobriety rather than the Jester's wit and ambiguity, is the norm in *The Secret of the Guild*, one that the Jester does not really challenge. Indeed, he is also a keen promoter of serious talk, an impression which is created when he removes the 'fool's cap' and then puts it on again. The theatre is suffused in illusion and ambiguity but, like Rousseau, Strindberg is a puritan at heart, and seeks to avoid such things. They are both cultural critics as well as linguistic pessimists, a pessimism that, in Strindberg's case, will culminate in the Chamber Plays of 1907. In *The Secret of the Guild*, meanwhile, the ending is given a religious twist: the sins of Jack's father, the Alderman, have come back to haunt him. He gains absolution through a woman who makes the sign of the cross over him, and thereafter we are shown the Jester 'breaking the whip, throwing the pieces across the floor, and wiping his eyes with his cap' (p. 146). The play thus adheres to the convention of comedy through its happy ending, even though it may be characterized as religiously austere rather than openly comical. The performer rids himself of the tools of his trade and the curtain falls.

Strindberg later savaged this play and claimed only to have written it to provide an excellent role for his wife. It ran for only six nights and, in 1884, when a new production was mooted, he displayed little enthusiasm, and suggested several radical changes: 'Cut, cut like hell ... The whole Jester business, all the proverb nonsense!' (*ASB*4, p. 306). In effect, he wanted to eliminate the very features that would justify the designation comedy. What remained of the play would merely have been a moralizing historical drama.

Playing with Fire

Playing with Fire is the one so-called comedy of Strindberg's that has been judged by posterity to best correspond with the genre. However, there is reason to question this view.[8]

When writing the play, he was using a formula outlined in his essay 'On Modern Drama and Modern Theatre' (1889) where he discusses traditional French comedy. There Strindberg rejects Victorien Sardou's 'pale character and worn out intrigues' while Molière's 'glorious vivisection' in *Le Tartuffe* is hailed as a model. He also finds something positive in the contemporary form known as *comédies rosses*, a genre used particularly by Henry Becque whose play, *La Nanette*, meets with Strindberg's complete approval. The basic tone of such comedies was sardonic with intrigues taken from 'the cynical world'.[9] Similarly, in *Playing with Fire*, the tone is cynical, but unattractively so since the moralist Strindberg is out to unmask this kind of cynicism.

The setting for *Playing with Fire* is a beach resort in summer where a young couple, Knut and Kerstin, are living on his parents' money. Kerstin is idle, while Knut devotes his time to some amateurish painting. A friend, Axel, joins the family, and an erotic current starts to flow between him and Kerstin. This is discovered by Knut, who declares himself willing to give up

Kerstin, provided that Axel marries her. Axel runs away. Although previously attracted to her, Knut now finds Kerstin's seductive tricks quite decadent, and has come to feel that the putrid atmosphere in the house emanates from her. When he flees, he does so, like Alceste in Molière's *Le Misanthrope*, to escape a morally corrupt atmosphere.

The ending is, therefore, hardly in keeping with traditional comedy, although it might have been so were it possible to overlook the fact that Axel is the truth-teller of the play. As it is, however, the fact that everything reverts to how matters were at the start of the play makes it more of a tragedy. As in *The Dance of Death*, the beginning is the end. The victor turns out to be the painter's wealthy father, a quarter of whose speeches consist of proverbs from *The Book of Psalms* and *Ecclesiastes*. Consequently, he has no individualized language, but merely serves up ready-made thoughts. He is also an accomplished schemer. He rose from the same roots as the *senex* of the classic era, and is also the trickster of the drama. For him, and nobody else, to emerge victorious is thus more tragic than comic.

But what of the tone of the remaining dialogue? This is often witty and entertaining, which explains the stage success of the play.[10] But it is necessary to observe that the conversation is conducted on different levels with different degrees of candour. The most sincere character is Axel, who emerges as a truth-teller, although he restrains himself for as long as possible. When he finally gives way and erupts with his truth-telling, matters almost run out of control, as when the Student lets fly at the corruption in the world and literally talks the Young Lady to death, in the final scene of *The Ghost Sonata*. It is consequently worth paying attention to the discrepancy between what is actually said, and the manner in which it is said. Take, for example, Kerstin's remark in the opening scene: 'Well, if I didn't know Knut as well as I do, and if I hadn't known that these artists are a peculiar kind of people, there would be times when I couldn't tell where I belong' (p. 222). 'If I didn't know': several lines in *Playing with Fire* begin in this manner, and their irony soon becomes evident: the character who speaks knows only too little of what she is talking about, which becomes highly entertaining to the audience once they understand this. The female characters are particularly ignorant; nevertheless, the Mother does express a dangerous truth without realizing that it is true:

MOTHER:	So, your friend returned again last night!
SON:	Your friend? He's Kerstin's friend! She's quite crazy about him! I thought they were going to kiss last night, when he arrived!
MOTHER:	Don't tease so, Knut, for the one who plays with fire ... (p. 220)

But Knut is not the only one who plays with fire, assuming that in fact Axel only comes close to kissing Kerstin. In this instance it is Knut who plays with fire by treating a possibly very explosive truth in such a teasing manner. His language is cynical and ambiguous. Moreover, without understanding how close to the truth she actually is, Kerstin says: 'You have such a horrid way of jesting, so it's impossible to know when you're being serious!' (p. 221). This is where we find the core of the comedy and Knut is boring further into this core when, in a moment of self-knowledge, he exclaims: 'Through assumed candour we tried to forestall the danger. To make fun of it.' What Knut actually does here is question what characterizes the very essence of the comedy: the jocular, ambiguous tone of the conversation. Hence, as well as giving the play a tragic conclusion, and by showing the consequences of frivolous and ambiguous speech, Strindberg is in effect doing something that we are quite unprepared for: he invites us to a comedy, but offers us a vivisection and an immanent criticism of comedy as a genre.

Crimes and Crimes

It is remarkable that Strindberg calls what was the fourth of his dramas after the Inferno crisis a 'comedy', a description that does not seem to correspond to the contents of the play. He includes ingredients that would seem impossible in a comedy, such as the death of a child and an autopsy. The memory of a botched termination is also recalled. These ingredients are more suited to tragedy, as is the development of the principal character, the dramatist Maurice. He experiences great professional success, is seized by hubris and severely punished. He also deserts two women, Jeanne, the mother of his dead child, Marion, and the unfortunate Henriette, in both cases seemingly with no sense of guilt. This might be acceptable as in some respect a 'happy' ending if we considered that even Jeanne had attempted to curtail his freedom. It is thus possible to imagine the two women as projections of a composite 'Woman' as in expressionist drama.

Strindberg's outlook after the Inferno crisis was religious and sometimes even Christian. The Christian view[11] is represented in *Crimes and Crimes* by, among others, the Abbé, and is already evident at the start of the drama which opens in a cemetery where a woman in black is moving between the gravestones which bear the inscription: 'O Crux ave! Spes unica' ('O Cross, Our Only Hope'). Gravestones such as these can still be found in the cemetery of Montparnasse in Paris, where the scene is set. This was also the inscription which Strindberg chose for his own wooden cross at Norra Begravningsplatsen in Stockholm.

Such a scene hardly raises expectations of comic banter or amusing misunderstandings of the kind on which comedy thrives. There are misunderstandings in this drama, but of the fateful kind, and the tone is often accusatory. That we are dealing with obedience and not play is emphasized by a seemingly unimportant detail at the beginning of the drama. Maurice's child is 'playing' in the cemetery with discarded flowers but is admonished by a Keeper and told to stop, since such behaviour is forbidden by the regulations. 'In that case', the Abbé remarks, 'we must obey' (SV40, p. 138).

'To play' or 'obey': this is the same alternative presented to Olaus Petri in the opening scene of *Master Olof*, where he was likewise confronted by a situation in which he was compelled to make an existential choice. Moreover, of relevance whenever Strindberg employs the word, is the fact that in nineteenth-century Swedish, 'play' (*leka*) also meant to 'create', to work as an artist. And of further relevance to the paratextual conditions of this play is the fact that Strindberg coupled *Crimes and Crimes* with the strongly moralizing fairy-tale play *Advent*, and published them together with the title *At a Higher Court*. In so doing, he drew attention to a religious and moral discussion that makes it even more difficult to understand why he should have called *Crimes and Crimes* a comedy.

The dialogue in *Crimes and Crimes* is more poignant and not as lighthearted as we occasionally encounter in *Secret of the Guild* or more frequently in *Playing with Fire*. 'Only a fire engulfing the whole world could erase my shame', exclaims Maurice (p. 230), and when Henriette observes that 'the world has not yet seen a faithful man' (p. 156), she has the same grand perspective as Maurice when he suggests that they show 'the world the kind of friendship that demands nothing' (p. 177). Likewise, in *Playing with Fire*, Axel, in a heated exchange with his daughter-in-law, says, 'let's show the world what honest people look like!' (SV33, p. 264). In all these examples, the world is the spectator and the difference between the comic and the pathetic is almost negligible.

However, the dialogue of *Crimes and Crimes* contains a multitude of reproaches and accusations. Jeanne suspects 'that there is something frightful in store for me' (p. 141) and at an early stage she talks to the Abbé about 'ending it' in the river if Maurice deserts her. There is a sadness about Jeanne, which emanates from something other than the spleen that characterizes the figures in *Playing with Fire*. And when she speaks of her suffering, she evokes a metaphysical dimension that is entirely absent from the earlier play where the characters toy with truths and flirt with one another out of pure boredom. This kind of 'playing' is elevated to a more serious level in *Crimes and Crimes* when the proprietress of the *crémerie*, Mme Catherine, observes of Maurice that he 'toys with sin'. Indeed, had Strindberg wished to establish an intertextual relationship with *Playing with Fire*, he might well have called the play *Toying with Sin*.

Much care is taken over what is said in *Crimes and Crimes* – and yet Maurice's downfall is caused by carelessly spoken words. He gives the impression of having wished his own daughter dead, and thus initiates the gossip that ultimately leads to his terrifying night in custody. But later, when he again meets up with Jeanne in the cemetery, where she has been waiting for him for hours, and pleads with her to forgive him, he insists that she does so out loud. However, she offers 'to whisper it in your ear!' (p. 143), and finally kisses him instead. This scene is the creation of a dramatist with the eye of a director. It shows a certain respect for language, but also a distrust of it.

That what is said becomes dangerous by the very fact of being spoken is an old superstition that Strindberg had used before in the opening lines of *Advent*.[12] Here, he does so again:

JEANNE:	Don't say it! Not like that!	
MAURICE:	Yes, for that's how it is.	
JEANNE:	Yes, but don't say it.	(p. 144)

There is also a manual labourer eating in the kitchen of the *crémerie*, usually frequented by artists. He reflects on their language: 'I don't understand a word of what they're saying' (p. 142). This could be interpreted to mean that he does not grasp the actual content of their discussions about art, but perhaps even more that he does not understand their artists' jargon. If this is the case, it is a similar kind of comment to the one made by Kerstin about artists in *Playing with Fire*. Strindberg thus seems to conclude that it is the artistic milieu where all three of these comedies (and *Comrades*, too, for that matter) take place that gives rise to carelessness where words and thoughts are concerned. Consequently, it would seem that in his comedies Strindberg wants not only to unmask the genre's light-hearted superficiality, but also to express a scepticism concerning all artistic activity. The influence of Rousseau is one of the few constants in his life.

Finally there is more to be said about the ending of *Crimes and Crimes*. It is possible to imagine that the principal character is a dramatist, and it is equally possible that Strindberg has projected something of his own life on to him. But if so it is relevant to recall that during his recent period of mental and spiritual turmoil, Strindberg studied Dante's *Divine Comedy*, and in particular the *Inferno*, which eventually gave its name to these crisis years. The *Commedia* is, for Dante, a tale in which the main character, after having lived through his personal hell, meets God. Maurice is heading in the same direction, and this station of his journey, which turns into the drama of penitence depicted in *Crimes and Crimes*, might indicate that, just like Strindberg, he now intends to start writing religious dramas.[13] Certainly, having completed *Crimes and Crimes*, Strindberg never wrote another comedy.

NOTES

1. Strindberg also planned *Comrades* (1888) as a *komedi*. Otherwise he used alternative Swedish designations such as *lustspel* (roughly 'popular comedy'), *Folkkomedi*, *allvarsamt lustspel* (seriously minded popular comedy), or (for *Creditors*) *tragi-komedi*. If a *fastlagsspel* (Lenten play) is also included, this yields ten plays of a comic nature, out of Strindberg's corpus of sixty-three dramas. See Otto Oberholzer, 'Strindberg und die Komödientheorie', in Oskar Bandle, Walter Baumgartner and Jürg Glauser, eds., *Strindbergs Dramen im Lichte neuerer Methodendiskussionen* (Basel/Frankfurt am Main: Helbing & Lichtenhahn, 1981), pp. 97–118. Barbara Lide considers all Strindberg's comedies and related plays in her unpublished thesis *Strindberg's Comic Spirit: a Study of August Strindberg's Comedies and their Relationship to the Comic Tradition* (Urbana, Ill.: 1975).

2. For a presentation in English see Walter Johnson, *Strindberg and the Historical Drama* (Seattle: University of Washington Press, 1963), pp. 56–62.

3. See Torbjörn Nilsson's commentary in *SV*11, pp. 389–410.

4. This is underlined in the grotesque comedy embedded in several later works, including *The Dance of Death* and *The Pelican*.

5. *Strindberg and the Historical Drama*, pp. 66–7 and Barbara Lide, *Strindberg's Comic Spirit*, p. 269.

6. See Hans-Göran Ekman, *Strindberg and the Five Senses: Studies in Strindberg's Chamber Plays* (London: Athlone Press, 2000), pp. 64–86.

7. Further examples of such, almost metadramatic, aspects are discussed in Hans-Göran Ekman, 'Humor, dubbelmoral och Strindbergs kritik av Bellman', in Margareta Brundin *et al.*, eds., *20 x Strindberg. En vänbok till Lars Dahlbäck* (Stockholm: Almqvist & Wiksell, 2003), pp. 105–16.

8. See also Hans-Göran Ekman, 'Strindberg's *Leka med elden* as a Comedy', in Bandle *et al.*, *Strindbergs Dramen*, pp. 119–36.

9. See Barbara Lide, 'Perspectives on a Genre. Strindberg's *comédies rosses*', in Michael Robinson, ed., *Strindberg and Genre* (Norwich: Norvik Press, 1991), pp. 148–66.

10. For example in Luc Bondy's 1996 production with Emmanuelle Béart as Kerstin and Staffan Valdemar Holm's staging at Dramaten in 2002.

11. The religious aspect of *Crimes and Crimes* has led Göran Stockenström to use the term *religiöst salongsdrama* (religious parlour play). *Ismael I öknen. Strindberg som mystiker* (Uppsala: Almqvist & Wiksell, 1972), pp. 415–49.

12. The Judge is boasting about his success and his wife warns: 'Don't say that, someone might hear you!' (*SV*40, p. 15).

13. Barry Jacobs explores the notion of comedy and the religious contents of the drama in 'Strindberg's *Advent* and *Brott och brott*: Sagospel and Comedy in a Higher Court', in Robinson, *Strindberg and Genre*, pp. 167–87.

7

GÖRAN STOCKENSTRÖM

Crisis and change: Strindberg the unconscious modernist

In the inaugural programme for the Provincetown Playhouse, which opened on 4 January 1924 with a production of *The Ghost Sonata*, Eugene O'Neill acknowledged Strindberg as 'the precursor of all modernity in our present theatre' and insisted he remained 'among the most modern of moderns'.[1] The Provincetown Players rediscovered in what O'Neill called Strindberg's later plays elements of a theatrical aesthetic which they themselves advocated as the dominating form of modernism. Strindberg's view of man and his radically new stagecraft presented the necessary challenge to their own attempts to transcend realism and the Provincetown production of *The Ghost Sonata* was followed in 1926 by *A Dream Play*. Strindberg and the plays he wrote after his Inferno crisis thus paved the way for the experimental studio theatre in MacDougal Street under the banner of modernism, the general notion being one of revolutionary change from a mimetic realism, as defined by preceding generations of theatre practitioners in its use of language and dramaturgical techniques.

Strindberg's post-Inferno plays are first of all stories, remembered because of what happened and mattered to him. Below the tangled pattern of events, as well as behind the action, there are experiences, psychological realities of passionate importance to him. These accumulations of passion, sin and suffering were recorded by the dramatist and told in different ways upon the stage. His plays represent incomplete and imperfect actions, which always assert their place in the larger pattern of history. On stage his plays assume universal significance and simultaneously point inward to central meanings, yet trail behind them the roots of his Inferno experiences.

During a series of consecutive crises between 1894 and 1897 Strindberg's painful and bizarre psychic experiences entailed a loss of the usual foundations of the sense of a reality shared with others. External perceptions of reality no longer seemed to apply in the old way; it was as if the events in which he was engaged were mystically conjured up by some mysterious external force. Earlier models of explanation and understanding no longer seemed viable. Everyday reality was peopled with a plurality of shades and presences, and internal experiences (fantasies, dreams, hallucinations and visions) seemed to take on an objective reality of their own. The nature of phenomena was unstable and the centre of his experiences moved beyond the horizons of an identity anchored either in space and time or a communal existence.

In the chaotic fragments of reality to which Strindberg was now exposed, he needed to find an informing order. Thus, it became imperative to discover some system of rational explanation. This fundamental concern is reflected in his scientific speculations in *Antibarbarus* (1894) and *Sylva Sylvarum* (1896) where he sought a coherent vision that would explain the apparent chaos surrounding him in nature. Strindberg was familiar with the methods of empirical science, but the categories of law, purpose and causality were always incorporated within social and historical systems of thought, which served to locate the coherent pattern in the larger chaos that he described in *Sylva Sylvarum* as 'the great chaos and the infinite order' (SS27, p. 208). If man and nature were created *in effigiem deorum*, then the signs of the Creator could be observed and studied in all aspects of the cosmos. Matter is one, living and evolving, and in consequence all things originate in, flow and return to one. In the garden of nature rare similarities and strange correspondences were revealed wherever Strindberg turned his gaze. Powers, demons and spirits whispered their secret messages; God pointed and spoke. In contrast to the modern scientist, Strindberg believed in the unique, singular event as an act of divinity. 'If you wish to know the invisible, observe with an open gaze the visible' was a maxim from the *Talmud* that he often quoted and used as one of the mottoes for *The Occult Diary*, which he kept between 1896 and 1908. Around him in Paris in 1895–6 were various kinds of occultists and alchemists who attempted, through similar quasi-scientific methods, to prove the essential unity of the cosmos, which they also perceived in terms of separation and constant flux. Strindberg, himself an alchemist, was well versed in their traditions and shared their belief in the idea of original unity, the *prima materia*, out of which all things arise. He found reaffirmation for his own development among these occultists whose systems also worked in and through images to provide the primordial link between science and religion. His method was to observe the signs in nature and detect the correspondences between the microcosm and the macrocosm.

During the acute psychotic states of the Inferno crisis Strindberg noted all the unnerving events and experiences that seemed to threaten his sanity. The writing of the diary served to keep the great chaos without and within at bay. His powerful feelings of guilt made him experience and imagine life through an afflicted perspective of persecution and morbidity. His burden of sin was large, for he had previously used his writings to attack sacred authorities with a vengeance, smash sexual taboos and outrage public decency. In the process he had harmed many innocent people whom he had portrayed with virulence in both novels and plays. Above all he had deserted his first wife and their three children, and grievously injured them by his unfounded and exaggerated accusations in *A Madman's Defence*. In 1894 these ghosts from the past reappeared as Strindberg forsook his second wife and their newborn child for Paris. Strindberg's mode of dealing with his acute guilt feelings had always been to project his own sins and crimes on to his fictional characters, and to blame another. But the creative process, which served to overcome the paralysis of guilt and achieve closure with the past, was unavailable to Strindberg in these crisis years when science became an ineffectual surrogate during this period of literary unproductivity.

Strindberg's greatest fear was paranoia. There are many outward signs of this, reflected in his flight from one dwelling to another with, he imagined, imaginary foes in pursuit. These intervals of heightened anxiety were accompanied by physical sickness and suicidal thoughts, and the black magic of *envoûtement*, or the casting of spells, served as a temporary explanation for the strange events and shapes that haunted him; but he was eventually forced to assume that his crimes were being punished by spiritual powers, whether evil or good. His search for explanations in science, occultism and mythology finally brought him to the writings of the scientist and mystic, Emanuel Swedenborg (1688–1772), whose major works he studied in 1896-7.[2] For both men the rigorous language of natural science failed to evoke the inner truth that was concealed beyond the visible forms of nature and they turned instead to the hermetic and cabalist traditions. Thus Swedenborg, with his doctrine of correspondences, played a central role in Strindberg's religious reorientation. In another letter to publisher and theosophist Torsten Hedlund (31 October 1896), he concludes:

> We are in Inferno for sins committed in a previous existence. Therefore: pray for nothing save resignation! and desire nothing, absolutely nothing from life. If possible, find joy in adversity, because with every misfortune that occurs an entry in the deficit column is struck out … Swedenborg's description of Inferno is so close to earthly life without his having intended it, so exact that I am convinced … (*ASB*11, p. 376)

Strindberg is willing to accept punishment and suffering but unable to take responsibility for his own sins, which are referred to a previous existence, of which he has no personal memory. His solution to this dilemma was to take the Swedenborgian theology of a last reckoning with existence and transpose it from the spiritual to the human world. And by gradually shifting the focus from himself to the world, he was eventually able to view his present suffering as temporary. From this perspective life on earth becomes a purgatory and human beings are reincarnations, for whom suffering is the only form of atonement.

In its shifting versions and nuances Strindberg's Inferno mythology has many roots. Its centrality in his *œuvre* points to the garden of childhood, for it reflects a particular way of relating to the world, experiential and meaningful at the same time. It evolved over the years into an eclectic complex of ideas, which sometimes drew upon other systems, including gnosticism, alchemy, occultism and Pythagoreanism, as well as Swedenborgianism. As an existential myth it depicts man as an exile in the fallen world of matter, born into the world of sin and suffering to be punished and to atone for crimes committed in this or a previous existence. Man's life has only one purpose, redemption, and every aspect of the cosmos has a bearing on this process. Humanity must atone for its own guilt, and man's manifest destiny is to become a scapegoat, subjected to suffering for his own sins or for other people's. It is therefore no coincidence that the issue of God's goodness in a world characterized by evil was to become the dominant theme in Strindberg's post-Inferno writings.

Swedenborg's writings, such as *Earths in the Universe* (1758), helped Strindberg understand both his immediate physical suffering, as outlined in *Inferno* and the *Occult Diary*, and the suffering of the soul which accompanied his profound sense of personal guilt. But Strindberg's existential experiences are not simply the result of objective facts that require explanation. They involve a process which entails subjective experiences that require acceptance and understanding, and the result is relief and eventually healing. It was the acceptance of a benevolent providence that had a positive liberating effect on Strindberg. The notions that the disciplinary spirits he recognized in Swedenborg were loving, and that suffering meant atonement, affirmed his earlier hopes. His reading of Swedenborg allowed him to view the power of evil as limited and the prospect of eternal damnation as non-existent. Strindberg's fear that his experiences might be judged insane was replaced by the insight that he had been chosen to serve God, and the spirits, whom he called *makterna* (the Powers). His mission henceforth was an exalted calling like that of Paul to explain the ways of God to man, and this conviction allowed him to contain his guilt feelings while offering the hope of atonement through suffering and penance. Following the breakthrough in March 1897, the sluice gates of renewed literary productivity thus opened, and he was able to write *Inferno*. As Count Max observes in *Gothic Rooms*, 'You do not read Swedenborg, but you receive him through grace, for he can only be understood by those who have had similar experiences' (*SV*38, p. 61).

To characterize the profound change described in *Inferno*, Strindberg refers to the Swedenborgian concept of 'vastation'. This concept constitutes a central tenet in Swedenborg's doctrine of the spiritual world where, after death, human beings are transported to the spiritual world or the lower earth. Following their arrival the appearance of the newly fledged spirits remains unaltered, and they can still conceal their thoughts and feelings. They walk around as ghosts in their corpses, not even aware that they are dead. In time the veil of illusions is removed, and they can no longer hide the true nature of their thoughts and feelings. All the costumes they have worn, all the roles they have played, are stripped away, feature by feature. This dramatic unmasking entails the revelation of every action and thought from their inner memories. Every scene in their past lives passes by in review, and the true nature of their earthly existence is revealed from a divine perspective. In this process their exteriors are transformed into mirror images of their interiors and a correspondence between outer appearance and inner reality emerges, and they are subsequently dispatched to one of the many societies in heaven or hell. Strindberg now interpreted 'vastation' as analogous to his own redemption, a stage of spiritual purification by divine grace, transposed from the spiritual to the phenomenal world in the scourges visited upon him by the disciplinary spirits that he describes in *Inferno*. What remains of Swedenborg's doctrine after its transformation for poetic purposes is essentially that the world and humanity in all its aspects reflect spiritual realities, and its dramatic unmaskings, processions of shame and spectacular transformations provide Strindberg with both the themes and structure of his later dramatic art.

Strindberg described his 'vastation' as a process of 'spiritual purification' with reference to Paul's Epistles to the Corinthians and Timothy: 'To deliver such an one unto Satan for the destruction of the flesh, that the spirit may be saved in the day of the Lord Jesus' (1 Cor., 5: 5); and 'Of whom is Hymenaeus and Alexander; whom I have delivered unto Satan, that they may learn not to blaspheme' (1 Tim., 1: 20). In a note from late 1897, he comments:

> The word Satanism is given another interpretation by those who like me believe life on earth to be a purgatory where we are punished in order to restore the equilibrium between crime and punishment, partially educating us for the good through suffering. This point of view is strictly Christian and Christ himself speaks on many occasions of Satan as the prince and ruler of this world, and humanity subjugated to his power. In the most striking passage from *The First Epistle of Paul to Timothy* 1.20, one of my mottos to *Inferno*, the apostles seemed to have been ordained to put '*esprits correcteurs*' to punish and purify man. (SgNM, 9: 2, dated 24 November 1897)

In this instance he responds to a question concerning the renewed interest in Satanism in Paris at the time. This was consistent with his Inferno fantasy and still served to alleviate his guilt feelings. In the gnostic tradition that had long interested Strindberg, the evil spirits who kept man captive in the fallen world of matter had to be exorcised. They held that the flesh could not be resurrected and identified redemption with the awakening of the spirit through knowledge (*gnosis*). Once illuminated in pre-existence, spiritual man was held to be already resurrected and eternal. From this perspective, redemption is a recollection of the spiritual self, imprisoned and lost in the fallen world of matter. Strindberg's catchword to define religion was *Anschluss zu Jenseits*, reconnecting to the beyond as a process of recollection, and it was this mythical drama in its diverse phases that gave meaning to his mission, along with that of other scapegoats of history. His emphasis and tone may vary (he found support for his belief in gnosticism, Buddhism, theosophy, occultism and other related philosophical and religious systems), but the underlying fantasy of redemption remains the same.

In his scientific pursuits Strindberg had attempted to verify a vision of the world as ordered and unified. The artificial frontiers of naming and ordering reality now gave way to one central understanding. The world was not a great chaos in constant flux but a meaningful and coherent universe, displaying an infinite order behind all its disparate elements. In the phenomenal world all things existed concurrently and productively as part of the whole. The potential of madness, human persecutors or evil spirits was eliminated and replaced by 'the Powers', which tortured and punished Strindberg on the road to Damascus. His is thus not a conversion in the Christian sense, a new essence and being in the grace of Christ, and, lacking psychological healing, he would consequently fall prey to further periods of severe anxiety throughout his life.

But first he would tell his story as a *morala exemplum* in a series of works in which the conversion motif was central, initially in *Inferno*, *Legends* and the fragment *Jacob Wrestles*, and then in his return to the theatre with the first two parts of *To Damascus*. By articulating his central meaning through the biblical story of Saul/Paul, Strindberg was able to enact the mythemes of his own soul in which he offered both a new reading of his own experience and a critique of the materialism of late nineteenth-century European society. Hence, these autobiographical and confessional writings were succeeded both by a sequence of penitential dramas, *Advent*, *Crimes and Crimes*, *Easter*, *The Dance of Death* and *To Damascus III*, all of which centred around stories of individual pilgrimage, and the social critiques of *Gothic Rooms* and *Black Banners*, and the Chamber Plays of 1907 where, as in *A Blue Book*, the theme of redemption is represented in the journey from the

Isle of Life to the Isle of Death with its concomitant stages of illusion, unmasking and liberation, combined with a substantial element of social critique.

Like the angle from which he enters the fictional world of his characters, Strindberg's choice of settings and events may vary and will ultimately determine the rhetorical and dramaturgical devices he employs. Thus in *A Dream Play* or *The Ghost Sonata* his version of history is panoramic, with its focus on universal suffering and the pain and torments caused by the injustices of socio-economic and political systems. The dilemma of innocent suffering was increasingly to trouble a dramatist who tended to view man from his own perspective of Jacob wrestling with God. Each human being must bear his own responsibility and atone through suffering for his own sins, whether in this or a previous existence. Thus, innocent suffering, whether Strindberg's own or other people's, was interpreted as a divine scapegoat mission. To become a chosen vessel, to be subjected to suffering in order to help fellow human beings redeem their sins, was thus a calling in no way unique to Christ or Saul/Paul. Anyone may be asked to play that role in Strindberg's dramatic universe, like Agnes and the Lawyer in *A Dream Play*, or the Student and the Milkmaid in *The Ghost Sonata*. The central action on Strindberg's stage is not located in the externalized conflicts between different characters or between the internalized conflicts of characters and their masks, but rather between the soul and spirit of the human being, and his bondage in a material existence. The dualism between this material world of objects and the other world of soul and spirit is constantly reiterated by the suffering voices of humanity, half in and half out of this world. Strindberg communicates this to the audience in the nexus between dialogue and scenography, when Agnes asks the Glazier about the flower on top of the growing castle: 'Tell me Father. Why do flowers grow out of dirt?' (*MJoP*, p. 181). All the suffering that human beings have experienced throughout a lifetime of ignorance and misunderstanding demands an answer: why do human beings suffer? The laws of science provide no answer to such a question, and the Glazier avoids a response. Reaching the final station of her journey through the human inferno, Agnes already knows the Poet's answer: 'Surely suffering is redemption, and death deliverance' (p. 246).

In order to represent the human journey to enlightenment, Strindberg has to deconstruct the material mode of existence with its inherent illusions and claims to 'reality'. In his dramaturgy the world of physical objects is constantly pitted against the world of the soul. Strindberg created the term 'spiritual somnambulists' to characterize the nature of man's existence in the realm of desires and illusions (*SV*38, p. 61). Given this state of dualism, the only recourse for his characters when giving voice to their souls is through language, aphysical in nature. While the scenographic discourse remains realistic in the tradition of the illusionist theatre, the verbal discourse of the dialogue serves to make the physical environment illusory to his audience. Strindberg's characters are engaged in a process of casting off their bondage to the material mode, to awaken and find their true selves. His protagonists are souls *in extremis* but, as we learn from alchemy, only separated things can unite. For the process of separation, the moment of blinding on the road to Damascus, Strindberg favoured spectacular theatrical scenes of unmasking, that is, what he himself termed 'processions of shame' positioned at the pivotal turning point in the lives of his characters. Some of the more striking examples include the asylum scene in *To Damascus I*, the alchemists' banquet in *To Damascus II*, the ball scene in *Advent*, the first of the two ghostly scenes from the Auberge des Adrets in *Crimes and Crimes*, the Captain's dance and ensuing heart attack in *The Dance of Death I*, and the ghost supper in *The Ghost Sonata*, all of which have an identical dramaturgical function, however different they may be in terms of style and technique. Dramatically, their mode of operation is defined by the dramatist in terms of 'Vastation: [whereby] the past is represented again, but in the present moment' (*SgNM*, 3: 12).

When Strindberg had to clarify the style and nature of these scenes for his editor and publisher, he coined the term *hexscenerna* (literally 'witch-scenes') to evoke their style, which is at once real and surreal (*ASB*12, p. 212). The first scene of this nature was the asylum scene in *To Damascus I*, which is intimately related to Strindberg's interpretation of his own vastation.[3] To represent the ineffable on stage posed a dilemma in itself on account of the mimetic-objective nature of theatrical presentation. Far more difficult, however, was Strindberg's relation to an audience who could hardly be expected to share his vision of reality, in which the material, psychological and spiritual domains combined. In that way his dramatic universe becomes what Ingmar Bergman terms completely open and without limits.[4] Like Shakespeare, Strindberg articulated his central meaning through a larger framework, that of myth, to represent the before and after of the existential human journey. The moment of blinding on the road to Damascus represents the vertical connection to the divine which forever alters the significance of the experiences and actions that have formed the protagonist's character up to that moment. In Strindberg's play God is hidden and called 'The Unknown', but there is always something of him that appears and extends into the very depths of the action. When Shakespeare raises the ghosts of the dead and their crimes on stage, he asks the audience willingly to suspend their disbelief because his reality is theatrical. When Strindberg, on the other hand, confronts his audience with the spectres of the dead and the doubles of those still living, he actually asks them to change their belief in human identity, as it is anchored in time and space, in order to accord with his own personal vision.

Strindberg frequently employs the concept of 'half-reality' to describe his expanded concept of reality, comparing it to the veil of Maya or a dream. He characterizes *To Damascus I* as 'a fiction with a terrifying half-reality' (*SL*, p. 624), and in the opening scene the protagonist informs the audience:

> It's not death I fear but loneliness. All alone we meet someone. I don't know if it's someone else or myself that I perceive, but in the midst of loneliness we're not alone. The air thickens, the air congeals, and certain beings begin to take shape, invisible but tangible, and possessing a life of their own … Yes, for some time now I've noticed everything. Not, as before, when all I saw was objects and events, forms and colours. Now I see intentions and meanings. Life, which was just nonsense before, has become meaningful, and I see an infinite order, where previously I saw only chance and chaos. (*SV*39, pp. 17–18)

Incongruous as it may seem in relation to the protagonist's subsequent development, it is paramount for Strindberg to tell his audience that reality cannot be understood on its usual terms. Strindberg's later plays repeatedly present us with characters who question the nature of reality, as a fairy tale, or something read or dreamt. As his experience of the world and himself in terms of consistent identity began to disintegrate, the pathology of everyday living became infused with universal significance, and is often described in dramatic metaphors. Thus, in *To Damascus* the protagonist maintains that he is not persecuted by nightmarish hallucinations but by 'small, recurring events, real ones'. It is from this perspective we have to understand Strindberg's claims that his art remained realistic (*SV*37, p. 91; *Inf*, p. 148).[5] It was this sense of concreteness in his understanding of reality, its fundamentally half-real nature notwithstanding, which was to distinguish him from the German expressionists and many others.

In Strindberg's theatre all existing things correspond to spiritual realities while simultaneously serving as signs for the moral and religious education of the ego. In his post-Inferno plays such a vision of the world is created on stage through both textual and stylistic means, as well as through the specific dramaturgical techniques Strindberg employed. The latter are part and parcel of his dramatic repertoire, drawing upon a wide variety of theatrical traditions. They are always used with a specific object in mind in relation to an audience. They serve to make his private vision public on stage, and to universalize his message. As such, they are means toward a definite end and not dramatic experiments *per se*: 'No predetermined form is to limit the author, because the theme determines the form' (*SV*64, p. 13). The purpose common to his use of literary and theatrical conventions in relation to his audience is to reorganize their experience in terms of how they perceive the physical world and understand themselves, and their relation to their fellow men, to God and the universe.

The Unknown in *To Damascus*, Maurice in *Crimes and Crimes*, Elis in *Easter*, the Captain in *The Dance of Death*, the Gentleman in *Storm* and other characters serve as unwilling models in this quest. If Strindberg's focus is on universal suffering rather than the individual, such scapegoat figures as Adolphe in *Crimes and Crimes*, Eleonora in *Easter*, Agnes in *A Dream Play*, and the Student in *The Ghost Sonata* serve to mediate the suffering of humanity in order to enable them to see, or rather see through, the frontiers separating the material and spiritual realms, while a few characters who have capitulated to the material mode of reality like Hummel in *The Ghost Sonata* and the Mother in *The Pelican* are destroyed without penetrating the veil of Maya; but these are the exceptions.

In Strindberg's post-Inferno dramas the physical and the spiritual are constantly translated into one another's language in ever new, more complicated relationships. On the level of the text Strindberg clarified his intentions to his audience by the extensive use of myth and symbolic leitmotifs. On the dramaturgical level he used a variety of dramatic techniques to dislocate conventional expectations. If he was to succeed as a dramatist, he had to create within the audience a feeling of the illusionary nature of existence, at once within this world and out of it at the same time. His various dramatic techniques, both on the visual and the auditory level, can be subsumed under the general headings repetition, distortion and contradiction. This entailed new ways of using the stage and its relationship to an audience which resulted in profound changes in the nature of the theatrical event. *To Damascus I* he originally characterized as 'a new genre, fantastic, and brilliant', and stressed that it took place in the present and was based on 'real experiences' (*ASB* 12, p. 311). Four years later, after considerable success with several of his new plays, including the production of *To Damascus I* at Dramaten on 19 November 1900, he created the term 'dream play' and explained, in his frequently quoted preface to *A Dream Play*, that he was seeking to:

> imitate the disconnected yet apparently logical form of a dream. Anything can happen, everything is possible and probable. Time and space do not exist; on an insignificant basis of reality the imagination spins and weaves new patterns: a blend of memories, experiences, spontaneous ideas, absurdities and improvisations.
>
> The characters split, double, multiply, evaporate, condense, disperse, and converge ...   (*MJoP*, p. 176)

The motif of unmasking occupies a pivotal position in Strindberg's post-Inferno plays. The theme of a reckoning with existence is usually developed stage by stage as a continuous process by analogy with Strindberg's own experiences. At times different aspects of vastation are emphasized: the procession of shame in the asylum scene, the transformation of physical reality in correspondence with the spiritual reality of the protagonist in the alchemists' banquet in *To Damascus II*, the sloughing off of character masks and social roles and the bondage to the material realm in the ghost supper of *The Ghost Sonata*. In all of these, the differentiation of the material and the spiritual serves the purpose of enlightenment. As the Father tries to explain to his child in *A Dream Play*: 'flowers don't like the dirt, so they hasten up into the light, to blossom and die' (*MJoP*, p. 181). The natural process has been reversed: suffering is thus seen to be existential, reaching beyond individual lies, perversions and social injustices. The moment of blinding becomes the moment of seeing, the dilemma of Oedipus, but very few characters in Strindberg's dramatic universe truly want to awaken.

These metaphysical functions are assumed by various characters in Strindberg's dramatic universe. In *To Damascus I* various aspects of these interrelated functions are performed by the Confessor, the Beggar, and the Mother, while the Lady is called upon to serve a mediating role in relation to the audience as a scapegoat figure. In terms of the plot she also serves as a parallel figure to the protagonist, a common dramatic device used by Strindberg in a number of plays. In *To Damascus II*, the Dominican, the Beggar and the Confessor all serve as revelations of the Eternal One, in keeping with the idea of the Trinity. Strindberg presented legends on stage in order to teach his audience the ways of God to man. His characters' stories may vary, but in the dramatic web they all represent the same recurring theme. Maurice's destiny in *Crimes and Crimes* is not only shared by Henriette but paralleled in Adolphe's story, the tragic events that befall Jeanne and the experiences of Émile and the disciplinary spirit Madame Catherine. The same is true for Edgar, Alice and Kurt in *The Dance of Death*, who all undergo a similar fall in order to be reborn. In *The Ghost Sonata*, all the participants are bound to the realm of Kama-Loka, the state of flesh, desires and need. They share in the process of purification to liberate their souls from the illusions created by their pretence and beliefs in the material world. To represent aspects of this spiritual process Strindberg juxtaposes Hummel and the Mummy, the former identified totally by the physical matrix of life, the latter voicing the concerns of soul and spirit on behalf of suffering humanity. Strindberg's pessimism about the state of human affairs may have deepened, but his conviction that the world and humanity in all its aspects reflected spiritual realities remained the same. To Strindberg this essential truth was proved by every belief system, whether Swedenborgian, Christian, gnostic or Buddhist. Within this framework, he was to remain eclectic, and his religious syncretism became an expression of the larger framework of history.

Where *The Dance of Death* is concerned, O'Neill coined the term 'super-naturalism' to distinguish its dramaturgy from mimetic-objective realism. Here the evils of the flesh and the struggle between the spirit and the flesh are recorded in scrupulous detail, and the scenographic discourse is also borne out naturalistically in the tradition of illusionist theatre. Strindberg relies on the dialogue to underscore the illusory nature of the environment, punctuated as the action is by a dynamic and expressive *mise-en-scène*. As prisoners of the flesh, its self-deceptions and lies, the participants in this *danse macabre* share the same existential dilemma. Identity anchored in space and time, explained in terms of nature and nurture, becomes exceedingly precarious; God may be hidden, but his power extends into the heart of the action. Picked up by the scruff of his neck, Edgar is thrown to the ground during his solitary dance, a ritual of hubris and materialistic boredom. The Captain experiences death, motivated naturalistically by his heart condition, but subsequently we learn that he had a vision of life on the other side. Originally, Strindberg had drafted a spectacular scene at this point, similar in function and construction to the asylum scene in *To Damascus I* (*SgNM*, 3: 2; *SgNM*, 4). But this would have broken the natural confines of the action, and was later discarded. Unable to surrender to the infinite order of a new day, Edgar is thus made to fall back into the chaos of the old night, together with the protective illusions and lies that had formulated his character in life and Strindberg resolves his dramaturgical dilemma by introducing a pantomime scene at the beginning of the final act. In this magnificent scene Edgar renounces the illusions of his life one by one in an expressively choreographed ritual, a vastation in retrospect, so to speak. Thus Strindberg remains within the confines of his chosen style of representation, but the Captain's ceremonial pantomime becomes a crystallizing moment and is charged with thematic significance. By an intensification of the techniques of realism, Strindberg conveys his super-naturalistic intentions to an audience: something of extraordinary significance has happened to both Edgar and Alice, and they can celebrate their silver wedding anniversary with a different understanding of spiritual realities.

As well as experiences on the road to Damascus to use as a model of social evolution, history itself offered Strindberg an abundance of analogies. These found dramatic form in the history plays, eleven of which span more than five hundred years of Swedish history, and four with leitmotifs from world history. The success of his historical dramas on the stage was in a sense predicated on his audiences' awareness that they were witnessing a re-enactment of their past. By reinterpreting the facts and events of history, Strindberg hoped to prove the truth of his personal vision as chains of events in a divinely guided process.[6]

Strindberg's profound influence on modern theatre in general has been generally recognized, yet it was only by finding ways in which to represent his own idiosyncratic vision and personal experience on stage that he became the first modernist in the theatre. The psycho-expressionism of *To Damascus*, the existential closed space of *The Dance of Death*, the radical *mise-en-scène* of *A Dream Play*, and the grotesque distortion of reality in *The Ghost Sonata* have all opened new grounds for theatre in the twentieth century, whether expressionist, existentialist or absurdist.

But was Strindberg really 'the most modern of moderns', as O'Neill contended? Common to such a claim is the general notion of modernism having as its focal point the idea of revolutionary change, usually expressed through programmes and manifestoes. Since Baudelaire it has been axiomatic that the renewal of history constantly requires new artistic expressions. The continuing interest of Baudelaire and the symbolists in aesthetic innovation was, however, of no interest to Strindberg. Baudelaire's conception of universal analogies grew out of theoretical reflections and was drawn upon with great artistry to explore a changing perception of reality that was demanded by the historical situation. The correspondences that Strindberg observed between the phenomenal and spiritual world developed as a result of his existential experiences during the Inferno crisis and were ultimately based on scientific and religious concerns. He constructed a personal vision of God, man and nature out of a new existential situation. His one and only aim was adequately to express his story, in whatever forms he chose to tell it.

This resulted in a brand of symbolism peculiarly his own with no direct counterpart in *fin-de-siècle* literature. In the theatre it resulted in new ways of using the stage which effected profound changes in the very nature of the theatrical event. In contrast to Baudelaire, Strindberg did not attempt to analyse a historical situation and seek to find new forms adequately to express it. Instead, he interpreted history, both past and present, out of his own experiences on the road to Damascus. His use of dream structure in *To Damascus* and *A Dream Play* was consciously crafted in relation to an audience to represent reality as he perceived it, and why he persisted in calling himself a 'realist'. If Strindberg was 'the precursor of all modernity in our present theatre', he remains, in Sven Delblanc's words, 'an unconscious modernist'.[7]

NOTES

1. Eugene O'Neill, 'Strindberg and Our Theatre', in Oscar Cargill, *O'Neill and His Plays* (New York: New York University Press, 1982), pp. 108–9.
2. See Göran Stockenström, 'The Symbiosis of "Spirits" in Inferno: Strindberg and Swedenborg', in Marilyn Johns Blackwell, ed., *Structures of Influence: a*

Comparative Approach to August Strindberg (Chapel Hill: University of North Carolina Press, 1981), pp. 8–20.

3. See Göran Stockenström, 'His Former Dream Play *To Damascus*', in Oskar Bandle, Walter Baumgartner and Jürg Glauser, eds., *Strindbergs Dramen im Lichte neuerer Methodendiskussionen* (Basel and Frankfurt am Main: Helbing and Lichtenhahn, 1981), pp. 218–26.

4. See Frederick J. Marker and Lise-Lone Marker, *Ingmar Bergman: Four Decades in the Theatre* (New York: Cambridge University Press, 1982), p. 222.

5. Cf. Strindberg, *Inferno and From an Occult Diary*, trans. Mary Sandbach (Harmondsworth: Penguin, 1979), p. 148:

> A new art discovered, Nature's own! A natural clairvoyance. Why scoff at naturalism now that it has shown itself capable of inaugurating a new kind of art, full of youth and hope? ... Nature has awakened from her slumber of centuries. Nothing happens in this world that has not the approval of the Powers. Naturalism has come into existence. Therefore let there be naturalism, let there be a rebirth of the harmony of matter and spirit.

6. Cf. '*Charles XII* as Historical Drama', and '*Charles XII* as Dream Play', in Göran Stockenström, ed., *Strindberg's Dramaturgy* (Minneapolis: University of Minnesota Press, 1988), pp. 41–59, 223–45.

7. Sven Delblanc, 'Ett drömspel', in *Stormhatten. Tre Strindbergsstudier* (Stockholm: Alba, 1979), pp. 63–70. See also Göran Stockenström, 'Strindberg's Cosmos in *A Dream Play*: Medieval or Modern', *Comparative Drama*, 29:5 (1996), pp. 72–105, and Sven Delblanc, 'Strindberg and Humanism', in Stockenström, *Strindberg's Dramaturgy*, pp. 3–14.

8

ESZTER SZALCZER

A modernist dramaturgy

Upon emerging from the artistic and spiritual ferment of his Inferno crisis in 1898, Strindberg returned to writing for the theatre with a series of plays that represent a radical departure from the classical model of playwriting. This turn was anticipated by themes and dramatic devices in earlier works, including *The Father* and *Miss Julie*, where the characters struggle to keep afloat while on board a sinking culture. By the late 1890s, however, a new consciousness had found expression in ever-shifting forms of drama, in continually modulating experimental techniques, and in bold structural patterns inspired by music, painting and the natural world rather than a conventional narrative perspective. The preceding Inferno years, during which Strindberg abandoned the practice of drama for the sake of science, the visual arts and attempts at making gold, yielded a transformation in drama. This shift in his dramatic techniques can be understood in the context of *fin-de-siècle* modernity reflected in the arts generally as they groped towards new conceptions of the human being in relation to a rapidly changing environment. In an essay from 1894 entitled 'Sensations détraquées' ('Deranged Sensations'), Strindberg voices his transitional sense of himself and the world around him in an attempt to redefine both, as he perceives the pieces sliding apart and producing distorted images and fragmentary reflections:

> Or do I feel displaced since, being born in the good old times, when people had oil lamps, stagecoaches, boat-women, and six-volume novels? I have passed with involuntary haste through the age of steam and electricity, as a result of which I have possibly lost my breath and acquired bad nerves! Or is it that my nerves are undergoing an evolution towards over-refinement, and that my senses have become all too subtle? Am I changing skin? Am I about to become a man of today? I'm as nervous as a crab that has cast off its carapace, as irritable as a silkworm in its metamorphosis.
>
> (*SE*, p. 128)

'I know … but cannot say'

The post-Inferno plays *To Damascus*, Parts I-II (1898) and III (1901), *The Dance of Death*, Parts I-II (1900) and *A Dream Play* (1901) reflect the modern subject's confrontation with new challenges, which cannot be rendered by a plot that traditionally imitates an action 'which is complete and of a certain length'.[1] This new sensibility dismantles the conventional perception of the very notions that had made Aristotelian dramaturgy possible, including those of dramatic action, character, time, space, rational thought and discursive language. One of the most memorable instances that demonstrates the failure of the old dramaturgy to emulate the changing human experience can be found in the school scene of *A Dream Play*. Here the grown-up Officer, after a degree has been conferred on him, finds himself sitting on the school-bench among small boys:

SCHOOLMASTER:	Now, my boy, can you tell me how much two times two is? …
OFFICER:	Two … times two … Let me see! That makes two two!
SCHOOLMASTER:	Well, well … somebody hasn't done his homework!
OFFICER:	(*ashamed*) Yes, I have, but … I know what it is, but I can't say it …
SCHOOLMASTER:	You're trying to get out of it! You know, but you *can't* say. Perhaps I can help you! (*He pulls the Officer's hair*)
OFFICER:	Oh, this is dreadful, really dreadful!
SCHOOLMASTER:	Yes, dreadful, that's precisely what it is when a big boy like you has no ambition. [...]
OFFICER:	Yes, that's right, one must mature … Two times two … is two, and I can prove it by analogy, the highest form of proof. Listen, now! … One times one is one, so two times two must be two! For what applies to one must apply to the other!
SCHOOLMASTER:	This proof accords perfectly with the laws of logic, but the answer is wrong.
OFFICER:	What is in accord with the laws of logic can't be wrong. Let us put it to the test. One into one goes once, therefore two into two goes twice [...] No, I'm still not mature! … But how long must I sit here?
SCHOOLMASTER:	How long? Do you think that time and space exist? … Suppose that time exists, then you ought to be able to say what time is. What is time?
OFFICER:	Time [*Considers*] I can't say, but I know what it is. *Ergo.* I know what two times two is, without being able to say it. Can you tell me what time is, Sir?

SCHOOLMASTER: Of course I can! [...] Time? ... Let me see! ... While we
               are talking, time flies. Therefore, time is something
               that flies while I talk!
A BOY: [*getting up*]. Your are talking now, and while you're
               talking, I'm flying, consequently I am time!
SCHOOLMASTER: According to the laws of logic that is perfectly correct!
OFFICER: But in that case the laws of logic are absurd, because Nils
               can't be time just because he flew away.
               [...]
SCHOOLMASTER: But if logic is absurd then so is the whole world too ...
               and in that case why the hell should I sit here teaching
               all of you such absurdities! ... If someone will stand
               us a drink, let's go for a swim!

                                              (*MJoP*, pp. 216–17)

This brief scene embodies the quintessence of a modernist dramaturgy, and
reveals the shock of a disintegrating world order. It arrests the instant when a
previously shared set of values and perceptions, which had served as a basis
for the meaningful action of coherent dramatic characters, transforms into
nonsensical babble. Cognitive systems, such as logic, language and the concepts of classical physics, by which human beings had previously made sense
of the world, no longer function. These changes also had fateful consequences
for drama. In an irrational world a plot constructed of a causal chain of events
is no longer possible. Moreover, the characters find no reason to act, since
their actions have no serious consequences. In Greek tragedy the plot unfolds
through the inevitable actions of the protagonist. A tragic hero like Oedipus is
being born as he acts on the stage. The Officer in *A Dream Play*, however, is
incapable of any action that would identify him as a hero or would reveal his
character. The more the scene evolves, the greater his paralysis, and the more
confused he becomes regarding his own identity. It is as if Oedipus, having
reached the point of recognizing who he actually is, were suddenly to find
himself back at his starting point, in complete ignorance once again. This is a
universe that no longer recognizes itself in the patterns of classical drama
where the world of the play is constituted as the main character unfolds
through a series of actions.

In many of Strindberg's post-Inferno plays the protagonist stands outside
the world of a play-within-the-play, looking on as if watching a performance,
or journeys through his or her own life as if visiting a foreign planet. If they act
at all, the characters are divorced from their actions. It is precisely the notion
of character that is questioned, for example, in *To Damascus*, and this
questioning becomes a central theme that connects the episodes enacted for
the education of the main character, the Stranger, in his search for himself.

The exploration of guilt becomes a vital component in his search because he, like many other characters in the post-Inferno plays, cannot take responsibility for a life that seems forced upon him externally, and has nothing to do with his decisions or actions. Under such circumstances the classic notion of *hamartia*, the tragic failure of judgement upon which the hero's action is based, becomes obsolete. Life appears to him a punishment for some unknown guilt, possibly even contracted in some other life, or at best a game played with human puppets by a cruel god.

Similarly, the Officer in the school scene of *A Dream Play* is trapped in the nightmare of watching himself act and react mechanically in a dream, like a helpless puppet, unable to break the spell and change his plight. There are no external reference points against which actions might be measured. The objective plot of classical drama is replaced by a dream-within-a-dream structure in which the dreamer is lost in the maze of his, or her, own subjectivity. Even the most routine action (getting up and leaving, for instance) constitutes insurmountable hardship. Still sitting on the school-bench, the Officer cries out for help to his friend, the Quarantine Master:

OFFICER: Can you imagine, that fellow's had me sitting on a school-bench, even though I've got my doctorate!

QUARANTINE MASTER: Well, why don't you just leave?

OFFICER: You can talk! Leave? That's easier said than done!

(p. 218)

A dreamlike quality of life is also experienced by the characters in *To Damascus I*, which Strindberg in his preface to *A Dream Play* labels his previous, and thus very first, dream play. Here, the Stranger, a writer by profession, reports that 'there are moments when I doubt that life has more reality than my poems' (*SV*39, p. 17). And again, in *A Dream Play*, it is the Poet who equates reality with both poetry and dream as he sings a duet with the god Indra's Daughter:

DAUGHTER: The Growing Castle and the Officer ... I dreamt it all...

POET: I put it into poetry once!

DAUGHTER: Then you know what poetry is ...

POET: Then I know what dreams are ... What is poetry?

DAUGHTER: Not reality, but more than reality ... not dreams, but waking dreams

(p. 230)

'...seek out masquerades...'

The sense of dream and poetry replacing reality becomes a leitmotif in *A Dream Play*, one that is not only voiced by the characters repeatedly, but is also reflected in the structure of the play. The entire play is constructed of episodes in which groups of characters perform scenes which are observed by others who stand by as spectators. The Officer, for example, complains to the Quarantine Master that he keeps forgetting everything he knows. His friend, who is 'dressed as a blackamoor' (*MJoP*, p. 207), gives him a cryptic answer, 'I often wish I could forget, especially about myself. That's why I'm so fond of masquerades, fancy-dress parades, and theatricals' (*MJoP*, p. 209). He guides the Officer through several scenes in this spectacle, relating the stories of the people who enact their lives in dumb shows before them. But the technique of theatricalizing the characters' world is not unique to this specific scene. When in 1906 Strindberg added the prologue between Indra and his Daughter, he decided to frame the entire drama as a play-within-a play that was performed for the education of the latter, the goddess who descends from the ether to explore life on earth. Episode by episode she discovers how social interaction wrought by coercion, ignorance, miscommunication and exploitation perpetuates the suffering of humans. In each scene she witnesses the theme of discord is modulated. This scheme that thematically links the successive scenes, replaces Aristotelian, causal plot. As the Daughter enters the 'Growing Castle' within the walls of which she finds a theatre with actors, singers and dancers of all ranks, she is guided through the house of life. Eventually, however, she is unable to remain an impartial spectator, and is drawn into the spectacle to enact a variety of roles as she becomes involved with the denizens of earth as a friend, wife, mother, confessor and a variety of other roles. Finally she ascends again to heaven, leaving behind the spectacle and abandoning the actors doomed endlessly to re-enact their roles, seemingly without reason or conclusion.

As Richard Bark points out in his study of Strindberg's dream-play technique, a dreamlike atmosphere is created when a fictional character in a play (first level of fiction) becomes the spectator of a play-within-the-play (a second level of fiction).[2] The effect of such a juxtaposition of various fictional layers is an ephemeral sense of reality. The characters are neither rooted in a tangible reality nor victims of their fatal psychological drives. Rather, they are both actors and perplexed spectators in a grand cosmic theatre, or trapped in the dream of an unknown dreamer. This conception of life as a dream and the world as a stage becomes prevalent in Strindberg's writing in the 1900s. According to Lionel Abel the world view that produces such 'metatheatrical' patterns (i.e. drama structured as a play-within-a-play or performance-within-a-performance) implies a vision of 'an essential illusoriness of reality'. With the questioning of formerly implacable values, 'the reality of the world is mortally affected, illusion becomes inseparable from reality … As in tragedy the misfortunes of the hero must be necessary and not accidental, so in the metaplay life *must* be a dream and the world *must* be a stage.'[3] Thus, 'metatheatre' occurs in 'theatre pieces about life seen as already theatricalised'.[4]

In his post-Inferno drama Strindberg could no longer make use of the naturalist techniques he embraced in the 1880s. His changing perception of the world and the self produced not only anti-realistic dramatic structure, but also entirely different ways of creating dramatic character. In his dream plays people are shown as dynamic sets of relations as opposed to singular identities. The plot of *To Damascus I* (the first play Strindberg completed after his Inferno crisis) consists of the Stranger setting out to resolve the Oedipal riddle of who he really is by pasting together the fragments of his personality like pieces in a jigsaw puzzle. He does that by confronting a series of uncanny figures, in each of which he recognizes some aspect of himself and his past as if contemplating his own shadows. They are not independent beings in their own right, but exist only in relation to the Stranger. Strindberg experiments here with a treatment of character that erases the uniqueness of personality and dissolves identity in the plurality of reflections.

By such profound subjectification of both plot and character, Strindberg turns the traditionally objective dramatic form inside out. Despite their large casts, *To Damascus* and *A Dream Play* can be read as monodramas, since the diverse characters seem to embody fragments of a single subjectivity: that of the dreamer, the author or the central character. In both these plays the individual characters lack distinct identities, and thus constantly switch roles and metamorphose into different shapes. Theorizing his new technique in the author's preface to *A Dream Play*, Strindberg claims that the

> characters split, double, multiply, dissolve, condense, disperse, and converge. But one consciousness holds sway over them all, that of the dreamer … He neither acquits nor condemns, but merely relates, and, just as a dream is more often painful than happy, so a tone of melancholy and pity for all mortal beings runs through this uncertain tale.   (*MJoP*, p. 176)

The term 'all mortal beings' signifies, of course, only those whose lives are confined within the space–time of the dream, whose very existence depends on the dreamer's subjectivity. As the dream quality of the Daughter's journey is stressed by the repetitious split of her personality into a spectator of, and actor in, the grotesque scenes taking place in the metamorphosing scenery around her, she seeks in vain for a higher self, a unifying principle. Because she is unable to break out from the enchanted dream world, she loses her sense of identity. The 'silver thread' which connects her to her (divine) origins is broken. She sees herself dissolve in the constantly changing roles she assumes in the dream. By the end of her journey she arrives at the very place where she started, and there is no way of telling how much time has elapsed, if any. Likewise, in *To Damascus I* we are left uncertain whether the Stranger has moved through all the stations of his journey or whether we are made to contemplate the evolving internal landscapes of his mind – the mind of the writer who conceives reality by means of poetry. As in *A Dream Play*, it is a question of similarly recurring scenes, albeit with a more consistent mirror structure. From the starting point of the street corner, the episodes move through a series of locations up to the central scene in the asylum, where the Stranger is confronted with a group of ghostlike figures, including the like-nesses of people he has previously encountered. After being chastised by a Confessor, he sets out along the same route he had followed to get here, passing the same stations in reverse order. At the end, he is again discovered sitting on the same street-bench as in the beginning, writing with his cane in the dust of the street.

The characters in these dream plays have no proper names and the Stranger's Swedish name, *den Okände*, translates literally as 'the Unknown'. Moreover, while this technique has often been compared to that of the allegorizing morality plays of the medieval world, Strindberg's splintered, transient characters are thoroughly modernist and negate any stable moral and meta-physical system of the kind which formed the basis of medieval allegorical characters such as Everyman or Avarice. Nevertheless, the journey structure of medieval dramatic forms, which Strindberg indeed borrowed in his dream plays, enabled him to present his perception of the fleeting modern self through a metatheatrical form in which aspects of the central character are distributed among a variety of figures, whom he or she observes acting out their roles.

The characters of Strindberg's post-Inferno drama are thus trying in vain to reintegrate fragments of their past and present selves into a makeshift whole. In the school scene of *A Dream Play* time seems at first reversed: the Officer has regressed into childhood. But rather than just a backwards flow of time, Strindberg devises a dreamlike dimension in which the concept of time is obliterated altogether. The Officer's figure incorporates two distinct states of consciousness; he is aware of being a grown man and an immature child simultaneously. External reality as a measure of subjective truth is no longer an option. Thus the irrational and nonsensical are revealed as both the characters' existential and psychological condition.

But if the world of the play is irrational, then language, an instrument by which to grasp the rational order of things, has become dysfunctional. The Officer in the school scene insists that he has done his homework, he 'knows', but he cannot 'say' how many two times two makes. This is a world where things no longer operate according to the laws of formal logic, but function by way of the seemingly chance associations of dreams, where images, situations and emotional states emerge, disperse and re-emerge. Language devised to communicate rational thought is of no use in expressing a state of irrational being. Dialogue, which in traditional drama carries the interactions between characters to an inevitable and logical conclusion, is ridiculed: although language obeys the laws of logic (time flies – Nils flies – Nils is time) as before, it is completely incongruent with the experience of the individual. The associative 'logic' of dreams has replaced rational thought and discursive language.

'What shall I play?'

Dramatic character as a set of roles without a fixed identity appears in a different way in part I of *The Dance of Death*, a play from the same period as *To Damascus* and *A Dream Play*. It is less a 'dream play' and more a direct enactment of plays-within-the-play and roles-within-the-role. And although *The Dance of Death* is often seen as a somewhat anachronistic post-Inferno naturalist play or a bourgeois marriage tragedy,[5] the title already suggests that we should not take everything literally. The environment is highly metaphorical – a projection of the characters' mutual state of mind rather than a realistic setting. The action takes place in a circular fortress tower on an island surrounded by the sea. We soon discover that the island is known popularly as 'Little Hell', and that the fortress used to be a prison. Again, the play's theme, as well as the circular structure which it dictates, is expressed visually in the set. The title's reference to the medieval *danse macabre* brings to mind the allegorical mode of a morality play. In *The Castle of Perseverance*, for instance, Mankind's castle is situated in the centre of a circle surrounded by water and the action represents Mankind's progress from birth to death and beyond, to the Last Judgment of the soul.

The hermetically isolated world of *The Dance of Death* encompasses Alice and Edgar, the couple who are, in the opening scene, preparing to celebrate their silver wedding; their twenty-five years of misery spent joined together in an infernal relationship. The initial stage directions describe two separate realms in the circular room, one belonging to Alice, the other to Edgar. The rest of the room seems to be a neutral acting area open to both of them. Alice's world includes an upright piano and two laurel wreaths with ribbons hanging on the wall on either side of a portrait that represents a woman in theatrical costume: Alice herself, who used to be an actress before her marriage. Edgar's 'dressing-room', on the other hand, contains a coat rack for his uniform accessories and sabres. A captain in the coast artillery, Edgar is not simply a soldier; he also acts out the role of the soldier, always wearing the proper costume: a uniform fitting for the occasion, a helmet and a sabre when on duty and riding boots with spurs. The boots, which he never takes off, even when sick or apparently dying, symbolize his role. In the dialogue there is a strong emphasis on playing from the opening sequence:

CAPTAIN: Won't you play something for me?
ALICE: ... What shall I play?
CAPTAIN: Whatever *you* like.
ALICE: You don't like my repertoire.
CAPTAIN: Nor you mine.   (*MJoP*, p. 113)

Although the conversation refers to playing the piano, an allusion to a theatrical performance and repertoire, which the following scenes will reinforce, is unavoidable. Throughout the play, Alice and Edgar engage in an acting game in which they both assume several roles. Alice's favourite role within the role is that of the actress, but she also plays the role of the neglected wife and the abducted and imprisoned princess of fairy tales. Edgar plays not only the soldier, but also the monstrous vampire feeding on others' lifesap, and Bluebeard, renowned for murdering his wives. These theatrical and mythical references transport the dramatic interaction from the concrete and realistic level to the metaphorical. When a third person, Kurt, enters this world of make-believe, Alice and Edgar gladly embrace a spectator, and

4. Keve Hjelm and Margaretha Krook as Edgar and Alice in the opening scene of *The Dance of Death* at the Royal Dramatic Theatre, Stockholm, in 1983.

stage for him a series of scenes from their repertoire. Despite Kurt's growing discomfort at having been cast as audience to the couple's infectious playacting, he seems to appreciate the game, and declares that Edgar would be 'comic if he weren't tragic, and for all his pettiness there's something grand about him' (p. 145). Eventually, however, their stage world engulfs Kurt as well. He is given the role of the liberator prince, the lover in the triangle, and finally the treacherous friend and scapegoat. Another theatricalizing device in the play is Edgar's tendency to rewrite and dramatize his own past as well as other people's. He insists that Kurt was the matchmaker who brought Alice and him together, and that Kurt abandoned his children. These are not simply lies, but the fictionalization of past events, a cruel game that creates occasion for further playacting. This is how the vampire appropriates other people's lives in order to sustain his own.

The dialogue is built up from sequences in which the characters are either playing games and acting out roles, or talking about playing. Their games include playing cards as well as performance numbers such as Alice's playing on the piano or Edgar's dancing the 'March of the Boyars'. Much of the dialogue is constructed of recurring clichés as key-lines of the characters' roles within the role. Edgar, for example, creates the image of being a tough military man with phrases such as 'I've never been ill ... I'll just drop down dead like an old soldier' (p. 115), 'A soldier must always be ready for action' (p. 143), and 'Strike out and march on' (p. 174). Both Edgar and Alice are aware of the eternal repetition in their lives, their games and their verbal exchanges: 'Haven't you noticed that we say the same thing every day?' (p. 121), exclaims Edgar, and Alice realizes that 'everything comes full circle' (p. 141). Causal plot yields to an oscillating dialogue, a verbal duel in which the character who concocts the more shocking story holds power over the other. Language has no information value, nor does it communicate the ideas or emotions of the speaker. In fact, language is used to confound information and falsify feelings. Alice gets into the habit of 'translating' Edgar's speeches, meaning to decipher the subtext: the covert information and the hidden intent behind what is being said.

Together, Alice and Edgar are set apart from the flow of time and detached from the external world, or indeed from any reality outside the microcosm of their relationship. In order to feel that they are alive and connected, they put on masks and create dramatic scenes, which provide occasions for interaction. At the close of Part I they find themselves as they were in the opening scene, preparing to celebrate their silver wedding, which depicts their course of life dragging on in perpetual cycles, without any growth or essential change. When Kurt tells Edgar of his realization that 'you've invented a life for yourself and those about you', the Captain replies, 'There comes a moment when the ability to invent ... ends. And then reality is revealed in all its nakedness! ... It's terrifying' (p. 167). Thus, by playacting, Alice and Edgar constantly reinvent themselves in an attempt to conceal their sense of void, the terrifying reality of the empty self. But the actor needs both a spectator and an antagonist, which makes them mutually dependent on each other. The actor-vampires are imprisoned in a parasitic relationship balanced between mutual love and hate, between a constant need for each other and a drive to break away. They keep making the rounds of their 'Little Hell': their marriage turned into a theatre. As Edgar suggests,

> I've never been able to figure out whether life is serious or just a farce. When it's funny, it can be most painful, when it's serious, it can be quite tranquil and pleasant ... And then, when you finally take it seriously, along comes someone and makes a fool of you. (p. 174)

'...a net of nerves and knots...'

The radical shift in the conception of the self as reflected in these plays can also be detected in the work of other artists, philosophers and scientists of the period. Strindberg's new dramaturgy testifies to an ongoing cross-fertilization between various disciplines, media and fields of experience. By the turn of the nineteenth century the study of the psyche had developed into a new experimental science that responded to the modernist transition in culture by discarding the unified conception of the self and presenting it as a dynamic and multiple structure. Hippolyte Bernheim, Jean-Martin Charcot, Théodule Ribot and Alfred Binet are but some of those associated with the modern conception of dynamic psychiatry, whose work was known to Strindberg. Their efforts were paralleled by equally influential philosophical reinterpretations of the self and subjectivity, such as Eduard von Hartmann's then immensely popular theory of the unconscious in *Philosophie des Unbewußten* (1869) and Carl du Prel's *Die Philosophie der Mystik* (1885). These intellectual currents had a vital effect on Strindberg's rethinking of drama. And even though his sense of a shifting, splintered self was by no means an original idea, his contribution consisted of endowing that notion with a tangible dramatic expression that corresponded with experience.

Freud's remapping of the human psyche, presented in a scientific context but drawing on literature and myth, arrived at similar conclusions as Strindberg's dramatic experiments. Both men were engaged in the same modernist revaluation of the self, and each introduced a new language in his respective field. Strindberg's *A Dream Play* and Freud's *Interpretation of Dreams* (1900) were not only published within a year of each other; they also had much in common in their themes and their focus on the modern subject. If Freud regarded dreams as the subject's staging of unconscious desires in a symbolic language, Strindberg dramatized the clash of internal impulses in concrete stage images, drawing on the scientific discourse of his time. In describing the psychic apparatus as the interplay between various aspects of the subject in spatial-visual terms, Freud also suggested an innate theatricality: the splitting of the subject into actor and spectator. In some passages he explicitly claims that the ego 'can take itself as an object ... [it] can observe itself, criticise itself ... In this, one part of the ego is setting itself over against the rest. So the ego can be split; it splits itself during a number of its functions – temporarily at least.'[6] Yet, for Freud, the unproblematic reintegration of the parts was the norm, and aberrations would be healed by therapy. Strindberg, however, carried his findings to their ultimate ideological and artistic consequences. He, who in the Preface to *Miss Julie* had already seen 'character' patched together from scraps of a dissolving culture, developed in his late plays a new mode of theatre, which rendered the despair of the irrecoverably splintered and alienated modern self losing sight of a coherent identity, including that of the author. For him there was no recourse to a reassuring, ordered universe such as science might provide, nor to artistic techniques that would re-establish the illusion of that bygone order with its safe and stable identities.

What helped Strindberg dramatize the experience of modernity beyond the scientific and philosophical discourses of the times were his observations of nature, his sensitivity to music and above all his ventures into painting and photography. He compared the contingency of generative and regenerative processes in nature to the creative methods of modernist painters, and strove to apply the same principles in his own painting and photographic experiments. The rise of abstraction and the shattering of perspective in the visual arts compares to the departure from Aristotelian aesthetics in the theatre with regard to the treatment of time, space, action and dramatic character. Although as a playwright Strindberg would never abandon verbal expression as his primary resource, he created a completely poeticized language that operates simultaneously on both an acoustic-musical and a visual level, rather than on a conceptual one. The majority of the post-Inferno plays combine scenic imagery, sound effects and evolving spatial and temporal patterns to create a sensory experience. Causal plot construction, rational language and realistic character motivation are superseded by a 'dream-logic' of perceptual associations in which images, melodies and verbal fragments are interwoven in an intricate collage where a leitmotif emerges from a texture of repetitions with variations.

In *To Damascus I*, for example, the visual and musical patterns that elaborate the central theme take over the role of action as organizing principle. Recurring landscapes, figures and musical chords, all of which reflect aspects of the Stranger's subjectivity, punctuate his journey. As the episodes unfold, these perceptual effects accumulate and fill up the originally blank canvas of the Stranger's self. The Lady's crocheting which she works on throughout the play becomes a tangible metaphor not only of the Stranger's volatile self ('it looks like a net of nerves and knots', he says (SV39, p. 64)), but also of the dramatic technique applied in the play. In *A Dream Play*, the dynamic image of the growing castle and the set pieces used to indicate the continuous metamorphosis of space serve as a visual background for the enacted events. The effect is that space seems always the same, yet at the same time different, alien, ephemeral. The rhythmic recurrence of locations, lines, and character groupings increases the uncanny effect of simultaneous sameness and difference – a distinct experience of the modern subject.

As these plays leave discords and contradictions unresolved, they reject the tradition of completeness so highly valued since Aristotle. The result is a departure from the hegemony of a single viewpoint as an organizing principle imposed on the material. Linear plot is replaced by a prismatic treatment of scenic space and by what Strindberg called 'polyphonic' musical structures, where characters and their speeches are traversed by shifting points of view, allowing multiple voices to be heard.[7] In the church scene of *A Dream Play*, for example, Indra's Daughter begins to play the organ. But instead of organ tones, human voices are heard. The Daughter, who literally and figuratively stands in for the Poet, serves as a musical instrument – the suffering of the people resounding through her. This is just one of many instances where conventional dialogue gives way to a plurality of often discordant voices. Strindberg's questioning of a stable, authoritative self and its underlying dramatic conventions effects the diffusion of the authorial voice. Groping towards ways of dramatizing his sense of a dynamic self, Strindberg prepares the ground for drama to emerge as a more pluralistic discourse.

NOTES

1. Aristotle, *On Poetry and Style*, trans. G. M. A. Grube (Indianapolis/Cambridge: Hackett Publishing, 1989), p. 12.
2. Richard Bark, 'Strindberg's Dream-Play Technique', in Göran Stockenström, ed., *Strindberg's Dramaturgy* (Minneapolis: University of Minnesota Press, 1988), pp. 99–101.
3. Lionel Abel, *Metatheatre: a New View of Dramatic Form* (New York: Hill & Wang, 1963), p. 79.
4. *Ibid.*, pp. 60, 62.
5. In his adaptation of Strindberg's play, Friedrich Dürrenmatt saw *The Dance of Death* as a bourgeois marriage tragedy which he developed into a 'comedy about bourgeois marriage tragedies'. See Dürrenmatt, *Play Strindberg* (New York: Grove Press, 1972), p. vi.

6. Sigmund Freud, *New Introductory Lectures on Psychoanalysis*, trans. James Strachey (New York: W. W. Norton, 1965), p. 58.

7. In a later addition to his Author's Preface to *A Dream Play*, Strindberg lays out his conception of the play's musical structure, claiming that its form is only seemingly incoherent. It is, in fact, designed as 'a symphony, polyphonic, now and then in the manner of a fugue with a constantly recurring main theme, which is repeated and varied by the thirty odd parts in every key' (*MJoP*, p. 300).

9

LYNN R. WILKINSON

The Chamber Plays

In 1907 and 1908 Strindberg wrote five plays for performance at his own Intimate Theatre, Intima Teatern, in Stockholm: *Thunder in the Air, After the Fire, The Ghost Sonata, The Pelican* and *The Black Glove.*[1] All were published in inexpensive editions by Ljus Publishing House and numbered as 'Chamber Plays', Op. 1 to 5. This represents the first occurrence in Swedish of the term *kammarspel* to designate a play but, as Strindberg himself acknowledged, he was inspired by Max Reinhardt's Kammerspiele, the small theatre adjacent to the large auditorium of the Deutsches Theater in Berlin, which opened in 1905 with a performance of Ibsen's *Ghosts* with sets designed by Edvard Munch. Strindberg also sent Reinhardt German translations of these works soon after they were written, and the latter's expressionist performances of these plays would make some of them part of the theatrical repertoire, at least in Germany and Scandinavia, where the terms *kammarspel* and *Kammerspiel* have come to designate a genre of plays with a restricted cast of characters, an emphasis on mood rather than plot, and intimate settings, often in interiors that suggest psychological space, as well as a social setting. Strindberg himself participated in this development, for he himself designated certain of his earlier plays, most notably *Easter*, as Chamber Plays.

In contrast to the situation in Northern Europe, in Great Britain and the United States the term 'chamber play', if it is known at all, refers to the five plays Strindberg wrote in 1907–8, works which are viewed as idiosyncratic at best and of interest mainly to Scandinavians and Strindberg scholars. Only one of the five, *The Ghost Sonata*, is somewhat familiar to English-speaking audiences. We have no tradition or genre of the chamber play, at least not one that harks back to Strindberg and his works of the 1900s. But if we take film into account, many of us are aware of at least one Scandinavian version of the chamber play or performance: in films such as *The Silence* or *Cries and Whispers*, Ingmar Bergman has transposed many of the elements of Strindberg's Chamber Plays to the screen. The juxtaposition is a suggestive one, for the Chamber Plays respond to changes in the technologies of communication and reproduction in the first decade of the twentieth century. At the beginning of *The Ghost Sonata*, for example, the Student makes a phone call, and throughout the five works, references to communicative networks tie them to the webs that connect city dwellers and perhaps even control their fates. As the association with Reinhardt's Kammerspiele suggests, one of the resonances of the term Chamber Play was spatial, the emphasis on intimate settings; Strindberg himself also compared the works to chamber music. But a third context also seems crucial: that of the *camera obscura* or, as in French, *chambre obscure*, the darkened interior into which the forms of the world intrude, appearing upside down on one of the walls. The *camera obscura* made possible the invention of the photograph; Marx and Engels also referred to its reversal of the image in a famous passage at the beginning of *The German Ideology* to describe a tendency, which appears natural, to view the world upside down so that relationships of domination were either reversed or obscured. The small worlds of the Chamber Plays, which may be dreams or illusions, recall the representations within the *camera obscura*. But the Chamber Plays respond to new technologies of representation and performance in more obvious ways, as well. The Intimate Theatre aimed to bring spectators closer than ever to performers, and in his writings to its actors, Strindberg stressed a more intimate style of acting, one which drew above all on the novel and pointed forward to the new performance styles that would emerge in tandem with the development of the close-up and other techniques of narrative film.

Patrick McGuinness draws a distinction that is also useful for understanding the relationship between Strindberg's Chamber Plays and later developments in Western theatre:

> I have argued the case for Maeterlinck's originality, but this 'originality' takes two distinct forms: that of having been the *first* to do something and that of having been the *only one* to do something. *L'Intruse* and *Les Aveugles* were, in their time, the *only* plays of their kind; they have now become the *first* of their kind. But *Pelléas* remains the *only* play of its kind.[2]

Of course, as McGuinness acknowledges, *Pelléas et Mélisande* has inspired several musical adaptations, beginning with that of Debussy, and has had a notable influence on performance culture broadly defined. A similar point might be made concerning Strindberg's Chamber Plays, especially in relation to film. But in the theatre, only two of the Chamber Plays point forward to later developments, at least outside Sweden: the apocalyptic misogyny of *The Pelican*, in which a demonic mother prompts her children to burn themselves alive, shares significant common ground with German expressionist drama;

and *The Ghost Sonata*, with its contradictory dialogue, inexplicable turns of events and half-human characters looks in hindsight like an ancestor of the theatre of the absurd.

Since the plays were originally published and performed individually and out of sequence, both at the Intimate Theatre and in Berlin, the reading or performance of individual plays in isolation does not appear to contradict Strindberg's intentions. But thematic continuities, as well as their numbering and common title, suggest that they can – and should – also be interpreted as a sequence. One might draw an analogy here with the way that the individual poems of Baudelaire's *Les Fleurs du mal* can be appreciated separately but are also part of an arrangement that has prompted some interpreters to look for a 'secret architecture'.[3] The comparison is not random; with their often lyrical focus on the experience of isolated individuals in the city, the Chamber Plays represent a late development of the urban aesthetics of Baudelaire's poetry, as well as its transfer to the stage.

Since *The Ghost Sonata* is the best known of the Chamber Plays, although in many ways the least typical, it can serve as a point of departure for a double-reading of the Chamber Plays as a group of discrete works and as a whole. The play comprises three distinct parts with three separate settings, and critics have disputed whether these should be called acts or scenes.[4] The first is set on a city street and brings together an Old Man in a wheelchair, a Student who rescued a child the night before, and a Milkmaid visible only to the Student, as well as several other, for the most part silent, characters who are all related in some way to the family that lives in the apartment on the first floor of the building in the background. The Student says he longs to see the interior of the apartment, but realizes that his dream is hopeless. The Old Man promises that he will, if only he follows orders. The second part of the play takes place in the so-called round room of the apartment, where a ghostly gathering called the ghost supper is taking place. Here the participants repeat gestures and phrases they have made or uttered countless times before, but the intrusion of the Old Man and the Student causes a stir. The Old Man, who had been the lover of the host's wife and is the father of the daughter of the household, unmasks his rival as a former servant and cook's assistant. Meanwhile, the wife and mother emerges from the wall of the house as a creature who combines features of an old woman, a parrot and a mummy, apparently an example of the living dead whose utterances are only partly human. At the end of this section of the play, the Old Man sees the Milkmaid, which terrifies him; he disappears behind the so-called death screen and dies. The third part takes place in an interior within the interior, in a space called the hyacinth room, where the daughter of the household lives. The Student enters to pay court to her, but very soon the frail young woman begins to complain about the burdens of life, especially housework. Their conversation is interrupted by the intrusion of the aggressive and resentful Cook, who also complains about the burden of housework, but whom the young woman accuses of starving her and her family. After the Cook leaves, the Student begins to recite the Old Icelandic lay to the sun, which the young woman had sung as she played the harp at the end of the second part of the play, but now his performance accompanies her death. Finally, a fourth perspective appears from behind the wall of the hyacinth room; it is a reproduction of Arnold Böcklin's painting *Der Toten-Insel* (The Isle of the Dead).

The ending of *The Ghost Sonata* has puzzled or annoyed many readers, spectators and performers, and some, like Ingmar Bergman in his 1973 production of the play, have simply chosen to omit it. But in the text and first performance, Böcklin's painting provides a clear link both to the interior of the Intimate Theatre and to the Chamber Plays as a sequence. In the theatre, a reproduction was hung on one side of the stage, while Böcklin's *The Isle of the Living* was displayed on the other. Moreover, on finishing *The Ghost Sonata*, Strindberg began work on a play entitled *Toten-Insel*, which opens with a kind of tableau vivant in which a dead man awakes in the world of Böcklin's painting, and of which he completed only two scenes.

The reproduction of Böcklin's painting, both in the Intimate Theatre and *The Ghost Sonata*, links the Chamber Plays to transformations in turn-of-the-century visual culture. Historians and theorists of silent film have long been aware of the parallels between the illusionism of nineteenth-century staging and silent film in the 1900s and 1910s. For Ben Brewster and Lea Jacobs, for example, naturalism in the theatre displaced an older pictorialism that emphasized the illusionism of theatrical spectacles. Pictorialism drew on performance traditions that dramatized paintings, such as the *tableau vivant*, or which saw the proscenium arch stage as an illusionistic space akin to a framed painting. The analogy was made explicit when a frame was con-structed around the stage at the Haymarket Theatre in London around 1880, emphasizing both the coherence of the world represented on stage and its separation from the everyday experience of spectators.[5] Brewster and Jacobs's analysis emphasizes the debts of some early silent films to the older pictorial tradition, which had emphasized large-scale acting while others, such as Victor Sjöström's *Ingmarssönerna*, incorporate naturalistic acting, as well as complex shots in deep focus that realize the dramatic potential of the pictorial tradition. Strindberg's Intimate Theatre and Chamber Plays likewise draw on both traditions. The two reproductions of Böcklin paintings on either side of the stage represent a kind of double framing, inviting spectators to view the performance as an illusion within a frame that is itself a framed illusion. In contrast, the sets of the plays are the streets and households of the contemporary bourgeoisie. They hark back to the drawing-room interiors of Ibsen and other late nineteenth-century dramatists.

In fact, echoes of Ibsen's plays and their interiors link *The Ghost Sonata* to the other Chamber Plays. The collapsed house and fire from which the Student rescued a child may well hark back to Ibsen's *Ghosts*, at the end of which a charity orphanage burns down, but it may also be another version of the blaze that destroyed the house in *After the Fire*, which may in turn be a result of the lightning in *Thunder in the Air*. It also points forward to the blaze that consumes the dysfunctional family in *The Pelican*. Both *After the Fire* and *The Pelican* suggest that incendiary blazes are cleansing, as well as destructive, but all five chamber plays give pride of place to buildings and interiors as psychological, as well as architectural, spaces. All five feature distinctly urban settings with buildings that house several families and whose thin walls compromise the inhabitants' privacy. Strindberg's houses, however, are thoroughly modernized. References occur throughout the series to the networks of modern life, such as railways and telephone lines, networks that sometimes appear to explain or represent the interconnectedness of life in the city, but at others are mythologized as a kind of fate.

Earlier approaches to *The Ghost Sonata* often emphasized its relationship to Strindberg's life but, more recently, critics and historians have explored its affinity with *To Damascus I* and *A Dream Play*. Common to these so-called post-Inferno plays is an emphasis on the fluid boundaries between dreams and waking experience, as well as other experiential categories, such as time, space or even human character. Richard Bark views *The Ghost Sonata* as the culmination of Strindberg's 'dream play technique', in which the writer has mastered the technique of representing the experience of dreams on stage, above all by showing a dreamer dreaming, as in the sequence in *The Ghost Sonata* in which the Student sees a milkmaid who is invisible to the other characters.[6] For Evert Sprinchorn, on the other hand, the play represents perceptions rather than people or things. Thus Strindberg employs a surrealistic language

> in which metaphors assume life. To say 'time hangs heavy' is one thing; to picture, as Dali has done, a watch hanging heavily is another. To say that the sweet young thing you once knew now looks like an old mummy is one thing; to have this woman imagine herself as a mummy and comport herself like one, as Strindberg has her do, is another.[7]

Again, the many references to food and servants who starve their employers have dismayed some critics, but such sequences do raise questions concerning work and social justice in otherwise apparently ethereal settings. In fact, the sickly young woman's complaints about housework in the hyacinth room at the end of the play suggest why she might choose to die. Others have been preoccupied by the question of the relationship between musical and literary form suggested by the title, *The Ghost Sonata*, which, according to Strindberg, harks back to Beethoven's Piano Sonata, Op. 31, no. 2, which Strindberg referred to as *The Ghost Sonata*, as well as his Piano Trio, Op. 70, no. 1, commonly known as 'The Ghost Trio'. Strindberg himself also emphasized the parallel between chamber play and chamber music, likewise intended for performance in small, even private spaces, but it is important not to insist on a detailed correlation of musical and literary form. If a three-part structure is common to sonata form and Strindberg's play, it also characterizes *Miss Julie*, written and first performed in 1888. And while it is possible to discern patterns that resemble leitmotifs, these occur for the most part across several, if not all, the Chamber Plays, which as a group are perhaps best viewed in terms of a theme and variations.

It is significant, however, that musical works are quoted either in the dialogue or as actual performances in all three parts of *The Ghost Sonata*. In the opening scene, the Old Man sends the Student to a performance of Wagner's *Die Walküre*; the second concludes with the young woman's performance of a stanza from the Icelandic lay to the sun, a performance which is echoed at the end of the play when sounds from the harp introduce the Student's recital of the same lines. These works find their place among others mentioned or performed in the series as a whole, from *La pluie d'or*, a waltz heard through a window at the beginning of Op. 1, to the piano music that seeps through the walls of Op. 4 and 5. Significantly, the music always comes from within the world of the play (in film terminology, it is diegetic), with the possible exception of Sinding's *Frühlingsrauschen*, heard on two occasions in Op. 5, with no discernible point of origin in the play. Music thus suggests the permeability of the interiors represented on stage, while the names and fragmentary performances of well-known musical pieces form part of a network of references to representations from other genres and the other arts. The appearance of Böcklin's *The Isle of the Dead* at the end of *The Ghost Sonata* is probably the most prominent in the entire series, but it is significant that the ghost supper in the second scene closely resembles a similar episode in Strindberg's own novel, *Black Banners*, published in 1907. Both in his writings for the Intimate Theatre and in the Chamber Plays themselves, Strindberg sometimes draws on the techniques and perspectives of narrative prose. In *The Ghost Sonata* the emphasis is on perceptions, as though from the perspective of a character or characters in a narrative work.

As I have argued elsewhere, the thematic similarities between the five Chamber Plays suggest that they can be read or performed as a sequence that tells a series of interrelated stories. Op. 1 and 5 both feature old men and younger wives and mothers who are punished for their failure to care enough for husband or child, thus reflecting Strindberg's anguish and resentment at his third wife's decision to remarry. The same two plays also reflect the old men's confrontation with, and acceptance of, death. The Old Man in *The Ghost Sonata* who dies at the end of the second scene can be seen as a variation on this theme. *Thunder in the Air, After the Fire* and *The Ghost Sonata* all feature *flâneurs* as central characters: thus in *The Ghost Sonata*, the Student gazes longingly into the interior of the apartment building he later enters; in the first and third parts of *Thunder in the Air*, the Gentleman stands on the street outside his apartment, musing about the goings-on behind the red curtains in an adjacent household; in *After the Fire*, on the other hand, a stranger confronts the ruins of his and the collective past. Here an individual returns after thirty years in America to find the building in which he grew up a smoking ruin; conversing with the inhabitants of the building, he discovers their pettiness and dishonesty. But if the blaze brings their faults into the open, the heat also forces the adjacent tree into early bloom, suggesting the renewing possibilities of fire. At the beginning of *The Ghost Sonata*, the Student has come from such a disaster, from which he has apparently rescued a child. In contrast, the younger generation in *The Pelican* reflect on their unhappy childhood and elect to immolate themselves in the apartment they grew up in. This play, which was especially popular in Germany in the early twentieth century, is marred by a virulent misogyny that demonizes the widowed mother, who has apparently starved her children, mistreated her husband and forced her daughter to marry one of her own lovers.

Short, lyrical dramas linked by common themes, these works represent the point of departure for any discussion of the chamber play as a genre. All five feature urban settings and expose the falseness, as well as the fragility, of the interiors that outsiders long to penetrate. Eschewing the obvious effects of musical accompaniment, the plays incorporate references to, and performances of, music in ways that throw into relief the intersection between language and other sounds, as well as the lack of privacy in the city. But music is only one among other arts and genres represented in the world of the plays, as Böcklin's *The Isle of the Dead*, displayed at one side of the stage in Strindberg's Intimate Theatre, confirms. Some interpreters view the world of the plays as a psychological space, a projection of the self. But, as the framing of *The Ghost Sonata* suggests, these are highly mediated works which lure the eyes and ears of the spectator inward through the faces of the city street into interiors that may be imaginary and that here, as well as in *Thunder in the Air, After the Fire* and *The Pelican*, are uninhabitable and even doomed.

Ironically, the performances of the Chamber Plays at the Intimate Theatre were not a success. The failure of works written specifically for the new theatrical space to win critical or popular approval seems to reflect the limitations of the theatre, its director, the actors and Stockholm audiences. Indeed, the small theatre, which closed on 11 December 1910, just over three years after it had opened, experienced many difficulties, not the least of which were financial, for the auditorium could accommodate only 161 spectators and performances often did not sell out. But the Chamber Plays posed particular problems. The small stage of the Intimate Theatre, which could not accommodate the set of the opening scene of *The Ghost Sonata*, was too limited for the other plays as well. August Falck, who had directed *Miss Julie* so successfully, did not seem to understand the Chamber Plays. Although many of the actors at the Intimate Theatre were talented, they were for the most part amateurs and apparently could not decide on a uniform speaking style. Moreover, Stockholm audiences were apparently not yet ready for these innovative short plays.[8] Not surprisingly, it was thus Max Reinhardt's guest performances in Stockholm in 1917, 1920 and 1921 that awakened Sweden to their potential.

In contrast to the Chamber Plays of 1907–8, *Easter*, which Strindberg also came to refer to as a Chamber Play, was performed at the Intimate Theatre to critical and popular acclaim. Like the later plays, it features at least one character whose experiences call into question the usual distinctions between waking and dreaming, the natural and supernatural. Its settings are evocative, for although it takes place in the interior of a family fallen on hard times, the changes in the light, reflecting changes in the weather, suggest shifts in the family's fortunes, as well as their perspectives on their situation. The play also has close ties to music, but in this case the music does not come from inside the world of the play. At the opening of each of the three short acts, movements from the string quartet version of Haydn's *Seven Last Words* are heard. Strindberg's designation of *Easter* as a Chamber Play may stem from his desire to make the most of the successes he had: that play seemed to belong in the Intimate Theatre to a far greater extent than the first four Chamber Plays (excluding the later *The Black Glove*). But it also reflects his attempts to define the Chamber Play as a new genre.[9]

Strindberg also grappled with this problem in a series of remarkable theoretical texts, written at about this time and collected in *Samlade Verk* in a volume entitled *Teater och Intima Teatern*. When he commenced *Thunder in the Air*, probably in January 1907, he had not written for the theatre since 1903. What prompted him to take up playwriting again? In the essay, 'The Concept of the Intimate Theatre', Strindberg emphasizes the importance of developments in Germany, notably the opening in Berlin of the Hebbel

Theater and the Kammerspiele under the direction of Max Reinhardt, but he also notes that he had been in the forefront of the movement towards smaller spaces and shorter texts with works such as *Miss Julie* and his one-act plays written around 1890. The essay also provides important information about what Strindberg meant by a chamber play. Of Reinhardt's Kammerspiele, he writes:

> This autumn Reinhardt ventured to open the Kammerspiel-Haus, the name of which suggests the secret program. Chamber music's idea transposed to the drama. The intimate plot, the meaningful motif, the subtle treatment. Last autumn the Hebbel Theater opened in almost the same spirit, and throughout Germany theatres have sprung up with the name 'Intimate Theatre'.   (*SV*64, p. 13)

And he goes on to note:

> If one now asks what the purpose of an Intimate Theatre is and what is meant by 'chamber plays', I can give the following answer: In the drama we seek the intensely meaningful motif, but with limits. In the treatment, we avoid all vanity, all calculated effects, occasions for applause, star roles, solo numbers. No one form should limit the author, because the motif determines the form. Thus stylistic freedom limited only by the concept of unity and a feeling for style.   (*SV*64, p. 13)

Strindberg had good reason to be reminded of *Miss Julie*, because the play had recently been performed with considerable success in the provinces, in a production directed by the young theatre director August Falck. It finally premièred in Stockholm, also to critical acclaim, on 13 December 1906. Moreover, preparations for the première of *A Dream Play* were also under way, and a revival of *Gustav Vasa* had recently met with success. Although Strindberg did not meet Falck until November 1906 they had been in contact earlier and, sometime that year, they agreed to open a small theatre in Stockholm, a showplace for Strindberg's own plays, but under the direction of the young actor-director. The Intimate Theatre opened on 26 November 1907 with *The Pelican*, although by that time Strindberg had completed the first four Chamber Plays. *Miss Julie* opened there on 12 December that year.

In his overview of the genesis and early reception of the Chamber Plays, Gunnar Ollén argues that Strindberg composed them for two audiences: those of the Kammerspiele and the Hebbel Theater in Berlin, on the one hand, and the Intimate Theatre in Stockholm, on the other. Strindberg had sent the plays to his translator, Emil Schering, even before they were published and on 20 June 1907, he noted in his *Occult Diary* that Reinhardt had accepted *Thunder in the Air* for performance at the Kammerspiele. Interestingly, Reinhardt's stage also harks back to the small avant-garde theatres of the 1890s, but with a difference. Its opening production of

Ibsen's *Ghosts* with sets by Edvard Munch gave a stylish new gloss to a play that had provoked outrage when first performed throughout Europe in the 1870s. Reinhardt now mounted *Ghosts* on a small stage adjacent to the foremost state-supported theatre in the German capital. Always attuned to the potential for theatrical effects, he distilled a new kind of spectacle from Ibsen's play, one that emphasized the interplay between sets and psychology over the scandals of hypocrisy and disease, and which demonstrated that many different kinds of play could be reinterpreted for performance on a small stage.

One sees a similar process of distillation in the Chamber Plays, which also recall *Ghosts* in the allusions to fire, old men swindling their friends out of fortunes and, of course, in the title *The Ghost Sonata*. Despite Strindberg's misogyny and even misanthropy, however, the Chamber Plays never lose their edge of radical cultural critique. But what is at stake in his production for his own small theatre is also the development within the new technologies of communication and mechanical reproduction of conventions of performance that would dissolve not only the outworn conventions separating audience and the stage, and even what is public and private in the everyday life of the early twentieth-century bourgeoisie, but also those of live performance within a conventional theatre.

Strindberg's theoretical writings from the period of the Chamber Plays also make explicit the connections to the new technologies and mass culture. In contrast to conventional theatres, movie houses are democratic, allowing working people to attend at their convenience and at a reasonable price. The seating arrangements in the Intimate Theatre attempted to imitate what Strindberg saw as the egalitarian policies of the cinema. In discussing acting styles, moreover, he compares performances to the projected images of a magic lantern:

> I have always found it difficult to come up with a fixed view of a theatrical performance. The art of the actor is the child of a series of moments, a projection of a magic lantern that disappears when the ramp lights are dimmed, something half-real that eludes one's grasp. (*SV*64, p. 102)

Further, good acting in a small theatre has more to do with the kinds of gestures described in a novel than with conventions of acting in a large theatre. Significantly, like other theorists of the silent film era, Strindberg points to Dickens as a model for a new style of acting:

> As for reading, the good actor doesn't need to read plays; novels are just as good, even better. I think Dickens would be a good teacher, since he both provides more thorough characterizations than any dramatist has time for and since he

supplies endless motives. But he also provides something else the actor can use. He accompanies every character's appearance with a wealth of gestures and facial expressions that are of unparalleled excellence. I have just reread *David Copperfield* and my admiration for the teacher of my youth now goes beyond words. Using only small characters the size of insects he manages to achieve the same kind of illusion one gets at the theatre, with its huge apparatus, or, more to the point, he gives me the hallucination of real experiences. (*SV*64, pp. 107–8)

The disadvantage of film culture, on the other hand, is that, like other forms of mass entertainment, such as the operetta, it can be banal and cater to the tired or lazy, who only want sensations.

The essays on Shakespeare included among the Memoranda to members of the Intimate Theatre present theatrical tradition as a kind of counterweight to the potential mindlessness of popular culture. Although Strindberg discusses a number of plays, including *Macbeth* and *The Tempest*, his essay on *Hamlet* is the most important for understanding the relationship of intimate theatre both to theatrical tradition and to popular culture. Like *Ghosts*, *Hamlet* lent itself to shortening, even to a kind of distillation. Goethe, Strindberg notes, had advocated radical cuts in the text, and he himself had seen a shortened version at the Royal Theatre in 1867 and found it very effective. Having studied the text recently, however, Strindberg notes that he now thinks it would be possible to perform the text in its entirety, but that such a performance would place demands on the spectator not unlike those made by opera, as opposed to operetta, on a good listener:

> But to be able to appreciate this mighty tragedy, one needs to prepare the way one does for attendance at an opera; one reads the text, tries to come to terms with the plot and its prehistory. And so that the audience isn't distracted by the chatter at intermissions, the play should be performed with only a couple of curtains; and in order to accommodate the twenty tableaux that should be shown in rapid succession, one should always use the kind of Shakespearean stage that was constructed in Munich in the 1890s. These are absolute requirements. A permanent, abstract, architectonic frame that can be a room, but also a street or square, when the curtains are drawn; when pulled to the side, one is in an open landscape. (*SV*64, pp. 58–9)

Strindberg's comments emphasize the very fluid boundaries between plays written for an intimate theatre and those such as *Ghosts* or *Hamlet* which lend themselves to performance there. His references to the importance of the setting, in this case a bare stage that could accommodate rapid scene changes without intermission, point to the common ground between Shakespearean drama, Strindberg's *Dream Play* and the Chamber Plays. The Intimate Theatre performed Strindberg's *Queen Christina* on a stage like the one described here, with curtains as backdrops to suggest various settings. But what links the three contexts is above all the musical structure of the drama. *Hamlet*, Strindberg writes, 'is a symphony, composed polyphonically with independent motifs that are woven beautifully together; there are elements of the art of the fugue' (*SV*64, pp. 58–9).

But if the performance of the complete version of the play demands that the serious spectator study the text before the performance, one of the functions of shortened versions and shorter plays may be to appeal to a less sophisticated audience. Strindberg had suggested something along these lines at the beginning of his preface to *Miss Julie*, when he compared the theatre to a *Biblia Pauperum* (a richly illustrated medieval work with pictures of biblical events), the function of which was to teach and to fascinate. With seating arrangements that Strindberg hoped would match the auditoriums of film theatres and works that made fewer demands on audiences, it seems that one of the aims of the Intimate Theatre was to occupy middle ground between the new performances made possible by mechanical reproduction and an older theatrical culture which catered for the privileged classes.

But elsewhere Strindberg suggests that film itself is a demanding medium that not only requires that the spectator actively interpret a sequence of images, but also brings into focus the discontinuous aspects of human personality. An actor's performance, he notes, is like a series of photographs that give the illusion of continuity:

> See, in a film projector, how many frames must be shown in succession in order to give the impression of a single movement, and still the image trembles. Every vibration is missing a transition. When thousands of instantaneous images are necessary for one movement of the arm, how many billions would be necessary to portray a movement of the soul? The poet's portrayal of human beings are therefore mere summaries, outlines, all incomplete and half false. (*SV*64, p. 65)

One hears in these lines echoes of the famous assertion in the Preface to *Miss Julie* concerning the illusoriness of character. Remarkably, this passage suggests that the characterless character is made possible by the invention of film and photography. Indeed, Strindberg's Preface acknowledged the importance of photography for the kind of staging appropriate for his play. But whereas the Preface to *Miss Julie* compared the ideal set – cropped and diagonal – with the cropped perspectives of photographs or impressionist paintings, now the reference is to film, which is also fragmentary and calls into question the continuity of time and the boundaries of the human and non-human worlds. Thus Béla Balázs's account of the close-up in which the camera lens brings into focus aspects of the human being previously invisible is pertinent to Strindberg's layering of character in the Chamber

Plays, which emphasize the theatricality of the human personality and call into question whether anything at all lies behind the successive masks assumed by human beings.[10]

Like film, the Chamber Plays also work with an accumulation of images that evoke the passage – illusory or not – of time. These plays hark back to *Miss Julie* and other works of that period not only because of similarities in literary structure and theatrical settings, but also because they are about memory. Whereas *Miss Julie* dramatized the coupling and uncoupling of an aristocratic young woman and a male servant in terms that echoed the dissolution of Strindberg's first marriage, *Thunder in the Air* represented the protagonist's coming to terms with the memory of his failed marriage. Similarly, the sequence as a whole looks back to the contestatory works of the late nineteenth-century avant-garde theatre and suggests how the provocative subject matter of plays like Ibsen's *Ghosts* had become part of the everyday life in early twentieth-century European cities. Moreover, like the sensationalist entertainments of popular culture, the Chamber Plays seem designed to leave the reader or spectator with a central impression or sensation but, unlike the mindless melodies of popular operettas, the music of the Chamber Plays is complex, often discordant and demanding.

NOTES

1. The titles of Op. 1 and 2 have been translated in different ways. I have used Eivor Martinus's *Thunder in the Air* and *After the Fire* in her versions of *The Chamber Plays* (Bath: Absolute Classics, 1991), for *Oväder* and *Brända tomten* throughout this essay.

2. *Maurice Maeterlinck and the Making of Modern Theater* (Oxford and New York: Oxford University Press, 2000), p. 256.

3. See, for example, Albert Feuillerat, *L'architecture des* Fleurs du mal (New Haven: Yale University Press, 1941), and James A. Lawler, *Poetry and Moral Dialectic: Baudelaire's 'Secret Architecture'* (Madison: Fairleigh Dickinson University Press, 1997).

4. Egil Törnqvist has argued that the three parts of the play are acts, not movements or scenes, and that *Spöksonaten* should therefore be considered a three-act, not a one-act, play (Törnqvist 1970, p. 30). The shortness of the five 'acts' in *The Black Glove*, however, suggests that Strindberg himself used the term in such a way that it may be futile to try to impose such distinctions.

5. For a summary of Brewster and Jacobs's argument (*Theatre to Cinema: Stage Pictorialism and the Early Silent Film* (Oxford and New York: Oxford University Press, 1997), see pp. 212–16. *Ingmarssönerna* is discussed pp. 133–6. On the relationship of the staging of the Chamber Plays, especially *The Ghost Sonata*, see Frederick J. Marker and Lise-Lone Marker, *Strindberg and Modernist Theatre* (Cambridge: Cambridge University Press, 2002). For the importance of technology to modernist culture, see Sara Danius, *The Senses of Modernism: Technology, Perception, and Aesthetics* (Ithaca: Cornell University Press, 2002).

6. For Richard Bark, dream plays evoke

> The impression of a dream [which] implies a transformation, a suspension of time and space and can be created in a play or onstage 1. when a character in a play finds him- or herself in a dreamlike situation as a participant in the dream fiction or 2. when a character finds him- or herself in a dreamlike situation but outside the fiction, instead contemplating the dreamlike as a spectator of a play within the play or 3. when the reader/spectator plays the role of the 'dreamer' of the dreamlike
>
> (*Strindbergs drömspelsteknik – i drama och teater*
> Lund: Studentlitteratur, 1981, p. 60)

7. Evert Sprinchorn, *Strindberg as Dramatist* (New Haven and London: Yale University Press, 1982), p. 259.
8. For an account of the Intimate Theatre in English, see Michael Meyer, *Strindberg: a Biography* (London: Secker & Warburg, 1985), pp. 471–546.
9. For a discussion of *Easter* as a chamber play, see Stephen A. Mitchell, 'The Path from *Inferno* to the *Chamber Plays*: *Easter* and Swedenborg', *Modern Drama*, 29:2 (1986), pp. 157–68.
10. See Balázs's account of Asta Nielsen's face, *Theory of the Film: Character and Growth of a New Art*, trans. Edith Bone (New York: Dover, 1970), pp. 64–5.

10

MATTHEW H. WIKANDER

Out of Egypt: Strindberg's historical drama

In the essay 'The Mysticism of World History' (1903), Strindberg sketched out a philosophy of history based upon patterns of analogous, parallel events in widely different places and times. The opening event of this wide-ranging sketch of world history is the exodus from Egypt. Similarly, his collection of short stories, *Historical Miniatures* (1905), opened with the birth of Moses and finished with the French Revolution. Also in 1903, Strindberg began a series of 'world historical plays'; the first of these was to be devoted to the exodus from Egypt, and the series was to culminate with the French Revolution.[1] 'The Mysticism of World History' treated the exodus from Egypt as one of a number of contemporaneous migrations. The Greek myths relate the voyages of the Argonauts; Semiramis, 'the legendary Assyrian queen', invades India, where the migration of the Hindus is already under way, giving rise to 'the tremendous conflicts depicted in the *Mahabharata*'. In China the emperor moves the capital 'just as Moses moves Israel's camp in the desert'. All of these 'migrations of peoples' accompany 'great upheavals in spiritual life', and Moses 'initiates his – conscious or unconscious – world historical epic by climbing Mount Sinai' and receiving 'the great secret of monotheism, the doctrine of unity, monism – one God, the father of all, in whose name every people will be united' (*SE*, p. 181).

Strindberg's fascination with the exodus is biblical, historical and personal. While his conversion experience in the Inferno period shapes the argument in 'The Mysticism of World History', the search for a single principle that would account for the chaotic turbulence of world history occupied him from the beginning of his career to its end. Just as Strindberg sought, through autobiography, to present himself both as a unique individual and as a case study (in his pre-Inferno years) and as a suffering sinner (in his later works) so, as a dramatist approaching world history, he sought to link the stories of individuals with larger national and transnational developments. Strindberg's most significant achievement in the area of historical drama is a series of plays that placed Swedish history within the larger contexts of European history and of his own notions concerning the workings of providence. Strindberg had hoped to complete a cycle of plays that would cover the history of his country from the time of Saint Erik right up to the threshold of his present. While this epic ambition was not fulfilled, the heritage of Swedish history plays he did complete is comparable only to Shakespeare's cycle of English history plays.

The comparison with Shakespeare is one which Strindberg himself relished and fully explores in the *Open Letters to the Intimate Theatre*. 'The difficulty in writing a historic drama is to find just the right mixture of the historic and the intimate', Strindberg argues in his notes on *Julius Caesar*. 'History in the large is Providence's own composition, and Shakespeare is a providentialist just as the ancient writers of tragedies were, so he does not neglect the historical but lets divine justice be meted out to the point of pettiness.'[2] In Shakespeare's English histories the playwright engaged a Tudor providentialist view of history, in which the Wars of the Roses were regarded as England's punishment for the deposition of Richard II. Shakespeare's history plays subject this easy providentialism to dramatic scrutiny. 'Pettiness' is a charge that might better be levelled against the works of providence in Strindberg's later history plays, where providence intervenes directly in the lives of individuals. Strindberg's view of providence endorses traditional Christian typology; the exodus he dramatizes figures the individual sinner's journey to salvation and also reflects a nation's journey from bondage to liberty and Christendom's eventual delivery from the constraints of time and history. In his conscious medievalism Strindberg adopts a less sceptical view of providence than Shakespeare, and places Swedish history within the framework of a divine plan.

The bulk of Strindberg's output in historical drama came after his Inferno experiences, in three major surges of creativity. After his return from Paris to Sweden he immersed himself in the study of Swedish history and in rereading Shakespeare. *The Saga of the Folkungs* (1899), *Gustav Vasa* (1899) and *Erik XIV* (1899) mark the first phase of Strindberg's attempt to infuse Swedish history with his views about divine providence; these were followed after a brief gap by the epic *Gustav Adolf* (1900), *Engelbrekt* (1901) and the remarkable threesome of *Queen Christina* (1901), *Charles XII* (1901) and *Gustav III* (1902). A final phase led to *The Last of the Knights* (1908), *The Regent* (1909) and *Earl Birger of Bjälbo* (1909). Taken together with *Master Olof* (1872), Strindberg's Swedish history plays cover an era from the mid-thirteenth-century (the time of Earl Birger) to the death of Gustav III in 1792. In addition there are the four world historical dramas, devoted to Luther, Moses, Socrates and Christ, all dating from 1903.

Just as Moses fulfils a great destiny in leading his people out of Egypt, so these historical figures act out the purposes of the divine will. 'A man of

Providence, a common soldier who proceeds blindly without knowing the commander's intentions, a great instrument, a token of contradictions and a rock of offence, a man full of pride and humility, of clear thoughts and unclear purposes': this description of Luther from 'The Mysticism of World History' applies to a whole host of Strindberg's historical figures (*SE*, p. 199). Master Olof, called to actions that would usher in the Swedish Reformation; Gustav Vasa, 'the wonder man of God'; Magnus Eriksson and Gustav Adolf, patiently expiating the sins of their ancestors; Strindberg's tormented Hamlet, Erik XIV; Queen Christina making her peace with Rome; Gustav III assassinated in a Sweden cast into revolutionary ferment by the news from France: these and Strindberg's other historical figures are national figures, but they are also agents of a conscious will working itself out in history.

'It has long been thought that the course of history has been governed by certain laws similar to those which prevail in the kingdom of nature', Strindberg declares in 'The Mysticism of World History' (*SE*, p. 220). Paradoxically, Strindberg's first great history play, *Master Olof* (1872), was written under the influence of Henry Thomas Buckle, whose *History of Civilization in England* (1857–61) explicitly repudiated both providence and free will in favour of a sociological approach to history. For Buckle history could be studied for moral laws that would correspond to the laws of nature. Strindberg's early admiration of Buckle provided him with a framework within which he could see national history and the histories of individuals as mirroring and refracting a larger pattern. In 'The Mysticism of World History', Strindberg uses Buckle's own terminology to arrive at an opposite conclusion:

> But the course of history shows such a combination of freedom and necessity that on the one hand one must to some degree recognise the freedom of the will, while on the other concede the existence of a necessity that restricts the efforts of the individual according to prevailing circumstances, and which thus brings about a synthesis ... The great synthesist who unites the opposites, resolves the contradictions and maintains this balance, is no human being and can be no other than the invisible legislator who alters the laws in freedom according to altered circumstances: the creator, the dissolver and preserver, he may then be called – what you will. (*SE*, p. 220)

Here Strindberg does not so much repudiate Buckle as provide an alternative explanation to Buckle's inquiries into the interaction of freedom and necessity in human history. Buckle, by proposing that history could function as an integrated scientific discipline and lead to certainties rather than speculation, provided the young Strindberg with a weapon against the complacent pieties of late nineteenth-century Sweden. More importantly, in focusing the dramatist's attention on the conflict between freedom and necessity in history, Buckle helped Strindberg to define the conflicts that have always animated great historical drama.

Master Olof (1872)

Master Olof was Strindberg's first great success in the theatre, and getting it produced occupied most of Strindberg's energy through the 1870s (it was finally performed in 1882). The play broke with the patterns of classical regularity, static declamation and hero worship that had characterized the earlier generation of Swedish historical drama. Strindberg drew inspiration from Georg Brandes, whose study of Shakespearean dramaturgy had 'very much the effect of a blast of dynamite' on Strindberg, 'removing the wall of rock that had hitherto stood between him and his genius', says Joan Bulman.[3] From Brandes, Strindberg learned that heroes can have flaws and tics, like Hotspur's speech impediment, and can be depicted in the round, making fools of themselves or squabbling with their wives, that comic and tragic plots could mirror each other, and that minor characters could offer thematic counterpoint and ironic commentary upon the great and famous.

Strindberg went further in his emulation of Shakespeare by invoking the world-as-stage motif so central to Shakespearean drama. The opening scene of Master Olof takes the form of a play-within-the-play, as the young Master Olof presides over a reading of The Comedy of Tobias. By citing 'the oldest extant Swedish play on a biblical subject', Strindberg suggests an ambitious parallel between his play and the foundations of Swedish drama.[4] The students quote Jeremiah in this 'little comedy about the children of Israel and the Babylonian captivity', as Olof describes it (p. 26). In standard Christian typological readings of Old Testament stories, the Babylonian captivity is a parallel episode to the bondage in Egypt, and both figure the soul's thraldom to sin. Lars Sparre demands that Olof stop playing and recognize the applicability of Jeremiah's words to himself. 'Did the Lord say that?', cries Olof, goaded by the prophetic text. As will become customary in Strindberg's plays, anniversaries and holidays mark significant events: Olof hears Sparre's call on Pentecost eve. Yet the play will dramatize Olof's ambivalence towards the Protestant cause, his wary attempts to balance the demands of church and state and his eventual backsliding. 'En Avfälling' (translated 'renegade' by Walter Johnson (p. 122), 'traitor' by Michael Meyer),[5] was an early title for Master Olof, signalling that the key event in the play would be Olof's capitulation and his failure to embrace martyrdom at the end.

Another early alternative title for the play was 'What is Truth?' Here Buckle's idea of the relativity of truth meets Strindberg's fondness for biblical parallels and allusions. (Pilate famously demands 'What is truth?' while washing his hands.) In a tavern scene Strindberg pays direct homage to both Brandes and Buckle, as drunken arguments about the Danes, the Lübeck financiers, Luther, Huss, Zwingli and America all set Olof's attempts at reform within a larger European context of Reformation European trade and colonialism. Strindberg shows his hero at home in a domestic quarrel, but Olof's wife Kristina is also an emblem of the people. 'Shouldn't I be happy when I've been released from bondage, when I've become your wife?', she asks. Like Moses, Olof has ascended the mountain top, and Kristina begs him to 'turn home now and then from the struggles you wage up on the mountains; I can't come up to you; come down to me for a moment' (pp. 84–5). In addition to Shakespearean and biblical elements in this characterization we find also a strong admixture of Ibsen's rigid and frosty Brand, who sacrifices his wife and son and allows his mother to die without reconciliation.

At the end of the play, Strindberg adverts to another of his favourite techniques, returning to the beginning. Olof stands in the pillory on the anniversary of the reading of *The Comedy of Tobias*. Vilhelm, one of the students from the first scene, enters, ready to see Olof go to his death, 'with your face radiant and your eyes raised to the sky while the people shout: So dies a martyr!' Everything repeats, and Olof must hear Gert's cry of 'Renegade!' as he '*collapses on the pillory, completely crushed*' (pp. 121–2). Instead of heeding the call to heroic martyrdom, he finds himself caught in a cycle of rebellion and reaction that evokes the stiff-necked people of the biblical exodus, who persist in their worship of Baal while Moses struggles on the mountaintop.

Penitents in Inferno

Early as it is, *Master Olof* shows all the elements of Strindberg's mature historical drama: the emphasis on holidays and anniversaries, the evocation of biblical parallels, the use of multiple plots commenting on each other ('that is my strength!' exulted Strindberg about 'parallel action' in his *Open Letters to the Intimate Theatre* (*LIT*, p. 59)), and the effort to place Swedish history within larger patterns of European, world and providential history. All these elements were then in place when Strindberg returned to historical drama in 1899, prompted by the success of a revival of *Master Olof*. In November 1897 Strindberg reminded Waldemar Bülow of the close connection between *Inferno* and the afterpiece (*Efterspel*) to the verse *Master Olof*, which was published as an epigraph to the German edition (*SL*, pp. 409, 617). This fragment features a 'Mystery Play', a conversation between God (the evil power), Lucifer (the force for good) and the Eternal One – a self-consciously medieval play-within-the-play – acted out before an old, complacent Master Olof and his two sons.

Strindberg emphasized the link between the Swedish middle ages and Shakespeare in his letter to the Intimate Theatre about *The Saga of the Folkungs*. His object was 'to represent the bloody saga of the Folkungs which very much resembles the War of the Roses in England' (*LIT*, p. 249). Walter Johnson cites Exodus 20: 5 ('For I the Lord thy God am a jealous God visiting the iniquity of the fathers upon the children unto the third and fourth generation') as

> undoubtedly Strindberg's point of departure, for that Old Testament idea fits Strindberg's King Magnus perfectly. He is the one member of the fourth generation of the great Folkungs. Add to that the biblical ritual sacrifice of the innocent and the atonement by the innocent.[6]

'The powers above are toying with mortals to show them they are children', Magnus explains, for he understands that he must expiate his ancestors' crimes (p. 103). 'It is fulfilled', he cries, Christ-like, at the play's close (p. 105).

After this play Strindberg returned to the period of *Master Olof* with his next two historical plays, *Gustav Vasa* and *Erik XIV*. He considered the three plays to be a trilogy (again in the Shakespearean mould). The first scene of *Gustav Vasa* shows Gustav's old friends and allies, the dalesmen who had supported his rising against the Danes, called out one by one to execution; in a stunning theatrical coup, their bloody coats are thrown into the room as we hear drumbeats offstage. Gustav does not appear until the third act, in his royal study. A painting of '*God visiting Abraham in the grove of Mamre*' dominates the room. '*The Abraham closely resembles the* KING', the stage directions report (p. 190). The dalesmen in the first scene remember Gustav as a 'wonder man of God', who delivered his people from bondage (p. 158), a type of Moses, and his son Erik compares him to the Norse gods Thor and Odin (p. 183). 'Providence wanted to test him and temper its man, to whom the building of the kingdom was entrusted, and for that reason it struck him with all the misfortunes of Job', Strindberg told the Intimate Theatre (*LIT*, p. 256). As the drumbeats of rebellion sound, Gustav is forced to conduct a Swedenborgian settling of accounts: 'Who is this mysterious man who's never seen?' the king asks as Nils Dacke's forces approach the palace. 'Perhaps a miracle man of God – in his way!' Olof rejoins (p. 226). 'I bend before the higher wisdom, which surpasses my understanding', Gustav announces (p. 216).

Erik XIV continues the story into the reign of Gustav's troubled son. But where Gustav haunts the first scene of his play like a mysterious, bloody agent of providence, Erik throws a tantrum and litters the stage with household items while he, too, remains unseen. Erik is 'a characterization of a character-less human being', Strindberg writes (*LIT*, p. 256). Erik is both a Prince Hal (a drunken torment to his father) and a Hamlet, a parallel that Strindberg emphasizes. In the play, Erik scandalizes the realm by marrying the commoner, Karin Månsdotter ('Ophelia = Karin' in Strindberg's view); he is 'insane or simulating insanity, like Hamlet, vacillating, judges and rejects his judgment' (*LIT*, p. 80). 'Have you ever noticed', Erik asks his confidant, Göran Persson, 'that there are matters we don't understand, and may not understand?' (p. 323). An inscrutable providence causes Erik to bungle through his rule, and the family destiny fulfils itself as his brothers depose him. Marc Roth has pointed out that Erik XIV participates in another Shakespearean convention, that of the player king. While Gustav Vasa is like an Odin, a Thor, a Moses and a Job, Erik flunks the demands of his role. He is humiliated at the trial of the Stures when his children wrap a doll in the text of his speech and he is forced to improvise inarticulately. Michael Kaufman makes the identification explicit: Erik is 'an abandoned doll, passively borne by forces he can neither control nor understand'[7].

Idealized heroes: *Gustav Adolf* (1900) and *Engelbrekt* (1901)

Gustav Adolf is 'my *Nathan the Wise*', Strindberg announced (*LIT*, p. 257). This play, epic in its length and sweep, anticipates the argument of 'The Mysticism of World History'. In its final scene, 'Scotchmen, Frenchmen, Russians, Turks, Hungarians, Calmucks, Italians, Jews' gather to pay respects to Gustav Adolf, who through the play undergoes transformation from a persecutor of Catholics to a spokesman for tolerance (p. 225). This ending is anticipated in the opening scene, set characteristically on a Midsummer Day, where we meet a Miller and his Wife, a Catholic and a Protestant, who function as recurring choral figures in the play. 'Pastor, pastor, that's our benediction', exclaims one of Gustav's soldiers overhearing the prayers of Jews and Mohammedans. Like a 'penitent in Inferno', in Martin Lamm's words, Gustav endures punishment for his ancestors' crimes and recognizes that 'the past comes back' (p. 198) to punish him.[8]

'Engelbrekt is one of Sweden's most beautiful memories, and I felt I should keep his character as high and as pure as Schiller kept his William Tell', Strindberg wrote of his next play (*LIT*, p. 253). The Schillerian idealizing impulse that transforms Gustav Adolf into an apostle of religious tolerance here makes Engelbrekt a blameless folk hero murdered by the spiteful and envious Måns Natt-och-Dag. The first reviews of this play were unanimously negative, leading Strindberg to fulminate: 'When they murdered my *Engelbrekt* during the fall of 1901, they seemed to have been led by the same stupid motive that Måns Natt-och-Dag had when he murdered his. I have forgiven that crime, but I have not forgotten it!' (*LIT*, p. 255).

'The villain': *Charles XII* (1901)

A Coastguard challenges a Man in rags in the ruins of an abandoned cottage; the Man is a former soldier in Charles XII's army, and the cottage was once his home. 'Stralsund has fallen', announces the Coastguard. 'No-o! And the villain?' 'Has fled!' 'Just as at Poltava! The villain always flees except when he wins', cries the Man (p. 109). For Strindberg, Charles's military campaigns impoverished and devastated his country, and the play offers a running commentary through choric figures like the Man, Luxembourg the Dwarf, a Malcontent and (at the end of Act Four), a host of 'shabby figures ... silent, ghostlike, curious, and fingering everything', who invade Charles's garden (p. 158). Strindberg here deploys, as Göran Stockenström has argued, the quasi-allegorical techniques of *A Dream Play*.[9] Charles staggers numbly through the wreckage of his country to his death. The play depicts Charles not in his early career, when he was a man of providence, but late in his life, 'divided against himself'. Providence has taken him 'by the ear and played blindman's buff with him' (p. 161). For Barry Jacobs, Charles undergoes a Swedenborgian 'vastation', and *Charles XII* is a 'nemesis play'.[10] Swedenborg himself is a character in the drama, and it is he who gets the ambiguous final words. When the king is shot, the bullet comes from above: either from the fortress, or, Swedenborg says, pointing to the heavens, 'From up *there*!' 'And if it didn't, it should have come from up there!' (pp. 165–6).

Player queen and player king: *Queen Christina* (1901)
and *Gustav III* (1901)

In these two plays, Strindberg eschews both the epic sweep of *Gustav Adolf* and the dream-play techniques of *Charles XII*. Rather, he seems to have adopted the focus on palace intrigue and amorous dalliance that characterizes the mid-nineteenth-century historical melodramas of Scribe. In a *Blue Book* essay, 'The Impossibility of Writing History', Strindberg inveighed against the practice of whitewashing historical figures; it is absolutely certain, he declared, that 'Charles XII was mad, and Christina a – – –'.[11] 'Whore, you mean!', cries Klaus Tott in response to her claim to be his 'queen of hearts' (p. 73). She treats her lovers like dolls – 'Exactly! Big dolls!' (p. 30) – and is foolishly overconfident. 'No one will murder me! Everyone loves me!', she tells her lover Magnus de la Gardie. 'You know, Charles I of England said exactly the same thing', he replies, 'amazed' (p. 30). In the final act, she appears in a *Masque of Pandora*, but this play-within-the-play dissolves into a tableau of 'strange people, all of them motionless, silent, and pale-faced' (p. 72). After this, Christina stops playacting and declares her conversion to Catholicism. 'Would it be possible for Gustav Adolf's daughter to desert her forefathers' faith?', asks Oxenstjerna. 'It is very possible that she will return to her forefathers' faith, to Engelbrekt's, Stures', and the first Vasas' faith ... from which you are apostates', she counters. 'I appeal to the spirit of my great father; I, too, for he gave his life, not for a faith forced upon anyone, but for freedom of faith, for tolerance!' Christina shames Oxenstjerna and Carl Gustav with this invocation not of the historical Gustav Adolf, but of Strindberg's champion of tolerance (pp. 79–80).

Gustav III takes the form of an intrigue drama, but, like *Queen Christina*, uses the world-as-theatre trope to reach out to a wider Swedish, European and providential context. The world of Gustav III, in the late eighteenth century, is a world of revolution. The news of the fall of the Bastille comes from France, and Gustav's reforms (like freedom of the press, dramatized in an opening scene at Horn's bookstore), show the king to be eager to emulate the Enlightenment in Sweden. But like Christina, Gustav is trapped in playacting. The whole play is rich with metatheatrical references to Shakespeare's *Julius Caesar* and Corneille's *Cinna*. Both plays deal with assassination attempts, successful in Shakespeare and forestalled by Augustus in Corneille. Since the most famous fact about Gustav III was his assassination after a masked ball (and since the historical Gustav played Cinna in his own court theatre), Strindberg's invocation of these earlier tragedies of assassination has an ironic resonance. Like Erik or Christina, Gustav improvises; like Charles, he is playing 'blindman's buff' with providence. At the end of the play, Anckarström (his eventual assassin) stalks Gustav, but the queen enters and puts herself in the line of fire. Unaware of Anckarström's presence, Gustav reminds the queen that despite the successes of his enemies, he was born with 'Caesar's luck'. 'Wasn't there someone called Brutus?' the queen reminds him. The queen and king act out a move from chess. 'The queen is the strongest piece and has the function of protecting the king', Gustav jokes, unaware that the queen's physical presence has saved him from checkmate this time (p. 265).[12]

The mysticism of history and the late historical plays

It is exactly like an enormous game of chess played by a single player who moves both black and white, is completely impartial, takes when he ought to, makes plans for both sides, is for himself and against himself, thinks everything out in advance and has only one aim: to maintain balance and justice, while ending the match in a draw!

Strindberg exclaims thus in 'The Mysticism of World History' as he watches China introduce Buddhism into Japan 'during Mohammed's life-time' (p. 191). The image of the chess game that concludes *Gustav III* becomes a central metaphor in Strindberg's understanding of history in his later plays. The historical plays inspired by the essay show the drawing of parallels and the insistence on a single, unifying intelligence guiding history that characterizes all Strindberg's post-Inferno historical drama. 'As usual in my historical dramas', Strindberg declares in his remarks about *Earl Birger of Bjälbo* (*LIT*, p. 265), 'I have placed Swedish history within the frame of world history.' Similarly, Strindberg's play about Luther, *The Nightingale of Wittenberg*, is set in 1492, and we hear rumours of great events taking place elsewhere in that year. In *Hellas*, the play about Socrates, a Jew and a Roman discuss whether Israel or Rome holds the key to the future, and they reappear in *The Lamb and the Beast*, the play about Christ, and continue the discussion. In these plays and his last plays about Swedish history, Strindberg fleshes out 'The Mysticism of World History'. His full expression of his theory of history in that essay, ironically, led to dramas whose construction is mechanical and whose choice of historical material, both Swedish and world historical, is dictated solely by the demands of the essay's vision.

Once Strindberg had made it explicit that the aim of the divine hand guiding human history was a united Europe, at peace with itself and embracing a single Christian faith, the tensions and conflicts that animate his greatest history plays dissipate. The last Swedish history plays show a weariness and cynicism about history that is matched in the *Blue Book* entries relating to history from about this time. Their titles are revealing: 'The Impossibility of Writing History' and 'Lie-History'. 'I am tired, of everything, and now I'll go – I'll go to Visingö. I'll walk in the forest, look at the lake, think about what I have lived through, try to be reconciled with the past and to prepare myself for what is ahead', says Earl Birger at the end of his play (p. 246). The earl's resignation mirrors the playwright's fatigue.

Alluding to a medieval, providentialist world view while, like Shakespeare, admitting its obsolescence, Strindberg was able in his best history plays – *The Vasa Trilogy*, *Charles XII*, *Queen Christina*, *Gustav III* and *Gustav Adolf* – to cast his historical figures against a biblical backdrop in which their struggles become emblematic and Swedish history a mirror of an exodus from bondage to freedom. The plays themselves enact Strindberg's struggle towards his theory of history. But once he had found a system, his plays came to be demonstrations rather than dramatic explorations of the conflict of freedom and necessity. Strindberg's Swedish monarchs only dimly apprehend the destiny that drives them, but in 'The Mysticism of World History'

Strindberg has identified the particular mission of Sweden. The 'current of civilization', he pronounces, moves always northward.

> Why does 'the spirit of the Lord dwell in the lands of the north,' or all the lands in the northern half of the globe? Why are prophets, heroes and lawmakers not born in the southern half, why did the tree of knowledge not grow beneath the equator and south of the meridian?

he asks (p. 196). The biblical text Strindberg quotes here (Zachariah 6: 7–8) does not at all support the use Strindberg makes of it, a suggestion (derived at least in part from Buckle) that people become more civilized as they are able to live in colder climates. Sweden, like Strindberg, enacts an exodus and emerges from bondage as its monarchs learn to submit to the divine will, and the divine will guides the world to a unity of belief that mirrors Strindberg's own 'creedless Christianity'.[13]

NOTES

1. According to Gunnar Ollén, Strindberg had originally proposed a trilogy 'dealing exclusively with world history: India, Egypt, Palestine, Greece, Rome, the Middle Ages, the Reformation, and ending with the French Revolution', in a letter to Karl Otto Bonnier in 1884 and had again mentioned such a project in 1889. See August Strindberg, *World Historical Plays*, trans. Arvid Paulson, intr. Gunnar Ollén (New York: Twayne Publishers and the American-Scandinavian Foundation, 1970), p. 5. For a translation of 'The Mysticism of World History', see *SE*, pp. 181–222.
2. *LIT*, p. 118.
3. Joan Bulman, *Strindberg and Shakespeare: Shakespeare's Influence on Strindberg's Historical Drama* (London: Jonathan Cape, 1933), pp. 47–8.
4. Strindberg's Swedish history plays are quoted from the Washington University Press edition, translated by Walter Johnson. In the case of *Master Olof*, Johnson used as his text the 1872 prose version of the play. The verse versions and the Epilogue are not available in English translation. Quoted is Johnson's note, p. 128.
5. August Strindberg, *Plays: Three; Master Olof, Creditors, To Damascus (Part 1)*, trans. Michael Meyer (London: Methuen, 1991). 'In the original', Meyer explains in a note,

    > Gert, offstage, cries 'Apostate!' on hearing of Olof's recantation. Many members of the audience will not immediately understand what this word means, and unfamiliar offstage words are notoriously difficult to catch. I have therefore altered the word to 'Traitor', and have put it in the mouth of Vilhelm, the young scholar, the only character left on stage with Olof.   (p. 10)

    There is some authority for this, in that Vilhelm is given this line in both the *Mellandramat* (middle version) and verse versions of the play.
6. Walter Johnson, *Strindberg and the Historical Drama* (Seattle: University of Washington Press, 1963), p. 80.

7. Marc Roth, 'Strindberg's Historical Role Players', *Scandinavica*, 18 (1979), pp. 123–39; Michael Kaufman, 'Strindberg's Historical Imagination: *Erik XIV*', *Comparative Drama*, 9 (1975), p. 327.
8. Martin Lamm, *Strindbergs Dramer I–II* (Stockholm: Albert Bonniers Förlag, 1924–6), vol. II, p. 179.
9. Göran Stockenström, '*Charles XII* as Dream Play', in Göran Stockenström, ed., *Strindberg's Dramaturgy* (Minneapolis: University of Minnesota Press, 1988), pp. 223–44.
10. Barry Jacobs, 'Strindberg and the Dramatic Tableau: *Master Olof* and *Charles XII*', *Scandinavica*, 43 (2003), pp. 71, 81.
11. *En Blå Bok II* (*SV66*, p. 790).
12. For fuller discussion, see Matthew H. Wikander, 'Historical Vision and Dramatic Historiography: Strindberg's *Gustav III* in Light of Shakespeare's Julius Caesar and Corneille's Cinna', in Birgitta Steene, ed., *Strindberg and History*, (Stockholm: Almqvist & Wiksell, 1992), pp. 201–7, and 'Strindberg's *Gustav III*: the Player King on the Stage of History', *Modern Drama*, 30 (1987), pp. 80–9.
13. Harry V. E. Palmblad, *Strindberg's Conception of History* (1927; rpt. New York: AMS Press, 1966), p. 90. A different view, stressing the provisional nature of 'The Mysticism of World History', is offered by Conny Svensson, *Strindberg om världshistorien* (Stockholm: Gidlunds Förlag, 2000), 'English Summary', pp. 272–8.

PART III

Performance and legacy

11

FREDERICK J. MARKER AND LISE-LONE MARKER

Strindberg in the theatre

Paradoxically, although the profound influence of August Strindberg on both modernist and postmodernist theatre is generally accepted as a critical truism, one of the sturdiest myths that has attached itself to Strindberg's work has been the notion that his plays – particularly the great experimental master-pieces of his post-Inferno period – are somehow 'unperformable'. Nothing could be farther from the truth, however, for despite the undeniable difficul-ties they present and the innovative thinking they demand in production, works such as *A Dream Play*, *To Damascus* and *The Ghost Sonata* have never lost their grip on the imaginations of directors, actors and designers. This enduring influence is, in turn, linked to the crucial effect that this writer's allusive (and elusive) dramaturgical method has had on the changing nature of the theatrical experience and the spectator's relationship to it.

For, although *Miss Julie* is probably still the play most commonly asso-ciated with Strindberg's name, the naturalist revolution it helped to ferment soon ceased to hold the playwright's interest. By the end of the 1890s he had become convinced that his ideal of a comprehensive revitalization of the theatre could only be achieved through the complete rejection of a con-ventional view of stage illusion and dramatic construction that no longer adequately expressed the mystical and visionary aspects of life that, to an increasing extent, he came to regard as the true fabric of reality. Even by the time *Miss Julie* had reached Paris and the Théâtre Libre in 1893, Strindberg himself had stopped writing plays altogether. When he resumed his theatre work at the end of the century, after having passed through the darkest period in his life, it was with a very different style of performance and a new revolution in mind. This revolution, fostered by a new generation of modernist innovators such as Gordon Craig, Vsevolod Meyerhold, Evgeny Vakhtangov and Max Reinhardt, would soon discover one of its strongest rallying points in Strindberg's dream plays and chamber plays. 'It is from him and through him that naturalism received the critical blow even if, moreover, it is also Strindberg who gave naturalism its most dramatic works', Pär Lagerkvist proclaimed in *Modern Theatre: Points of View and Attack*, a seminal reassessment of Strindberg's stature and significance that appeared six years after the playwright's death in 1912. 'If one wishes to understand the direction in which the modern theatre is actually striving, and the line of development it will probably follow, it is certainly wise to turn to him first of all.'[1]

German expressionism and beyond

To Damascus I, which appeared in print in 1898, was written at a time when concepts of theatrical illusion and stage setting were acquiring new meaning, radically at odds with the naturalistic objectivity promulgated by Strindberg himself only a few years earlier. In an interview published in *Svenska Dagbladet* (21 January 1899) to mark his fiftieth birthday, he makes his own solidarity with these new modernist trends perfectly clear. 'I don't want to use ordinary theatre decorations for my new plays', he told the Stockholm paper. 'All these old-fashioned theatrical rags must go! I want only a painted background representing a room, a forest, or whatever it may be, or perhaps a background could be produced by a shadow picture painted on glass and projected onto a white sheet.' For the world première of his first dream play, staged by Emil Grandinson at the Royal Dramatic Theatre (Dramaten) in November 1900, the symbolic journey of the nameless protagonist was enacted on a simple, raised stage-upon-the-stage, framed by a stylized arch in the spirit of von Perfall's so-called Shakespeare Stage in Munich. Glimpsed in the shadowy background a dreamlike succession of painted representational backcloths indicated the various 'stations' on the Unknown's pilgrimage. As Lagerkvist's modernist manifesto observes, the complex spatial and temporal dynamics of Strindberg's later dramas could not be adequately realized in performance until the more modern techniques of a new stagecraft – the cyclorama, advanced methods of lighting and back projections and not least the revolving stage – were introduced. Yet it is to Grandinson's credit that he pointed the way while having virtually none of these techniques at his disposal.

It was not until after Strindberg's death, however, that the major post-Inferno plays began to acquire a central place in the new theatre movement that Lagerkvist proclaims. Although *A Dream Play* and *The Ghost Sonata* were more significant in this respect, the influential Berlin première of *To Damascus I* in 1914 was the event that launched the veritable wave of expressionist performances of Strindberg that swept across Germany in the years around the First World War. Directed by Victor Barnowsky at his prestigious Lessing Théâtre, the focal point of this production was the compelling interpretation of the central character by Friedrich Kayssler. Very grand and spiritual as an actor, Kayssler's Unknown conveyed a deeply

5. Pointing the way: the asylum scene in Emil Grandinson's production of *To Damascus I* at the Royal Dramatic Theatre, Stockholm, in 1900.

human sense of suffering and guilt that called to mind his acclaimed performances as Faust in Max Reinhardt's productions of both part I (1909) and Part II (1911) of Goethe's drama. The protagonist's 'fantastical and hallucinatory' encounters with the other characters – all of them projections of his own inner guilt, Kayssler maintained – seemed to the German critics to oscillate 'between dream and waking, reality and vision'. Although the rather heavy expressionist scenery designed by Svend Gade necessitated the lowering of a black curtain between episodes, Barnowsky's skilful use of a revolve enabled him to sustain the desired impression on his audience of 'swiftly changing, lightly stylized pictures on the turning stage' (*Berliner Tageblatt*, 18 April 1914).

The impact of the Strindberg renaissance heralded by the Barnowsky revival of *To Damascus* was carried to Scandinavia and beyond by the touring productions of Max Reinhardt's smoothly coordinated ensemble. Reinhardt staged the first work in this cycle, *The Dance of Death*, at his Deutsches Theater in Berlin in 1912, a little more than four months after its author's death. His Strindberg campaign quickly gained momentum with successive productions of the first four of the Chamber Plays, *Storm* (1913), *The Pelican* (1914), *The Ghost Sonata* (1916) and *The Burned House* (1920). Most of these performances visited Scandinavia on tour, but none made a deeper impression there than his startling *The Ghost Sonata*, which first visited Stockholm and Gothenburg briefly half a year after its triumphant opening at his Kammerspiele in Berlin. By the 1920s, Swedish critics and directors would begin to raise vociferous objections to Reinhardt's 'Germanic' expressionism. But in 1917, with memories of the inauspicious premières of *A Dream Play* and *The Ghost Sonata* ten years earlier still fresh, this revolutionary reinterpretation of the latter play was greeted as a revelation. Its bleakness notwithstanding, Reinhardt's *Sonata* fired the modernist imagination with its consummate theatricality and emotional intensity – qualities that no one else (except perhaps Strindberg) had previously recognized in the Chamber Plays.

In the hands of Reinhardt's highly trained company, *The Ghost Sonata* emerged as a grotesque 'nightmare of marionettes', as critics called it. The driving force behind it was Paul Wegener's astonishing transformation of Hummel from the crafty and embittered old man Strindberg drew to a grotesque portrait of pure, diabolical malevolence – 'the incarnation of the Evil One, the symbol of destruction', as Norbert Falk wrote in *Berliner Zeitung am Mittag* (21 October 1916). From the outset, the emphatic use of expressionistic staging, lighting and sound effects established an unearthly atmosphere of darkness and dread that became, as it were, the outward manifestation of the inner spiritual darkness at the core of Wegener's demonization of Hummel. When the production came to Stockholm at the close of the same season, Reinhardt's picture of 'strange, spectral, sinister life' seemed fully as compelling to the Swedish critics as it had been to their Berlin colleagues. 'One sat totally absorbed, bewitched, seduced by this bizarre, fantastical vision that lay midway between genius and madness', Daniel Fahlström wrote in *Stockholms Tidningen* (4 May 1917).[2]

Even darker and more controversial were the twin productions of *A Dream Play* staged by Reinhardt in the autumn of 1921, first in Swedish at the Royal Dramatic Theatre in Stockholm and subsequently with his German company in Berlin. The initial German production of this play, directed by Rudolf Bernauer at his influential Theater im der Königgrätzerstrasse in 1916, had approached it as harmless fantasy, thereby subverting its dangerous modernist perceptions about the collapse of language, meaning and the differentiation between dream and so-called objective reality. In stark – and no doubt deliberate – contrast to this earlier popularization, Reinhardt's reinterpretation of *A Dream Play* projected a starkly pessimistic image of 'a shivering, desperate, shrieking humanity' struggling, in Siegfried Jacobsohn's words, in an atmosphere 'so distorted, so gloomy, so full of fantastic life and motion, that it might be Van Gogh's'.[3] Spotlights isolated individual figures and groups in pools of sculpted light while, in the surrounding primordial darkness, cries were heard and pale, wraith-like figures glimpsed 'with faces and demeanour united in anxiety, hatred and wrath' (*Svenska Dagbladet*, 29 October 1921). In general, from its expressive staging and choreographed mass scenes to the futuristic musical score provided by the Bulgarian composer Pantscho Wladigeroff, every aspect of Reinhardt's version contributed to the unified emotional impression of what one of his script notes for the Stockholm production terms 'the senseless chaos of an aggressive, murderous, and dying world'.[4]

The sense of deep human despair that even the Daughter of Indra experiences as the Lawyer's mortal wife became the leitmotif that resonated throughout Reinhardt's *mise-en-scène* – especially in the Berlin performance, in which Helene Thimig's blond, vulnerable Daughter and Eugen Klöpfer's poignant, Christ-like portrait of the Lawyer shared the focus of critical attention. In the performance's closing scene, this prevailing tone of unmitigated hopelessness was firmly underscored. After reciting her parting words to the Poet to music, the Daughter stepped on to a low altar of burning logs upon which all the other characters had laid their offerings; then, as the Growing Castle burst into flames, she too sank into the all-consuming fire. This harsh final image met strong opposition from the Stockholm critics, who were generally dismayed by the pessimism of the interpretation and its insensitivity to the play's lucid undertone of reconciliation and consolation.

By contrast, postwar audiences and critics in Berlin, for whom the appeal of Bernauer's escapist treatment had faded, embraced Reinhardt's nightmare vision of human suffering and anguish as a truer mirror of a daily existence overshadowed by poverty, labour unrest, political turmoil and the chaos of military defeat.

By the beginning of the 1920s, the musical, visionary power of Strindberg's late plays that Reinhardt's smoothly coordinated productions revealed had begun to attract much more widespread interest. The young Per Lindberg, the first in a succession of modernist Swedish directors devoted to Strindberg's plays, began his efforts in 1920 by using the ultramodern resources of the new Lorensberg Theatre in Gothenburg to extricate two of Strindberg's most popular historical dramas, *Master Olof* and *The Saga of the Folkungs*, from the naturalistic tradition of 'accurate' interiors and 'authentic' accessories in which both works had been located during the playwright's lifetime. Lindberg's defiance of these history play conventions anticipated in turn one of the most challenging of the new stagecraft experiments in Strindberg – Evgeny Vakhtangov's theatricalist rendering of *Erik XIV* at the First Studio of the Moscow Art Theatre in March 1921. Here, Michael Chekhov played the sensitive, ineffectual protagonist, trapped in a masked, moribund, crumbling court that stood in grotesque juxtaposition to the robust, realistically conceived world of the common people.

Some avant-garde attempts to perform Strindberg in the 1920s ended less successfully. The American première of *The Ghost Sonata*, presented by the Provincetown Players at their tiny theatre in Greenwich Village early in 1924, is remembered today chiefly for its programme containing Eugene O'Neill's widely reprinted tribute to Strindberg as 'the precursor of all modernity in our present theatre'. Despite O'Neill's exhortations and the innovative stage designs of Cleon Throckmorton, neither this production nor the Provincetown group's subsequent attempt to stage *A Dream Play* two years later succeeded in persuading the New York critics to take Strindberg's work seriously. Nor did *A Dream Play* fare any better in Paris, where the rebellious Antonin Artaud and his Théâtre Alfred Jarry staged it in 1928. Artaud's disruptive, pop-art version (*Le Songe, ou Jeu des Rêves*) survived only two afternoon showings, both of which, made the object of Surrealist outrage, collapsed into bedlam, brawling and verbal abuse traded freely between stage and auditorium.

In search of the poet within

Approaching them as neither outlandish avant-garde experiments nor nihilistic allegories of universal anguish, Olof Molander's Swedish productions of the dream plays in the 1930s established a new style of Strindberg performance that conclusively displaced what he called 'German Reinhardt-inspired romantic expressionism'. In his consciously revisionist revival of *A Dream Play* at Dramaten in 1935, exactly fourteen years after Reinhardt's guest production of it on the same stage, reality and dream seemed to merge into what some referred to as Molander's surrealism. 'Here one is in the midst of the dream, yet it seems to us at the same time more real than reality, uglier, more unsettling, more bitter, more beautiful. It is a condensed reality', Bo Bergman, the only Stockholm critic who had reviewed both Reinhardt's revival and the world première of the play in 1907, observed in *Dagens Nyheter* (26 October 1935). The 'condensed reality' to which this comment refers was grounded, precisely as Martin Lamm's critical interpretations of Strindberg's plays were grounded, in autobiography, in the identification of actual places and events in the playwright's life that lie encoded in his writing.

The spine of Molander's reinterpretation was thus its identification of the Dreamer, in all three of his voices, with the playwright himself. His presence was felt in the young, eternally expectant Officer, in the mature Lawyer whose bearded, careworn face bespoke the sufferings in which he dealt, and especially in the ageing Poet who, actually made up to resemble Strindberg, sat at the feet of Indra's Daughter – his muse and his own creation – to learn of the interchangeability of poetry and dream. In contrast to Reinhardt's version, in which the Poet was viewed on the same plane as all the other examples of tormented humanity, Molander presented him as the personification of the omniscient artist-dreamer for whom 'there are no secrets, no contradictions, no scruples, no law'. As a result, this suggestion of a Strindberg persona, standing both within the play and outside of it, introduced an ironic dimension of reflective compassion that counteracted the bleakness of Reinhardt's terrifying vision.

In the role of the Daughter, Tora Teje was a majestic, brooding figure in black who likewise often seemed to stand outside the action, as if watching a play-within-the-play being enacted for her. The presence of this sympathetic onlooker intensified the strongly oneiric dimension that Molander imparted to the moments of profoundest humiliation in the play. Such a moment was the scene in which the Officer finds himself seated on the school-bench again, obliged to relearn long-forgotten lessons and repeat old mistakes. Trapped in a nightmare of recurrences, Lars Hanson's Officer became both the dreamer and the player in a dream sequence watched by the Daughter. 'In this scene [Hanson] expressed a *wonderment* that came from the depths of his spirit', Vagn Børge later recalled. 'The lines were spoken as if by a sleepwalker, seeking clarification because he is half aware that he is dreaming.'[5] It was not least his exceptional mimic ability that made Lars Hanson the ideal Strindberg actor, capable of exploiting to the fullest the ironic doubleness of a scene that Molander later characterized as 'a play-within-the-play, *performed for the Daughter*. Narrated by the Officer! ... It is his nightmare that arouses her empathy.'[6]

Ultimately, however, it was the powerful overall effect of Molander's *mise-en-scène* for *A Dream Play* that made this production so seminal. Its basic style, which he himself characterized as 'hyperrealistic', was shaped by his determination to anchor the play firmly in the matter-of-fact reality of Strindberg's personal experiences, unencumbered by the gratuitous shock effects he ascribed to Reinhardt. Sven Erik Skawonius designed a rhythmic, oneiric flow of fragmentary settings, each built up of selected bits of sharply etched reality. Skawonius' shadowy dream images were predominantly black and white, each with a strongly lighted focus – a table and chair, an announcement board with hymn numbers for the cathedral scene, the omnipresent cloverleaf door in varying contexts, and so on. These skeletal sets were in turn collated with a succession of stylized back projections, created on the basis of sketches by the modernist painter Isaac Grünewald. Beyond the minimalist settings for individual scenes, one saw at times only impenetrable darkness. At other times, however, Grünewald's projected visions filled the cyclorama with suggestive period glimpses of Stockholm and its surroundings – the summer-house landscape of the archipelago, the old opera house and Jacob's church and, at the beginning and the end of the play, stylized images of the red horse guard barracks that Strindberg saw from his window and called the Growing Castle. Particularly to Swedish audiences of the day, these allusions to a recognizable time and place seemed to shed new light on Strindberg's play, dispelling the dark, alien impression left by Reinhardt's *Traumspiel*.

Although a great deal would change in the six subsequent revivals of *A Dream Play* staged by Molander over the next thirty years, the poignant simplicity of his handling of the play's closing moments remained a constant. His script for his first production calls for no fewer than twenty characters to swell the final *défilé*, which moved to the strains of Chopin's 'Funeral March' as Grünewald's image of the now-completed Flowering Castle filled the cyclorama. The burning of the castle was reduced to a hint of red back lighting that changed to pure blue as the Daughter disappeared and the castle projection vanished. It was replaced on the cyclorama by a jumbled collage of faces as the Poet with Strindberg's countenance remained standing and watching, alone on the deserted stage. As a kind of mystical benediction, a cross rose above the small altar in the background, bearing the inscription that Strindberg had chosen for his own grave: *Ave crux spes unica*.

Molander's ongoing exploration of *A Dream Play* through production after production may justifiably be regarded as the central achievement of

6. Situating Strindberg: setting for the opening scene on the street corner in Olof Molander's 1937 production of *To Damascus I*.

his long directing career. (He staged his seventh and last revival of the play at Det Norske Teatret in Oslo in 1965, the year before his death.) In differing permutations, the suggestive commingling of dream and reality that characterized the epoch-making 1935 revival remained the hallmark of most of his later excursions into Strindberg's post-Inferno period. Thus, in his very next season at Dramaten, his staging of *To Damascus I* conveyed a startlingly surreal doubleness, in which tangible, recognizable reality was collapsed into the steadily more insistent presence of an oneiric shadow world. As the insistence of this inner reality grew stronger, so too did the surprise and incomprehension of Lars Hanson's Unknown, until the Strindberg persona he drew seemed at last the bewildered dreamer of his own life dream.

Just a few months later, however, Molander demonstrated his extraordinary versatility with a revival of *The Saga of the Folkungs* in which both the oneiric simplicity of *A Dream Play* and the moody introspection of *To Damascus* were replaced by sheer theatrical pageantry conceived on a colossal scale. During the following decades, he went on to direct other important Strindberg revivals that included *The Ghost Sonata* (1942), *To Damascus II* (1944), *The Great Highway* (1949) and an ambitious final attempt in 1965 to stage a condensed version of all three parts of the Damascus cycle on the small studio stage of the Stockholm City Theatre. The essence of Molander's method in his best productions – call it surrealism or 'hyperrealism' or what you will – was not to impose a directorial concept on a given text but to compose a theatrical transcription of its inner dramaturgical rhythm. 'At first, Strindberg's inferno dramas put the strangest visions into the heads of Europe's directors, who … began to throw themselves into levels, projections, and other devices for all they were worth', Ingmar Bergman wrote in a programme article for his first professional Strindberg production, a revival of *The Pelican* on the Malmö City Theatre studio stage in 1945. 'Molander gives us Strindberg without embellishments or directorial visions, tunes in to the text, and leaves it at that. He makes us hear the poet's anxiety-driven fever pulse.'[7]

Some postmodernist experiments

Despite both the warmth of this homage and the Molander 'reminiscences' to be found in his own earlier productions, the later Bergman performances of Strindberg in Munich and at Dramaten over the past thirty years have scrupulously avoided both the elaborate visual effects and the biographical and religious symbolism associated with the Molander tradition, choosing instead to define theatrical 'reality' in terms of the direct and unimpeded confrontation between the audience and the living actor. Like Reinhardt and Molander before him, Bergman (the subject of a separate chapter in this volume) has created a body of work that has redefined the problem of performing Strindberg in a way that has profoundly influenced many other theatre artists.

This being said, however, Strindberg's plays have also continued to inspire a robust range of independent creative responses, not the least notable of which have been productions in recent years by non-Scandinavian directors. Giorgio Strehler's hypnotic performance of *Storm* at his Piccolo Teatro in Milan in 1980 was, for example, a very personal approach to this infrequently staged chamber play. The small, bare stage furnished with a minimum of objects and the emphasis on camera-like close-ups of the actors' faces and gestures recalled the Bergman style, but the theatrical effects were pure Strehler. The climactic quarrel between the Gentleman and his ex-wife Gerda concluded in a rainstorm of real water; flashes of lightning showed the audience brief glimpses of the old man's dream life (his daughter being carried off by a seducer, his own gravestone); characters and their movements were sometimes duplicated by reflected images seen in a background wall of mylar panels that suggested the facade of the house where the Gentleman lives (he says) in solitude. With these and other effects, Strehler reinforced the sense that the world of this play and its inhabitants was ultimately the solipsistic inner world of the central character's private agony.

Two other masters of theatricality, Robert Lepage and Robert Wilson, have come forward in the past ten years to present highly individualistic versions of *A Dream Play* that relied chiefly for their effect on the use of elaborate visual imagery and spectacle. Neo-expressionism is perhaps the term that best describes the colourful mechanical wizardry achieved by Lepage in his Swedish-language production in Målarsalen, Dramaten's intimate and flexible studio space, in 1994. In this unusual experiment – in marked contrast to Bergman's exquisitely graceful and spacious restaging of *A Dream Play* eight years earlier – virtually the entire action was confined to a claustrophobic, three-sided cube suspended above water. As this cube-universe turned, tilted and spun on its hydraulic axis, lighting changes and richly decorative projections designated the shifting scenes and moods in the performance.

Transformation, surprise and inversion were the ruling metaphors in Lepage's rotating cubist universe, where nothing was allowed to remain constant for long. A window became a trapdoor in the floor; the floor became a wall, the wall a ceiling. Often there was no ceiling, and characters peered over the top of the high walls at the action beneath them. At the outset, after making her descent through green-black darkness into the 'third world' of earth (where 'the people dance dizzily/ On the borderline between folly and insanity'), Indra's Daughter thus awakened on the floor of what seemed and sounded like a stable stall (the horse guard barracks, perhaps) where she looked out through a small, brightly lighted aperture at the Growing Castle. The box then turned, and she suddenly found herself yet deeper within this dungeon world, where a child in an officer's uniform waited to be freed. Three actors appeared as different aspects of the Officer – as a young boy, a young man and an older man (played by the same actor who first appeared as the Officer's father). Eventually, all three were brought together to sit at the same desk during the Schoolmaster's withering arithmetic lesson.

These ingenious surprises in Lepage's cascade of images ultimately came to seem arbitrary, however, dictated by a purely intuitive logic that had its basis in the geometrical configurations of his spectacular but reductive concept. Within its confines, both text and acting seemed to matter less than visual effectiveness. 'Technology impedes the actors, who are obliged to adjust their energy to the gyrations of the cube', Leif Zern observed in *Dagens Nyheter* (14 November 1994). Lepage's belief that 'the future of theatrical art will depend on ancillary art forms' has, Zern concluded, little to offer 'those who dream of a theatre that springs from the encounter between actor and text'. And, as we know, Strindberg was surely among those believers.

Robert Wilson, perhaps the foremost exponent of the amalgamation of theatre with the other visual and performing arts, launched his 'installation'

7. Postmodernism: Indra's Daughter (Francesca Quartey) and the Poet (Gerhard Hoberstorfer) in Fingal's Cave, in Robert Lepage's production of *A Dream Play*, 1994.

of *A Dream Play* at the Stockholm City Theatre in 1998 and later brought it to New York and London as 'a new interpretation of August Strindberg's masterpiece'. In fact, however, his strange transfiguration was less an interpretation than a non-interpretative visual montage that paraphrased, contemplated, deconstructed and often even mocked *A Dream Play*. Thus, in the scene he calls 'ceremony in which the lawyer is refused graduation', four academics dressed in formal riding attire enacted an absurd mechanical dance before three life-size stuffed cows. During the Theatre Corridor ('opera stage door') scenes, the most conspicuous figure was a stuffed white stallion (a Jungian symbol of sexuality, one reviewer presumed to suggest). A highly exoticized Daughter of Indra moved through her adventures on earth with the glacial control of a slow-motion gymnast. The Growing Castle that she entered at the beginning and the end was, in this case, an old, dream-grey frame house with porch and shutters that was (like the play) undergoing extensive interior renovation. 'Out of Strindberg he makes a world of his own, drawn from the turn of the [previous] century and the American east coast', Lars Ring wrote in *Svenska Dagbladet* (15 November 1998). 'Obvious interpretations do not exist here; the audience must understand or proceed on its own intuition … Wilson builds architecture from the text, a structure of spaciousness and time.'

When this experiment reached New York, however, critics were less tolerant of its languid pacing and affected poses. 'As a concession to Mr. A. S.'s anguish', Michael Feingold wrote tartly in *The Village Voice* (6 December 2000),

> Wilson occasionally has one of the posed figures scream or cackle for no reason, or interrupts Michael Galasso's graceful music with an ear-splitting crash, but these things fade away so smoothly in the general atmosphere of pointless gestures and lavender light.

Yet Wilson's work builds on his assumption that 'what we see is as important as what we hear – it should, and should not be there just to serve the text'. Hence, his followers are prepared to watch a play differently, heeding his exhortation to 'see the text and hear the text and hear the pictures and see the pictures'.[8] Strindberg, the great revolutionary who laid claim (not unjustly) to the invention of a new kind of play, in which form was in itself the direct expression of its inner emotional meaning, might well have found such an argument appealing – provided the pictures to which the audience were asked to 'listen' remained *his* images. In the case of this reimagining of it, however, *A Dream Play* ('a stymying thorn for directors', as the *New York Times* called it) served chiefly as a springboard for Wilson's formidable theatrical virtuosity.

From the work of Lindberg, Vakhtangov, Reinhardt, and the expressionists of the 1920s to reinterpretations by directors such as Strehler, Lepage and Wilson in our own time, the Strindberg productions we have been considering are all stylisations that reflect a broader, ongoing creative process, inspired in particular by the challenge of the post-Inferno works and aimed at perceiving them from a new perspective, for a new audience and a new age. This process is one in which the apparent statement of a given text must continually be transformed, through the encounter of actor and audience, into living representation. 'The nature of the audience changes, and consequently the nature of the author changes', Strehler once remarked. As for Strindberg's part in this dialectic of repeated reinterpretation and renewal, his response can be heard in his famous statement (in his Third Letter to the Intimate Theatre) that 'to be "your own contemporary" must be the task of the artist who is ever growing, ever renewing himself'. It has been, above all, the major performances of his post-Inferno dramas that have continued to show us the remarkably resilient contemporaneity that he was determined to retain.

NOTES

1. Pär Lagerkvist, *Modern Theatre: Points of View and Attack*, trans. Thomas R. Buckman (Lincoln: University of Nebraska Press, 1966), p. 20.
2. For further details, see Frederick J. Marker and Lise-Lone Marker, *Strindberg and Modern Theatre: Post-Inferno Drama on the Stage* (Cambridge University Press, 2002), pp. 122–9.
3. Siegfried Jacobsohn, 'Vignettes from Reinhardt's Productions', in Oliver M. Sayler, ed., *Max Reinhardt and his Theatre* (New York: Brentano's, 1924), p. 325.
4. Quoted in Kela Kvam, *Max Reinhardt og Strindbergs visionære dramatik* (Copenhagen: Akademisk Forlag, 1974), p. 120.
5. Vagn Børge, *Strindbergs mystiske Teater* (Copenhagen: Ejnar Munksgaard, 1942), p. 283.
6. Cf. Richard Bark, *Strindbergs drömspelsteknik: i drama och teater* (Lund: Studentlitteratur, 1981), p. 128.
7. Programme quoted in Lise-Lone Marker and Frederick J. Marker, *Ingmar Bergman: a Life in the Theatre* (Cambridge University Press, 1992), p. 60.
8. Robert Wilson, 'See the Text and Hear the Pictures', Claes Englund and Gunnel Bergström eds., *Strindberg, O'Neill and the Modern Theatre: Addresses and Discussions at a Nobel Symposium at the Royal Dramatic Theatre, Stockholm* (Norsborg: Entré, 1990), pp. 61–2.

12

EGIL TÖRNQVIST

Bergman's Strindberg

Ingmar Bergman (1918–2007), born into a clerical Stockholm family in the last year of the First World War, was a director already in the nursery, where he staged plays, also by Strindberg, in his puppet theatre and made up stories with the help of his *laterna magica*. At seventeen he wrote his first play and in the 1940s some twenty others were to follow, a few of which were published and staged. In recent years he has returned to writing dramatic dialogues for an unspecified medium. Like his renowned autobiography, *The Magic Lantern* (1987),[1] several of these texts are linked to people very close to him, especially his parents.

With his forty feature films, one hundred and seventy stage performances, some forty radio, fifteen television and several opera productions, not to mention his work as a playwright and screenwriter, Bergman has proved more versatile than any other writer-director to date. There is a great amount of overlapping between his work in the theatre and in the film studio. His films, he has said, 'are only a distillation of what I do in the theatre'.[2] In fact, 'no other film director after the breakthrough of the sound film has been so influenced by the theatre'.[3]

The total number of his Strindberg productions amounts to twenty-eight, eighteen for the stage, eight for radio and two for television. Like Olof Molander, his predecessor as Sweden's leading Strindberg director, he has shown a certain preference for the post-Inferno dramas. And like Molander, he has often staged the same plays more than once, *A Dream Play* and *The Ghost Sonata* both no fewer than four times, *The Pelican* three times, and *Miss Julie*, *Playing with Fire* and *Storm* twice.

This alone is a sign that among the writers who have meant much to him, Strindberg holds a special place.[4] 'Strindberg', he has said, 'has accompanied me all my life.'[5] Acquainted with his work already at the age of twelve,[6] Bergman soon became a Strindberg devotee. He 'expressed things which I'd experienced and which I couldn't find words for'.[7] As a student of literature at Stockholm University, he found the lectures of Martin Lamm, the leading

Strindberg scholar at the time, 'absolutely crucial'[8] and wrote an essay on *The Keys of Heaven* which reads 'like a directorial stage copy',[9] not surprisingly since by this time he had already begun directing plays.

It was in 1935, aged sixteen, that Bergman truly discovered Strindberg's power in the theatre. In the programme notes for his 1945 production of *The Pelican*, he states his indebtedness to Olof Molander, who 'has made us see the magic in Strindberg's plays':

> First it was *The Dream Play*. Night after night I stood in the wings and sobbed and never really knew why. After that came *To Damascus*, *The Saga of the Folkungs*, and *The Ghost Sonata*. It is the sort of thing you never forget and never leave behind, especially not if you happen to become a director and least of all if you ... direct a Strindberg drama.[10]

Here was a dramatist who, given a gifted director, could exert a powerful emotional impact on his spectators, something of utmost importance to Bergman; as he has often told an audience: 'It is in your hearts, in your imagination, that this performance should take place.'[11] The film medium supports him in this aim, for 'no form of art goes beyond ordinary consciousness as film does, straight to our emotions, deep into the twilight room of the soul'.[12]

Affinities

The kinship between Strindberg and Bergman has often been pointed out, but usually in passing. Some aspects of this kinship are examined a little more fully here.

With *To Damascus* Strindberg created the first subjective drama in world literature. A fusion of parts I and II was staged by Bergman at Dramaten in 1974. An overwhelming part of this trilogy is a projection of the protagonist's thoughts and emotions. The varying locations and weather conditions represent above all inner realities. Tempered by the realism of the medium, much of this has been carried over into many Bergman films. The diffuse borderline between dream and reality found in *To Damascus* and other plays by Strindberg, which results in a feeling that life is a dream, is found in much of Bergman's work as well. In the teleplay *After the Rehearsal* (1984) he lets Henrik Vogler, his *alter ego*, state: 'Everything *represents*, nothing *is*.' Vogler refers not only to life on the stage but to life in general. This experience of life as dreamlike is undoubtedly one of the main reasons why we may speak of a close kinship between Strindberg and Bergman. When quoting from the 'Author's Note' to *A Dream Play*, first in his TV version of this drama, then at the end of *Fanny and Alexander* (1982), Bergman clearly indicates this.

Long before *To Damascus*, Strindberg showed a tendency to create characters who could be seen not only realistically as separate individuals but also allegorically as conflicting drives within one and the same ego. Olof and Gert in *Master Olof*, Mrs X and Miss Y in *The Stronger*, Mr X and Mr Y in *Paria*, Jean and Julie in *Miss Julie*, Gustav and Adolf in *Creditors* are such characters. With Bergman we find similar 'allegorical' protagonists in Antonius Block and his squire, Jöns, in *The Seventh Seal* (1957), Ester and Anna in *The Silence* (1963), Elisabet and Alma in *Persona* (1966) and Karin and Maria in *Cries and Whispers* (1973). In this way the surface layer of interhuman conflicts is supplemented, and problematized, by a deeper, intrahuman layer.

The subjectivism characteristic of *To Damascus* is also found in *A Dream Play* and *The Ghost Sonata*, where the world as experienced by the protagonist is the issue. The Student in *The Ghost Sonata* makes this explicit when he first asks himself, 'Where does anything fulfil its promise?', and then answers his own question: 'In my imagination!'

Likewise, both on stage and screen, Bergman frequently filters the action through someone's mind. This someone functions as an identification object for the audience. On stage this is done by isolating a figure from the rest of the characters and making him or her observe their words and actions. On screen, where the subjectivism is much easier to handle and to clarify to the audience, it is done in the form of dream sequences, flashbacks or even miraculous events, as when the woman sculpture in *Fanny and Alexander* suddenly begins to move her arm or Agnes in *Cries and Whispers* remains alive after death. The sculpture does not really move her arm, but Alexander experiences it in that way. Agnes does not really survive death, but Anna wishfully believes she does. And since we visually share their experiences, their subjectivism is transferred to us and in this sense objectified. In truly Strindbergian spirit, Molander made the supernatural almost natural by mingling one with the other. Bergman has continued this tradition.

In *Miss Julie*, Bergman has remarked, 'the man and the woman never stop swapping masks'.[13] Role-playing towards others and for oneself is a *sine qua non* in much of modern drama, and Strindberg frequently demonstrates both forms. When this role-playing is revealed, we have a scene of unmasking. A striking example is found in *The Ghost Sonata*, where Hummel, after he has unmasked the Colonel, tells him: 'Here come the guests – keep calm, now, and we'll go on playing our old roles.' As the title implies, a similar pattern is found in *Persona*, where the blunt confrontation between Alma and Elisabet is followed by a return to their normal, masked existence. Elisabet, who has refused to speak for months, returns to her role as an actress, and Alma to hers as a nurse, as is indicated when she puts on her uniform again.

8. Hummel unmasking the Colonel in Ingmar Bergman's 1973 production of *The Ghost Sonata* at the Royal Dramatic Theatre, Stockholm.

Vampirism is a major theme with Strindberg. When Hummel in *The Ghost Sonata* takes hold of the Student's hand, the latter remarks: 'you're taking all my strength away'. When Bergman rehearsed this passage for his third production of the play, he called Hummel's gesture vampiric, for the Old Man is figuratively sucking the Student's blood.[14] In *Persona* such vampirism is shown directly. Elisabet sucks the blood from Alma's wrist which, however, is voluntarily stretched out to her. As in *The Stronger*, in *Persona* we are confronted with two women, one speaking, the other silent. And in both play and film we cannot be sure which of the two women is the stronger. Similarly, we cannot say for certain in either work whether, or to what extent, the vampirism is real or imagined.

The most common way of establishing contact with others is through language. Yet, as a stage and screen director, Bergman distrusts language as a means of communication in any deeper sense. In accord with Hummel's remark in *The Ghost Sonata* that languages are 'codes' invented 'to conceal the secrets of one tribe from the others', he often demonstrates how language masks reality. This idea underlies the unintelligible words on the blackboard in the exam scene of *Wild Strawberries* (1957), later expanded in *The Silence*, where the principal characters are confronted with a language, construed by Bergman, which is as unintelligible for them as for us. The inability to understand each other's language is, in either case, a metaphor for the inability truly to understand one another. While Anna in *The Silence* tries to communicate via the senses and without words, the unintelligible language becomes for Ester, the professional translator, a challenge. Like the Student in *The Ghost Sonata*, she is a seeker who tries to decipher the meaning of life.

The search undertaken by Bergman's protagonists is sometimes thematized in the form of a journey. In *The Seventh Seal* we accompany Antonius Block on his way home to his waiting wife – and death. Similarly, in *Wild Strawberries* we accompany Isak Borg on his last journey. Strindberg's pilgrimage plays have undoubtedly been of importance for these films. When Bergman once, with regard to *Winter Light* (1963, sometimes entitled *The Communicants*), declared that 'everything became stations on the road for the priest',[15] he presumably did not only have Christ's *via dolorosa* in mind but also that of the Stranger in *To Damascus*.

Bergman has been called 'the most energetic pursuer of the Strindbergian chamber play'.[16] Keenly interested in 'the intimate in form, a restricted subject, treated in depth, few characters, large points of view' (*SL*, p. 734), he applied Strindberg's term to some of his own films:

> *Through a Glass Darkly* and *Winter Light* and *The Silence* and *Persona* I have called chamber plays. They are chamber music. That is, you cultivate a number of motifs with an extremely limited number of voices and characters. You extract the backgrounds. You place them in a kind of haze. You create a distillation.[17]

Just as *The Ghost Sonata* by its very title implies a relationship with sonata form, so the title of *Autumn Sonata* (1978) has the same implication, a title which, in fact, was anticipated when Bergman played with the idea of calling *Persona* 'A Sonata for Two Instruments'.[18] Even more explicit is the title of his last teleplay, *Saraband* (2003), referring to the movement in Bach's Cello Suite in C minor that forms the musical leitmotif of the play. *The Ghost Sonata* ends with a 'coda', a swift recapitulation of earlier themes and a development: the faith in a benevolent God which is the prerequisite for the Student's intercession for the Young Lady. In the same way, *Through a Glass Darkly* (1961) ends with a 'divine proof' – the idea that God is love – and this, says Bergman, forms 'the actual *coda* in the last movement'.[19] Just as Strindberg calls *A Dream Play* 'a symphony' (*MJoP*, p. 300), so Bergman calls *The Seventh Seal* 'an oratorio'.[20]

Of all Strindberg's plays, *A Dream Play* and *The Ghost Sonata* have proved the most seminal for Bergman. The viva and congregation sequences in *Wild Strawberries* are familiar variations of the school and congregation scenes in *A Dream Play*. Waiting is a leitmotif in *Through a Glass Darkly*, initiated already in the early play-within-the-film, where Karin waits in vain for Minus much as the Officer in *A Dream Play* waits in vain for Victoria. And just as everybody in Strindberg's drama is waiting for the enigmatic door hiding the riddle of life to be opened, so Karin in *Through a Glass Darkly* waits for God to appear behind the enigmatic wall. *Fanny and Alexander* ends with Helena's reading from the 'Author's Note' for this play to her grandson Alexander, Bergman's *alter ego*. The grey crocheted shawl wrapped around her at this moment indicates that she has mentally already begun rehearsing the Doorkeeper's part in Strindberg's play. The passage she is reading, which praises the gift of imagination, offers a key to the television series with its interweaving of dream and reality.

In his next television production, *After the Rehearsal* (1984), Bergman's grown-up *alter ego*, Henrik Vogler, is actually rehearsing *A Dream Play*. The director is first seen from above. On his table is a green lamp, his prompt book and a green copy of Strindberg's play in the familiar first Collected Works edition. This initial, 'celestial' shot imitates the opening of the drama that is on his mind: Indra's Daughter's descent to Earth. Likewise, when turning his lamp on and off, Vogler is apparently recalling the alternation of light and darkness, 'day and night', in the corridor scene of *A Dream Play*. But whereas 'a merciful Providence', allowing time to pass quickly, is responsible for the flashing light in Strindberg's play, it is Vogler himself who causes the flashing in Bergman's, a sign of his desire to attenuate his waiting for death. When he relates to Anna how, as a boy, he witnessed the hairpin sequence in *A Dream Play* from the wings of the theatre, he replays the sequence, turning himself into the Lawyer who first describes, then breaks, the hairpin, symbolic of the man–woman relation. Bergman includes this passage because, while referring to the relationship between the Daughter and the Lawyer, it prefigures the imagined relationship between Anna and Vogler who, walking around the stage, indulge in fantasies about how their relationship might continue. Like the marriage scene in *A Dream Play*, their behaviour telescopes the development from early infatuation and harmony to disagreement and divorce. But whereas Strindberg shows all this as acted out, Bergman shows it largely as narrated.

Agnes, the Christ figure in *Cries and Whispers*, shares her name with Indra's Daughter once the Daughter has taken human shape, and strikingly resembles the Young Lady in *The Ghost Sonata*. In *Cries and Whispers*, the first part of the Chaplain's intercession for Agnes, once she has died, recalls the Student's intercession for the recently dead Young Lady. The second part resembles the Poet's appeal to Indra's Daughter. Crammed with sceptical 'ifs', it undermines the ritual of the first part. No longer praying that God take mercy on the dead woman, the Chaplain asks her to intercede by Him for the living. To speak with the author of *A Dream Play*: it is not the dead but the living who are pitiable. Another striking correspondence is that between the Milkmaid in *The Ghost Sonata* and the servant, Anna, in *Cries and Whispers*. The mute Milkmaid has an obvious counterpart in the highly taciturn Anna; both incarnate what in a medieval morality play would have been called Good Deeds. Bergman indicated the parallel visually by having the 1973 Milkmaid played by the same actress and dressed in the same way as Anna.

Strindberg on Bergman's stage

How then has Bergman handled Strindberg's dramas on stage? Opposing the idea of a director's theatre that renders the dramatist peripheral, he claims to be a humble elucidator of the play text, loyal to its spirit, if not to its letter. In 1968 he declared: 'I cannot and will not direct a play contrary to its author's intentions. And I have never done so. Consciously, I have always considered myself an interpreter, a re-creator.'[21] This statement begs several questions: Can the author's intentions be deciphered? Is it possible to speak of a proper interpretation? Is what was relevant for the author also relevant for the director and his audience? Fortunately, Bergman's statement does not agree with his practice and decades later he recognized the liberties he had sometimes taken with Strindberg's plays. Unnecessarily defensive, he now pointed out that the author was himself not 'fussy' when others wished to alter his dialogue.[22]

The late Strindberg's faith in an after-life that would justify this life was not shared by Bergman when he launched most of these productions; instead they stressed his belief in human love as the only salvation in the single life granted us. When they have nevertheless seemed convincing, it is not because the director has been true to the spirit of the text. It is rather because he has been able to transubstantiate it in such a way that his own vision has come to penetrate it. The subtitle given to the published version of his 1970 production of *A Dream Play*, 'An Interpretation by Ingmar Bergman'[23] adequately summarizes his own very distinctive and important contributions to the Strindberg plays he has directed.

Just how this transubstantiation has been achieved can be seen in some of Bergman's productions based on *Miss Julie*, *A Dream Play* and *The Ghost Sonata*.[24] His 1985 *Miss Julie* at Dramaten in Stockholm was his second stage production of the play. Four years earlier he had staged it at the Residenztheater in Munich, a production which has been thoroughly documented.[25]

In so far as he pitted the life-denying Julie against the life-affirming Jean, Bergman's presentation entailed a loyal reading of the text. But in his interpretation of the third character, the cook Kristin, he differed from both Strindberg and earlier directors. Kristin was depicted not as 'a female slave ... subservient and dull' as Strindberg characterizes her in the Preface (*MJoP*, p. 63), but as a young, sensual, forceful woman who 'rules not only her kitchen, but also Jean'.[26]

In the kitchen which resembled those in Swedish manor-houses around 1890 there was a strong suggestion of midsummer. There were also naturalistic touches, such as the smell of kidney from Kristin's frying pan. Jean's glancing at a newspaper was a directorial addition, presumably inspired by his later reference to the suicide story he had read about in the paper. The suggestion here was that Jean's reading was topical and incidental in contrast to Kristin's constant reliance on the Bible. Another significant directorial addition was Jean's prayer at table, a piece of role-playing enacted merely to satisfy Kristin.

Bergman provided Jean with low boots; when compared with the Count's high riding-boots, these seemed indicative not only of the servant's social position but also of his tendency to identify himself with his master, of his aspiration to end up a count. The low boot was figuratively turned into a riding-whip, symbol of mastership, when Jean was telling Kristin how Julie, having forced her fiancé to jump over his riding crop, suddenly saw her engagement broken. When describing this event, Strindberg had originally written: 'But the third time he grabbed the crop out of her hand and hit her with it across the left cheek.' He later replaced the last eight words by: 'broke it across his knee'. The director restored the original line and added another, Kristin's 'That's why she paints her face white now', inspired by Jean's remark about 'the powder on the smooth cheek'. Bergman here found a way of exteriorizing Julie's state of mind by providing her cheek with an ugly scar, which in the beginning was hidden behind a thick layer of make-up. During intercourse the make-up came off and the scar became visible.

Strindberg's use of drinking habits to demonstrate a desired social status begins when Kristin intends to serve Jean beer, while he finds wine more appropriate on festive occasions. At this early point Jean pretends to be a wine connoisseur with a refined, aristocratic taste. Later we learn that his expertise in this area stems from his time as a wine waiter. Bergman ironically illustrated this by letting Jean fill his own wineglass, waiter fashion; he was at this point at once master and servant, socially and psychologically in a middle position.

Strindberg's 'Ballet' became in Bergman's version almost a play within the play. Unlike Strindberg, he had Kristin enter the kitchen while the people of the estate were still carousing there. The intention was apparently to demonstrate Kristin's strength. One by one, the intruders left the kitchen, driven out by her austere apparition.

After the intercourse, Jean's sexual urge is again aroused. According to the text, he unctuously flatters Julie as he attempts to seduce her. Sensing his hypocrisy, she tears herself loose from him. Bergman left the dialogue intact but had Jean behave quite differently from what the acting directions suggest. As a result, there was a strong discrepancy between Jean's romantic flow of words and the raw, sexual urge demonstrated in his actions. Similarly, Julie's line about the possibility of love was coloured by her sexual excitement. What the audience witnessed was, in fact, a hypocritical version of the copulation between the thoroughbred Diana and the Gatekeeper's mongrel.

To Bergman it was of paramount importance that Julie's decision to die should be seen as a manifestation of strength, not of weakness. To this end her position was substantiated in various ways. Instead of letting Jean hand her the razor, as in the text, Bergman's Julie picked it up herself. By replacing part of the hypnosis passage, which he considered dated, with the mirror scene, Bergman further strengthened the idea that Julie consciously makes her own decision. And by increasing Jean's cowardice and have him speak the final 'Go!', not as a command but in an appealing, servile manner, he further weakened his share in her death.

At the end Jean, in black, could be seen closely behind Julie, in white, his arms in much the same position as hers, so that the two seemed to be one. Instead of making Julie imagine that the razor is a broom, as Strindberg has it, Bergman had Jean hand her a mirror, instructing her in how to commit suicide. To Julie, looking into the mirror at this moment signified a courageous confrontation with her own self. Her use of it glaringly contrasted with Jean's adjusting of his hair – his mask – with the help of his pocket mirror when, in the added epilogue, he prepared to make himself presentable for the Count.

9. The Poet at his desk in Ingmar Bergman's 1970 production of *A Dream Play* at the Royal Dramatic Theatre, Stockholm.

Bergman's first production of *A Dream Play*, in 1963, was made for the small screen. With its twenty-eight scenes and thirty-six actors and actresses, it was the largest production undertaken to date by Swedish television. Although on the whole well received, Bergman found it in retrospect somewhat of a failure. The teleplay opened with the 'Author's Note' to the play superimposed on Strindberg's face. Substituting Strindberg for Indra and abstaining from the Prologue in Heaven, Bergman immediately made clear that his performance was a fantasy on the part of the author, whose *alter ego* is the Poet in the play.

Strindberg's face dissolved into a cloud out of which Indra's Daughter emerged. She approached a barred gate in the foreground. Since we, the viewers, were found on this side of the bars, the impression was communicated that *we* were inside a prison. In accordance with the central idea of the play, i.e. that humanity is imprisoned in life and that the Daughter, the Christ figure, has come to set it free, Bergman in this way broke down the barrier between screen and off screen and drew the viewers into the action. His Daughter was significantly blonde, 'haloed' and wore a white, high-collared dress, indicating her pure, innocent, divine nature. Like Strindberg, Bergman opted for a circular composition. At the end, his Poet entered a cloud which dissolved into an extreme close-up of Strindberg's face.

The idea of the author as the dreamer of the play was to return in Bergman's first stage production of *A Dream Play* at Dramaten in 1970, but this time it was not Strindberg but the Poet who was the dreamer. The director used a very simple permanent setting with a minimum of properties which facilitated swift and smooth scene changes. Advertised as *The Dream Play*, Bergman's 'interpretation' retained the fifteen scenes that can be distilled out of Strindberg's play but a number of references to oriental religion, confusing to a modern Westerner, were omitted and the dialogue was condensed and rearranged; the opening and closing speeches were, for example, given to the Poet rather than to Indra's Daughter. The omissions and the swift scene changes resulted in a performance which lasted about forty-five minutes less than usual.[27]

Present on stage throughout, the Poet, in black, replaced Indra's Daughter as the person witnessing the various scenes. As the dreamer, he was constantly eavesdropping on his characters, indicating that he was not only the creator of the text but also the shaper of the performance.

Indra's Daughter was split in two: the Divine Daughter and the earthly Agnes. The Daughter appeared in a long white robe with a mantle attached to it, whereas Agnes wore a simple blue or grey dress with a white collar, completely unadorned, a representative of mankind, deprived of the possibility of return to a consoling celestial origin.

The performance opened not in Heaven, as with Strindberg, but on Earth, with a symbolic situation. In the grey light the characters gathered on the empty stage like shadows, then began a treadmill walk to the sound of a barrel organ. The celestial world of the Prologue was transformed into the world of theatrical illusion as the Bard, rather than Indra, and his Daughter were applauded for their 'theatrical performance'. Strindberg's independent divinities were turned into products of the human brain, theatrical inventions, poetic fantasies.

The Coalcarriers' scene, where class differences are emphasized, was integrated into the Fairhaven scene, that is, transposed from the Mediterranean to anywhere. When the blackened coalcarriers entered, the movements of the white-dressed holiday makers at Fairhaven were frozen. In this manner, Strindberg's literal and figurative black-and-white pattern was retained.

In Bergman's reduced version there was no burning castle at the end. Instead, there was a purely symbolic fire: a large, non-figurative, red design. No doubt he meant to exercise the spectators by presenting them with an enigma, which was interpreted by the critics in widely different ways. The altar, not prescribed by Strindberg but usually figuring in stage productions, was replaced by the Poet's table, where the characters sacrificed their attributes, that is, took leave of their roles in token of the fact that these were merely products of the Poet's imagination. Furthermore, this production was reductive in another respect. Apart from effectively condensing Strindberg's dialogue and largely ignoring his stage directions in favour of a Shakespearean empty stage, the director transformed his metaphysical perspective, in which the existence of a divine plan is assumed, into an immanent, metatheatrical, Pirandellian conception,[28] in which the 'divinities' posed as actors to a stage audience. Metonymically representing humanity at large, this audience was linked with the real audience. As a result, a *theatrum mundi* was created. The stage was all the world and the characters such stuff as dreams are made on.

Bergman's high opinion of *The Ghost Sonata* explains why he has staged it no fewer than four times. In his 1973 production at Dramaten, he placed the house facade of Act I not up stage, as Strindberg has it, but in the auditorium. On either side of the proscenium frame, half turned away from the audience, were the inhabitants of the house. By their position they became mediators between the audience in the auditorium and the characters on stage which represented the street in front of the house. At the same time a beautiful *art nouveau* building was projected on the black screens in the rear. As the Old Man and the Student watched the house in the auditorium, the spectators watched the house they were describing on the screens. The result was a dreamlike mirror effect. This was further heightened by the similarity between the stage, enclosed by concave screens, and the horseshoe shape of the auditorium, turning the whole locale into a *theatrum mundi*.

Act I was dominated by greyish tints. In Act II the characters appeared in costumes which were realistic in cut but so glaring that they looked like dresses for a fancy-dress ball; here the world of illusions was at its strongest. In the final act the costumes were pale; the masquerade was over.

A fundamental idea behind this production was 'the fact that the Young Lady is slowly turning into another Mummy'.[29] To convey this idea, Bergman had the same actress play both mother and daughter, when necessary assisted by a mute stand-in. The idea that the Mummy had once been what the Young Lady is now and, conversely, that the Young Lady is an embryonic Mummy was indicated in various ways: by costume, stage position, movement, gesture and voice. Similarly, the outward resemblance between the Old Man and the Student conveyed the idea that the Student incarnates an earlier stage in the Old Man's life and that, conversely, the Student is destined eventually to turn into another Old Man. Taken together, the male and the female couples thus presented a picture of the fate of humanity.

The references to Buddha in the text were omitted, partly because they would be alien to a Western audience, partly because Bergman's version did not allow for any divine superstructure. Instead, the Colonel, who at the ghost supper had appeared in a pompous red uniform, was in the final act turned into a 'Buddhist monk' with a shorn head, a simple gown, a mild voice and a radiant face. Similarly, the Mummy's parrot-like costume, at first intensely red at the hem, became almost colourless in the final act. Sapped of her lifeblood, she now looked like a living corpse.

Innovative, too, was Bergman's positive characterization of the relationship between the Colonel and the Mummy. By giving lines from the Student's concluding prayer for the dead Young Lady to them, Bergman provided a spiritual gap between his dark revolt and their pious acceptance, the latter strengthened by the choreographic pattern: the Mummy's hand rested tenderly on the Colonel's shoulder; he in turn lovingly held the hand of the Young Lady; both of them were looking at her. Strongly lit from above, the three formed a secular holy trinity which recalled the ending of *The Seventh Seal*.

The conception of life underlying this production was very different from that of the late Strindberg; in the director's own words: 'the only thing that can give man any salvation – a secular one – is the grace and compassion that come out of himself'. In line with this view, the projection of *Toten-Insel*, called for by Strindberg at the end, was omitted. Surprisingly, Bergman 'had the feeling that we had Ågust with us when we made changes in the final scene'.[30]

In his fourth production, again at Dramaten in 2000, the play was subtitled 'fantasy piece' just as at the first performance in 1908. Bergman now harked back to the view he held in his Malmö version of 1953, that the Student is the dreamer of the play. This was now indicated not by means of a gauze between stage and auditorium but by having the Student crawling from the dark auditorium, as if born out of its dark 'womb', on to the stage of life as Everyman.

At the close, the Milkmaid, seen by the Student from the auditorium, performed an upward-striving dance, Bergman's non-verbal substitute for the Student's prayer to Buddha. The message was clear. The death of the Young Lady meant a separation of body and soul, the former doomed to annihilation, the latter in the Student's imagination blessed with survival. No *Toten-Insel*, no angelic harp, no 'Song of the Sun', not even a secular family reunion. And yet consolation, however subjective, in the final vision of the spiritualized Milkmaid, 'born' by the Student and the audience together. His hope, our hope.

When Bergman staged his first *Ghost Sonata*, in 1941, he was the Student's age. When he staged his fourth version, in 2000, he had reached the age of the Old Man. If any play can be said to have been his companion through life, it is this one.

NOTES

1. The dates following Bergman titles refer to the year of first publication or, with regard to films and teleplays, of premières.
2. Vilgot Sjöman, *L136: Diary with Ingmar Bergman*, trans. Alan Blair (Ann Arbor, Mich.: Karoma, 1978), p. 102.
3. Leif Zern, *Se Bergman* (Stockholm: Norstedt, 1993), p. 59.
4. My comparisons in the following concern only Strindberg's dramatic *œuvre*, the part that Bergman has been actively involved with. See further Egil Törnqvist, *Bergman's Muses: Aesthetic Versatility in Film, Theatre, Television and Radio* (Jefferson, NC: McFarland & Co., 2003). For comparisons with the prose works, see Hubert I. Cohen, *Ingmar Bergman: the Art of Confession* (New York: Twayne, 1993).
5. Stig Björkman, Torsten Manns and Jonas Sima, eds., *Bergman on Bergman: Interviews with Ingmar Bergman*, trans. Paul Britten Austin (New York: Da Capo, 1970), 1993, p. 23. Translation here improved.
6. Introduction to *The Fifth Act*, trans. Joan Tate and Linda Haverty Rugg (New York: The New Press, 2001), p. 11.
7. *Bergman on Bergman*, p. 24.
8. *Ibid.*
9. Birgitta Steene, *Ingmar Bergman* (Boston: Twayne, 1968), p. 19.
10. Quoted from Henrik Sjögren, *Ingmar Bergman på teatern* (Stockholm: Almqvist & Wiksell, 1968), p. 38.
11. Egil Törnqvist, *Strindberg's The Ghost Sonata: from Text to Production* (Amsterdam: Amsterdam University Press, 2000), p. 187.
12. *The Magic Lantern*, p. 73.
13. *Bergman on Bergman*, p. 18.
14. *Strindberg's The Ghost Sonata*, p. 139.
15. *L136*, p. 42.
16. *L136*, p. 13.
17. *Bergman on Bergman*, p. 168; translation here improved.
18. *Svensk filmografi*, vol. VI (Stockholm: Svenska Filminstitutet, 1977), p. 289.
19. *L136*, p. 24.
20. Peter Cowie, *Ingmar Bergman: a Critical Biography* (London: André Deutsch, 1992), p. 141.
21. *Ingmar Bergman på teatern*, p. 293.
22. Henrik Sjögren, *Lek och raseri. Ingmar Bergmans teater 1938–2002* (Stockholm: Carlsson, 2002), p. 342.
23. August Strindberg, *A Dream Play: an Interpretation by Ingmar Bergman*, trans. Michael Meyer (London: Secker & Warburg, 1973).
24. See Egil Törnqvist and Barry Jacobs, *Strindberg's Miss Julie: a Play and its Transpositions* (Norwich: Norvik Press, 1988), pp. 163–85; Egil Törnqvist, *Between Stage and Screen: Ingmar Bergman Directs* (Amsterdam University Press, 1995), pp. 23–58; and Törnqvist, *Strindberg's The Ghost Sonata*, pp. 117–45 and 189–228 (transcription).
25. Lise-Lone Marker and Frederick J. Marker, *Ingmar Bergman: a Project for the Theatre* (New York: Frederick Ungar, 1983). The text of the stage version is given on pp. 101–47. Other Bergman productions are documented in the chapter

entitled 'The Strindberg Cycle', in Lise-Lone Marker and Frederick J. Marker, *Ingmar Bergman: a Life in the Theater* (Cambridge University Press, 1992), pp. 59–142.

26. Bergman in *Ingmar Bergman: a Project*, p. 17.

27. In his introduction to Bergman's *A Dream Play*, Meyer claims (p. xvi) that this drama 'in its original form, scarcely any longer seemed theatrically valid' to Bergman in 1970. Nevertheless, in his fourth production of the play, in 1986, he chose 'to play the text with no changes or deletions, just as the writer had written it'. See *The Magic Lantern*, p. 36.

28. Bergman staged Pirandello's *Six Characters in Search of an Author* in 1953 and again in 1967.

29. *Strindberg's The Ghost Sonata*, p. 130.

30. *Lek och raseri*, p. 342.

13

FREDDIE ROKEM

Strindberg and modern drama: some lines of influence

Strindberg's legacy is apparent in many aspects of the drama and theatre of the twentieth century. In the years following his death the lineage was quite clear, and the majority of the expressionists were acutely conscious of the impact of his work on them. The following generation, including Eugene O'Neill, also traced important aspects of their artistic pedigree to Strindberg's *œuvre*, but the immediate impact was somewhat fainter, and after the Second World War, his direct influence had faded still further. By then, however, criticism was in the process of establishing Strindberg's significant place on the map of the modern theatre.

Two such critical studies are Peter Szondi's groundbreaking work *Theorie des modernen Dramas* (1956) and Martin Esslin's no less important study, *The Theatre of the Absurd* (1961). Szondi clearly identified some of the key features that have laid the basis for our understanding of Strindberg's international impact on European drama and theatre, contextualizing his contribution both from a theoretical and a historical perspective, while Esslin made some interesting claims for the Strindberg canon and its importance for a major development of twentieth-century drama and theatre. Both books present a comprehensive overview of the development of modern drama, and in both of them, Strindberg occupies a central position.

Some fifty years on, however, a further assessment is possible, one that no longer needs to distinguish between those dramatists who have drawn more from Strindberg than from any other playwright (like Eugene O'Neill and Lars Norén); those who have more or less unconsciously integrated something from his work or technique (like Harold Pinter); and those who have, in one way or another, tried to avoid Strindberg's influence (like Jean-Paul Sartre, Heiner Müller and Tom Stoppard). For, no matter where one begins, Strindberg's work is so closely identified with the public consciousness or the collective unconscious of our time that he cannot be avoided.

Indeed, among Strindberg's major contributions to the formation of modern drama and theatre are the forms of sensitivity that made it possible to rethink the notion of such a public consciousness. Strindberg's influence on the notion of the public/collective sphere and its relationship to the inner/ private life of the individual has been of major and enduring importance. Throughout his career, he sought to understand how something as private as a consciousness, an individual's inner thoughts and feelings, are endowed with a public dimension, and become meaningful in a broader public context. In so doing, he developed a mode of artistic expression for what, in the later twentieth century, would be discussed in terms of a crisis of subjectivity

According to Szondi, the crisis that had begun with the drama of Ibsen, where the action is dominated by the past rather than the present, and the past is thematized as a central feature of the dramatic action, had continued with Chekhov's displacement of the interpersonal with what Szondi terms 'reveries of remembrance and utopian thought' (p. 45).[1] However, the most radical change towards what Szondi termed an 'epic dramaturgy' had occurred with Strindberg, where,

> the interpersonal is either sublimated or seen through the subjective lens of a central *I*. Because of this internalisation, (always) present, 'real' time loses its position of absolute dominance: past and present flow into each other, the external present calls forth the remembered past. With regard to the interpersonal, the action is reduced to a concatenation of meetings that are simply markers for the actual event: internal transformation (p. 45)

A clear and obvious expression of this development is the so-called '*I* dramaturgy', the basic style of expressionism which, according to Szondi, 'shaped the image of dramatic literature for decades to come, [and] actually began with Strindberg. In his case it was a dramaturgy rooted in autobiography' (p. 22).[2] The ways in which Strindberg mobilized and exposed his own private life for artistic purposes are unique, in particular for the directness and openness with which he practised this form of exposure.[3]

By introducing a figure like Hummel into *The Ghost Sonata*, 'who knows all about the other characters and, thus can become their epic narrator within the dramatic fable' (p. 47), Szondi suggests that Strindberg introduced a new kind of witnessing position in drama through which the borderline between the private and the public is redefined. This dramatic situation, which leaves us with a kind of silence that Szondi himself did not appreciate, consists of a recollection whereby a witness presents his or her testimony to a listener inside the fictional world, or directly to the spectators. Much of modern drama can be seen as such an ongoing negotiation between a witness and the victim about whom the testimony is given.

In Strindberg's mature plays there are many moments of traumatization situated at the margins of an extended or vaguely defined and gradually disintegrating family that cannot really be told or narrated, as in *The Ghost Sonata* and *A Dream Play*. This form can already be found in the major naturalistic plays like *The Father* and *Miss Julie*. However, it is particularly in the later plays that the privacy of the family is exposed to the public, social sphere to an extent which previous dramatic writing had only very rarely achieved (for example in Büchner's *Woyzeck*, which only became more widely known in the first decades of the twentieth century). In his mature work Strindberg developed a set of dramatic tools which enabled him to render the intimacy of the disintegrating family publicly by exposing the suffering and the despair of the individual through an outside, but involved, epic narrator, who serves as a mediator between that mute suffering and the spectators.

Szondi's theoretical model constructed a legacy of dramatic writing that leads from Strindberg, through a crisis of form, to Brecht and the Epic theatre, while Esslin's complementary approach depicts an historical heritage which culminates in what he termed the Theatre of the Absurd, i.e. a theatre of something called 'the absurd'. This form of theatre focuses on the endeavour to communicate what Esslin terms 'a total sense of being' (p. 394),[4] which is aimed at presenting a truer picture of reality. In Strindberg's *To Damascus*, *A Dream Play* and *The Ghost Sonata*, Esslin adds,

> the shift from the objective reality of the world of outside, surface appearance to the subjective reality of inner states of consciousness – a shift that marks the watershed between the traditional and the modern, the representational and the Expressionist projection of mental realities – is finally and triumphantly accomplished.
>
> (p. 342)

While Szondi identifies a stylistic change that leads to a crisis or ruptures which modern playwriting attempts to confront or rescue, Esslin views the Theatre of the Absurd as an endeavour to make the most of the stylistic changes that the drama of the first decades of the twentieth century underwent in order to serve new philosophical, existential objectives. For both these writers, Strindberg occupies a central position in the development of modern drama.

An example of the way that Esslin isolates the process whereby an 'intuition in depth', as he calls it, becomes a poetic, dramatic image, particularly as it was influenced by Strindberg, can be found in his discussion of Arthur Adamov, one of the early absurdists. In this respect Esslin quotes from Adamov's diary where he notes that it was only after reading *A Dream Play* that he began to discover the stuff of drama around him, finding it in

> the most ordinary everyday happenings, particularly street scenes. What struck me above all were the lines of passers-by, their loneliness in the crowd, the

terrifying diversity of their utterance, of which I could please myself by hearing only snatches that, linked with other snatches of conversation, seemed to grow into a composite entity the very fragmentations of which became a guarantee of its symbolic truth. (p. 94)

The impressions provided by this kind of street scene, which consist of fragments of overheard conversations, for which the eavesdropper lacks the full context, mixed with memories from previous chance encounters in the public arena, could be used to characterize not only certain aspects of the Theatre of the Absurd, but also extend far beyond it. Somewhat paradoxically, a street scene combines the exact, objective impressions with a subjective consciousness, thus returning us to the dialectics between the private and the public.

The notion of the street scene has had a seminal importance for the modern theatre, particularly from the perspective of the two major Western theories of acting of the twentieth century: the Stanislavski method and Brecht's theory. Both of them try to confront the complex dialectics between different forms of identification and distancing that develop from having witnessed a street scene.

Brecht's essay, 'The Street Scene: a Basic Model for the Epic Theatre' (ca. 1938), outlines the sources of epic acting on the basis of someone witnessing an event in the public arena. And for the Stanislavski method, which was more systematically developed from around 1907 onwards, the notion of the street scene has also been of seminal importance. These two theories of acting and the numerous variations that have emerged from them have no doubt also had a crucial influence on modern drama. The gesture of witnessing – my own more inclusive term for what Szondi calls 'the epic I' – that is implied by the street scene situation, holds a very prominent position in Strindberg's work. Indra's Daughter/Agnes in A Dream Play, who is the most emblematic of all Strindberg's many witnesses, has descended to earth to see whether humanity's suffering is really as great as it claims. And by becoming what modern anthropologists have called a 'participating witness', she absorbs something of that suffering before returning to her original heavenly abode. Hummel, on the other hand, who is also a witness, is in many ways diametrically her opposite, because he not only observes the victims, but also causes their sufferings, while she enters into different modes of empathy. Nevertheless, the first scene of The Ghost Sonata in the city square clearly denotes a street scene.

Brecht's model for an epic theatre clearly echoes these Strindbergian gestures of witnessing. Brecht begins his discussion as follows:

It is comparatively easy to set up a basic model for epic theatre. For practical experiments I usually picked as my example of completely simple, 'natural' epic theatre an incident such as can be seen at any street corner: an eyewitness demonstrating to a collection of people how a traffic accident took place. The bystanders may not have observed what happened, or they may simply not agree with him, may 'see things a different way'; the point is that the demonstrator acts the behaviour of driver or victim or both in such a way that the bystanders are able to form an opinion about the accident.[5]   (p. 121)

For Brecht, epic theatre is based on catastrophic situations witnessed in the public arena, which the actor learns to transmit to a group of bystanders, the spectators, who in turn are supposed to form an opinion about what has occurred. The actor is a story-teller whose authority is based on the fact that he has watched the accident carefully and is now giving us a report or, to use the term which becomes central to Brechtian theory, 'demonstrating' the behaviour of the different participants. And while this demonstration is not, as is sometimes claimed, unfeeling, a certain distance to what is being shown is necessary if a complex balancing act that recalls the situation in several of Strindberg's later plays is to be achieved.

Stanislavski places a much greater emphasis on the emotional aspects of acting, something which Brecht clearly does not totally repress. But he also has some interesting things to say about the street scene. In *An Actor Prepares*, the fictional student-narrator, Kostya, relates that one day on his way home from acting class he saw a large crowd on one of the boulevards. 'I like street scenes,' he continues, 'so I pushed into the centre of it, and there my eyes fell on a horrible picture' (p. 159).[6] Kostya goes on to describe in detail how an old man had been killed by a street-car. His wife and children towered over the victim, the conductor showed what was wrong with the machinery of the street-car, while 'the rest of the crowd looked on with indifference and curiosity' (p. 160). Here then is the catastrophic street scene situation and, some weeks later, Kostya reports that it has become transformed into something stern and majestic in his memory. Thinking about it he is suddenly reminded of another, earlier accident he had also witnessed. This accident, in which a monkey belonging to an Italian was killed, had for some reason made a much deeper impression on him. And, Kostya concludes:

> It would seem that this scene had affected my feelings more than the death of the beggar. It was buried more deeply in my memory. I think that if I had to stage the street accident I would search for emotional material for my part in my memory of the scene of the Italian with the dead monkey rather than the tragedy itself.   (p. 161)

And when Kostya takes up this issue in one of the acting classes, Tortsov (Stanislavski's *alter ego*), draws the following conclusions:

Each one of us has seen many accidents. We retain the memories of them, but only outstanding characteristics that impressed us and not their details. Out of these impressions one large, condensed, deeper and broader sensation memory of related experience is formed. It is a kind of synthesis of memory on a large scale. It is purer, more condensed, compact, substantial and sharper than the actual happenings. Time ... not only purifies, it also transmutes even painfully realistic memories into poetry. (p. 161)

The actor transforms his encounters with death into 'poetry', i.e. acting, through the synthesis of memories from a series of such street scenes. Different accidents that he or she has witnessed, and which repeat themselves, gradually become superimposed, thus enabling the actor to re-enact on stage the essential emotion memories relevant to a particular play. And the way in which Stanislavski describes this process is indeed very similar to the experiences that Indra's Daughter undergoes in *A Dream Play*.

A significant aspect of the Strindberg legacy is connected to the dialectics between the public and the private. One very important aspect of this legacy is its application in the major theories of acting, which in turn have influenced contemporary playwriting. Moreover, there is a significant dialectical interaction between these two poles. Street scenes are public events, just as the theatre is. The actor studies public events, like accidents in the street, in order to transpose them to another public event: the performance, which takes place in front of and for an audience. What is 'accidentally' public in the street accident is purposefully so in the theatre. The actor studies how to create the appearance of 'accidence' in his deliberate public presentation or demonstration. But these are only the most apparent similarities. What at the same time actually takes place is a personal or private tragedy: someone has caused the death of another person by an accident which could have been avoided. The street scene presents a private event in the public arena. This is a tension which Strindberg explored, and which has become crucial for modern drama and theatre.

The street scene and the theatre are also profoundly similar in this respect because the theatre as a form of artistic creativity gradually began to emphasize the public form through which the private lives of the heroes are presented. As an awareness of the public aspects of twentieth-century art developed, the privacy of the characters presented became more exposed. The development of film, a medium with a different sociology from theatre because of the conditions of watching, clearly points in this direction. Looking more closely at the theatre, however, it seems that the theatre of psychological realism, in which Stanislavski's methods have been applied, makes an obvious connection between the private and intimate spheres of the individual hero and their public or more official presentation in the theatre in front of an audience, where the spectators serve as a representative of society at large. But Brecht, as is evident above, also places great emphasis on the different forms of 'privatization' that his protagonists, as figures more directly involved in the public arena, undergo. And in this respect there are clearly differences between psychological realism, expressionism and the epic theatre as to where the line between the private and the public is drawn, and how the dialectics between them is activated. Strindberg explored a number of variations with regard to this dialectics, something which indicated to his successors just how flexible and complex it is.[7]

There is another aspect of the dialectics between the private and the public which is also connected to Strindberg's attitude to women, something for which he has been severely taken to task by succeeding generations and particularly by the feminist movements of the last third of the twentieth century. Some of Strindberg's pronouncements about women have no doubt had quite a negative influence on the way he has been received. He made public the most intimate details of his marriages in order to justify his own position and behaviour. Trying to understand this aspect of Strindberg and his work, it is important to note that two of his three wives (Siri von Essen and Harriet Bosse) were actresses, and that he wrote some of his most memorable roles for them. This, as well as his infatuation with the young actress, Fanny Falkner, during his later years, was no doubt also deeply connected to his interest in practical matters of the theatre, including the art of acting. Strindberg wrote many of his plays for these women; thus, while trying to satisfy their 'needs' as actresses he was also paradoxically quite cruelly exposing some of the most intimate particulars of their relationships. Miss Julie or Tekla are saturated with direct and indirect references to Siri von Essen, and Indra's Daughter/Agnes and Eleonora in *Easter* to Harriet Bosse.

What is it that fascinates Strindberg in these women? He was apparently captivated by the fact that the art of acting is somehow connected with deception and make-believe, and in accordance with traditional misogyny, this was precisely the characteristic he found in them as human beings. Women are perceived as actresses, deceivers and tricksters who expose themselves to the public eye on the social 'stage', just as the female characters in his plays do. Tekla in *Creditors*, a play with a very elaborate metatheatrical dimension, Miss Julie in the play that bears her name, and Laura in *The Father* are constantly deceiving and seducing their male partners by acting different roles, which is why they are so despised by the men in these plays. Meanwhile, Indra's Daughter in *A Dream Play* is acting her life on a kind of social stage where she is aware of being watched by her various male partners, exactly as Tekla, Julie and Laura are placed in a situation where they are watched and scrutinized. Again, this is what Strindberg did to his wives by writing these roles. What he apparently understood, but acted very aggressively on, is that his production of texts for the stage and for these women is part of a celebrity and consumer culture where his women are exposing their private selves to the public eye.

It is possible to regard Strindberg's depiction of women from another perspective, as representatives of supernatural forces, or as characters profoundly connected to such forces. From this perspective, his plays have also had an impact on modern drama and theatre. The theatre as an artistic medium has never shied away from representations of the supernatural. Creatures and phenomena that as a rule are classified as belonging to different spheres of religious belief have featured on stage from classical times until today. On stage the power and influence of these creatures can be 'tested' in various ways while, as a rule, their ontological status is not seriously questioned, because the primary presupposition of such representations is their fictional status. And even if Strindberg was during certain periods of his life a believer in God, his plays confront the theatrical issues of belief and representation, rather than the theological ones.

The *deus ex machina* represents the most common appearance of the supernatural in the theatre and it consists of the sudden and unexpected appearance of a God or a divine figure on stage, usually at the end of the performance, in order to unravel the otherwise insoluble predicament of the humans. This kind of supernatural intervention was prominent on the Greek and classical stages and continued to be an important theatrical device in medieval as well as baroque theatres. But such godlike figures have also made their appearance on twentieth-century stages, and Strindberg's contribution was to remodel this device to suit the modern theatre. The fictional universe of *A Dream Play* is divided between the heavenly sphere and the material, everyday world. It presents the journey and the investigations of a divine figure, Indra's Daughter, in the world of human suffering. The longing of Indra's Daughter for heaven is set in constant opposition to her imprisonment in this world, where, temporarily at least, the *deus ex machina* no longer functions as, for example, in *Waiting for Godot*. But in contrast to Beckett's play, *A Dream Play* contains a mechanism of redemption for Indra's Daughter, just as, at the close of *Miss Julie*, Julie enjoys a kind of redemption when Jean is transformed into a glowing messenger of death by the sunlight which illuminates him. Here the young Julie and Jean give way to the divine figure of redemption now represented by Jean and the vengeful, almost divine father figure of the Count who speaks unseen from above. Likewise, *The Ghost Sonata* presents a struggle between a young couple and the supernatural forces represented by Hummel in his wheelchair. Here too, the light of the sun figures prominently, until the girl dies, and Böcklin's painting *The Isle of the Dead* fills the stage.

In these three plays the final release of a young woman from the bonds of this world and her unification with some form of metaphysical principle, as a *deus ex machina*, is at the same time both thematically and iconographically conceived as an ascent to, or through, a heavenly light. This ascent is administered by a young man (the Poet in *A Dream Play*, the Student in *The Ghost Sonata*, or Jean), all of whom are potential partners for these young women, while an older man, often a father figure, observes the final departure of this young woman. In *A Dream Play* and *Miss Julie* the godlike father figure does not appear on stage, while in *The Ghost Sonata* he is very much present in Hummel.

The modern theatre is saturated with examples of the *deus ex machina*, and in some cases they are female figures. One interesting example is the Habima-theatre production of *The Dybbuk*, which premiered in Hebrew in 1922, when the theatre was still working in Moscow, where it had been founded some five years previously. The play depicts the yearnings of a young woman, Leah, to join her beloved, Hanan, who had died in a fit of mystical fervour when he learned that she had been betrothed to someone else. During the wedding ceremony with this other man, the voice of Hanan enters the body of his beloved, possessing her and speaking through her mouth. In an attempt to exorcise this spirit, Leah dies and is unified with her true beloved in the next world, thus accomplishing a mystical union of the male and the female forces.

Luigi Pirandello's *Six Characters in Search of an Author* (1921) approaches the device of the *deus ex machina* from a different perspective, draining it almost completely of any religious, mystical or theological substrata but, like the late Strindberg, still preserving its powerful female aspect. Pirandello's play presents a metatheatrical, self-contained aesthetic universe where the six Characters and Madame Pace enter the 'real', i.e. fictional world of the theatre from their otherworldly sphere of extra-theatrical reality where, according to the premises of the play, their lives have already been lived. In his stage directions for the first entrance of the Characters, Pirandello took great care to stress their otherworldliness, pointing out that they wear masks in order 'to bring out the deep significance of the play' and that they should be 'designed to give the impression of figures constructed by art'. Even if these Characters are supposedly more 'real' than the fictional reality of the play into which they seek to have their lives transformed by the actors, Pirandello, in his stage directions, emphasized that they 'should not appear as ghosts, but as created realities, timeless creations of the imagination, and so more real and consistent than the changeable realities of the Actors'.[8] Such 'timeless creations of the imagination' are closely related to divine figures, but the paradox is that these Characters have, through their own lives, already enacted the banal family melodrama which they now wish to see transformed into a work of art through the Director and the Actors.

The *deus ex machina* and its iconographic figurations are ubiquitously present in modern drama, as well as in the contemporary theatre. What Strindberg was able to demonstrate is how the device can be transformed to serve a modern world where its theological basis has been undermined. In pre-modern forms of the theatre, the boundaries between human characters and other kinds of creatures, whether divine or monstrous, were relatively clear. The modern theatre dismantled these boundaries, and created a more complex and more chaotic mixture between the natural and the supernatural. In such plays as *The Threepenny Opera*, where Brecht explicitly called the last scene a *deus ex machina*, or *The Good Person of Szechwan*, where the gods appear with a specific mission, these issues are confronted, but from a slightly different perspective. Likewise, Robert Wilson's scenic images, including the illuminated backstage area which appears in almost all his productions, bear strong traces of this device.

The twentieth-century theatre has emphasized the metatheatrical and even the nihilistic dimensions of the *deus ex machina*. With Hamm's total blindness in *Endgame* nothing remains of the divine machinery but the wheelchair which is inherited from Strindberg's Hummel, a pair of sunglasses, a broken toy dog and a few old jokes. The traditional Jewish joke about the tailor, which Hamm likes to tell his so-called 'progenitors', Nag and Nell, could perhaps be interpreted as a parable of the development of the contemporary theatre, in its descent from Strindberg. A man brings a piece of cloth to the tailor and after several attempts to make these trousers fit the customer (or perhaps the spectator) becomes angry with the tailor and screams:

> God damn you to hell, Sir, no, it's indecent, there are limits. In six days, do you hear me, six days, God made the world! Yes Sir, no less Sir, the WORLD! And you are not bloody well capable of making me a pair of trousers in three months.

The tailor retorts:

> But my dear Sir, my dear Sir, look – (disdainful gesture, disgustedly) – at the world – (pause) – and – (loving gesture, proudly) – at my TROUSERS!⁹   (pp. 102–3)

The theatre is striving to reproduce this act of creation. In the meantime the tailor has become a postmodern director collecting his materials from the garbage piles of history. The first seven days have passed a long time ago which means, to develop the tailor's argument, that the result may eventually become much more perfect than the world is. And while what could be a child is possibly approaching, Hamm chants: 'You cried for night; it falls: now cry in darkness … Moments for nothing, now as always, time was never and time is over, reckoning closed and story ended' (p. 133). Theatre history has not yet reached this condition, and hopefully will not. But we have to bear in mind

10. From Ole Anders Tandberg's staging of *Advent* at Malmö Dramatiska
Teater in 1997.

that this is one of the ways to end the story, with Hamm saying to himself: 'You ... remain' (p. 134). Szondi's interpretation of *Waiting for Godot* appropriately sums up many of these issues:

> Constantly pressing toward the abyss of silence, retrieved from it over and over again but only with great effort, this hollow conversation still manages to reveal the 'anguish of man without God' in this empty metaphysical space – a space that gives importance to whatever fills it. At this level, of course, dramatic form no longer contains any critical contradictions, and conversation is no longer a means of overcoming such contradictions. Everything lies in ruins – dialogue, form as a whole, human existence. Negativity – meaningless, automatic speech and unfulfilled dramatic form – is now the only source of statement. What emerges is an expression of the negative condition of a waiting being – one in need of transcendence but unable to achieve it.   (p. 54)

This is also where the legacy of Strindberg to modern drama and the modern theatre lies.

NOTES

1. Peter Szondi, *Theory of Modern Drama*, ed. and trans. Michael Hays (Cambridge: Polity Press, 1987). References to this translation are identified in the text with page numbers in parenthesis.
2. This aspect of Strindbergian drama was already analysed at some length by C. E. W. L. Dahlström, *Strindberg's Dramatic Expressionism* (Ann Arbor: University of Michigan, 1930), but without the broader contexts introduced by Szondi.
3. See in particular Michael Robinson, *Strindberg and Autobiography: Writing and Reading a Life* (Norwich: Norvik Press, 1986).
4. Martin Esslin, *The Theatre of the Absurd*, revised and enlarged edition (Harmondsworth: Penguin Books, 1968).
5. Bertolt Brecht, *Brecht on Theatre* (London: Methuen, 1982).
6. Constantin Stanislavski, *An Actor Prepares* (Harmondsworth: Penguin Books, 1965).
7. For a more detailed analysis of the private/public dialectics see my article 'Acting and Psychoanalysis: Street Scenes, Private Scenes, and Transference', *Theatre Journal*, 39:2 (1987), pp. 175–84.
8. Luigi Pirandello, *Six Characters in Search of an Author*, trans. John Linstrum, in *Three Plays* (London: Methuen, 1985), p. 75.
9. Samuel Beckett, *The Complete Dramatic Works* (London: Faber & Faber, 1986).

SELECTED BIBLIOGRAPHY

Titles listed here are items of immediate relevance to the essays in this collection, with the emphasis on material in English and Swedish, but including a selective number of established studies which have helped shape the course of Strindberg studies. Although they cover most areas of Strindberg's multifaceted project, readers interested in exploring the vast body of commentary on Strindberg and his writing are referred to the three-volume *International Annotated Bibliography of Strindberg Studies* by Michael Robinson, published by the Modern Humanities Research Association, where these and other works are discussed in greater detail.

Editions and translations

There is no critical English edition of Strindberg's works to compare with the Oxford editions of Ibsen and Chekhov, in part, no doubt because of the sheer variety and volume of his production. The closest is Walter Johnson's University of Washington Press series of translations of most of the plays (17 vols., 1955–83) together with the *Open Letters to the Intimate Theatre* (1966). There are, of course, many other translations of the plays (though generally of the same restricted canon that includes *The Father, Miss Julie, The Dance of Death, A Dream Play* and *The Ghost Sonata*, and sometimes extends to *Creditors, To Damascus I, Crimes and Crimes, Easter*, and the other chamber plays). Those by Elizabeth Sprigge (twelve plays, including *The Bond* and *Swanwhite*, 1963), Arvid Paulson (*Seven Plays*, 1960; *Eight Expressionist Plays*, 1965; *World Historical Plays*, 1970), Michael Meyer (twelve plays, including *Playing with Fire, Erik XIV* and *The Crown Bride*, 2 vols., 1975), Evert Sprinchorn (twelve plays, including *Playing with Fire* and *The Pelican*, 2 vols., 1986), Harry Carlson (five plays, 1983), Eivor Martinus (3 vols., including *Motherly Love, Pariah, The First Warning, The Great Highway* and the Chamber Plays 1987, 1990, 1991, 1998), Michael Robinson (Five plays, 1998), Joe Martin (seven plays, including *Charles XII*, 1997) and Gregory Motton (in progress) are the most current. Of earlier versions, those by Edwin Björkman (5 vols., 1912–16) and the four volumes published for the Anglo-Swedish Literary Foundation (1929–39), are both the most wide-ranging and comparatively dependable.

All these translations were made directly from the Swedish whereas many earlier versions were often done from the German and vied with one another in inaccuracies and omissions. This is notably the case with the prose works, where several of the most relevant still await translation. Of the novels and stories, the versions of *The Red*

Room (Elizabeth Sprigge (1967)) and *Hemsöborna* (Elspeth Harley Schubert (1959)) remain relevant, as does Mary Sandbach's excellent edition of *Getting Married* (1972). There are also respectable translations of *The Scapegoat* (Paulson, 1927) and *The Roofing Feast* (Paul, 1987). Of the autobiographical fictions, the early versions by Claud Field of *The Son of a Servant*, Ellie Schleussner of *A Madman's Defence* and the anonymous version of *Legends* (1912) are seriously defective and sometimes bowdlerized. Volume 1 of *The Son of a Servant* is available in a version by Evert Sprinchorn (1966), who has also revised Schleussner's 1912 translation of *A Madman's Defence* (1967), but the complex publishing history of Strindberg's original text means that even Anthony Swerling's otherwise fine translation of the 1895 French edition now needs replacing. *Inferno* has been translated by Evert Sprinchorn (1968, together with *Alone*) and Mary Sandbach (1962), the latter reprinted in Penguin Classics together with a selection from *The Occult Diary* (1979). Both editions have valuable introductions.

A collection of essays, including several of the Vivisections of particular relevance to the naturalist dramas of the 1880s, have been translated by Michael Robinson (1998) as has an extensive, annotated edition of the letters, which are central to many discussions of Strindberg's life and work (2 vols., 1992). Field's selection from *A Blue Book*, entitled 'Zones of the Spirit' (1913) is at best unfortunate.

Details of the principal Swedish editions of the works and letters on which these translations and the scholarly works listed below generally depend are given in the note on references. Particular bibliographical and critical issues are raised by the fact that Strindberg sometimes wrote in French (e.g. *Giftas II*, *A Madman's Defence*, *Inferno* and *Legends*), and left the translation into Swedish of their often heavily revised text to others. Consequently, which text has primacy or is deployed to underpin an argument is not without interest.

General studies, including biographies

Ahlström, Stellan, *Strindbergs erövring av Paris. Strindberg och Frankrike 1884–1895*, Stockholm: Almqvist & Wiksell, 1956. Documents Strindberg's attempts to establish himself as a writer and dramatist in France, including the staging of *Miss Julie* by the Théâtre Libre and *The Father* and *Creditors* at the Théâtre de l'Œuvre. French summary.

Berendsohn, Walter A., *August Strindbergs skärgårds och Stockholmsskildringar. Struktur- och stilstudier*, Stockholm: Rabén & Sjögren, 1962. Stylistic and structural studies of the depiction of Stockholm and its archipelago in numerous works in several genres. A conscious early attempt to break with the prevailing biographical trend in Swedish Strindberg studies.

Blackwell, Marilyn Johns, ed., *Structures of Influence: a Comparative Approach to August Strindberg*, Chapel Hill: University of North Carolina Press, 1981. A varied and variable collection of seventeen essays which relate Strindberg and one or other of his works to other writers, painters and composers in Scandinavia and abroad.

Boëthius, Ulf, *Strindberg och kvinnofrågan. Till och med Giftas I*, Stockholm: Prisma, 1969. Examines the evolution of Strindberg's ideas about women and their sexual and social roles from his sympathetic portrayal of their emancipatory desires in several early works to the hostility apparent in the first volume of *Giftas*. Boëthius demonstrates how Strindberg's notions changed in response to his personal situation and documents the debate about the nature and status of women both in contemporary Sweden and within a Scandinavian context then dominated by Ibsen, Bjørnson and Georg Brandes.

Brandell, Gunnar, *Strindberg in Inferno*, trans. Barry Jacobs, Cambridge, Mass.: Harvard University Press, 1974. A pivotal work in Strindberg studies, first published in Swedish in 1950, which seeks to unravel both the nature of the psychoses Strindberg experienced in the mid-1890s and the network of interlinking religious, scientific, alchemical and occult ideas that he explored in remaking himself as a writer.

Strindberg – ett författarliv, 4 vols., Stockholm: Alba, 1983–9. Overall this is presently the most reliable life and letters study of Strindberg's career taken as a whole.

Carlson, Harry G., *Out of Inferno: Strindberg's Reawakening as an Artist*, Seattle and London: University of Washington Press, 1996. A wide-ranging study of the way in which Strindberg renewed himself as a writer in the mid-1890s. Carlson stresses the role played by his highly developed visual imagination, especially in his post-Inferno work, and the inspiration he derived from a modish medievalism and a variety of occult and alchemical tendencies, with their techniques for rendering the invisible visible or transforming matter from one form into another.

Fahlgren, Margaretha, *Kvinnans ekvation. Kön, makt och rationalitet i Strindbergs författarskap*, Stockholm: Carlssons Bokförlag, 1994. Examines the crisis in patriarchal society during Strindberg's lifetime and the patriarchal structures of thought and feeling that inform the way in which women are defined in his essays and represented in his literary works, especially *A Madman's Defence, The Father, Miss Julie, By the Open Sea, Kristina* and *A Dream Play*.

Friese, Wilhelm, ed., *Strindberg und die deutschsprachigen Länder. Internationale Beiträge zum Tübinger Strindberg-Symposium 1977*, Basel and Stuttgart: Helbing & Lichtenhahn, 1979. A collection of eighteen conference papers, mainly concerned with the reception of Strindberg's plays in Germany and Austria.

Houe, Poul, Sven Hakon Rossel and Göran Stockenström, eds., *August Strindberg and the Other: New Critical Approaches*, Amsterdam and New York: Rodopi, 2002.

Johnson, Walter [Gilbert], *August Strindberg*, New York: Twayne, 1976. A short and sensible general introduction.

Kärnell, Karl-Åke, *Strindbergs bildspråk. En studie i prosastil*, Stockholm: Almqvist & Wicksell, 1962. An illuminating study of Strindberg's imagery with reference to his prose works.

Lagercrantz, Olof, *August Strindberg*, trans. Anselm Hollo, London: Faber & Faber, 1984. An error-strewn translation of a revisionary and sometimes controversial Swedish biography (1979) which does not dwell upon Strindberg's presumed neuroses or his problematic marriages but emphasizes his achievement as a conscious artist whose creativity extends from his work into his life.

Lamm, Martin, *August Strindberg*, 2 vols., Vol. I: *Före infernokrisen*, vol. II: *Efter omvändelsen*, Stockholm: Albert Bonniers Förlag, 1940–42. The cornerstone of the biographical approach which dominated Strindberg studies in Sweden until the 1980s. Discusses Strindberg's work in its entirety, often with reference to then unpublished manuscript sources. Lamm established an image of Strindberg as man and writer which dominated not only scholarly practice but also the staging of his plays in Sweden for several decades.

Lindström, Hans, *Hjärnornas kamp. Psykologiska idéer och motiv i Strindbergs åttiotalsdiktning*, Uppsala: Appelbergs Boktryckeri AB, 1952. An informative comparative study which documents how, in the mid-1880s, Strindberg turned away from a socially engaged literature and became deeply concerned with psychological ideas, the unconscious, psychopathology and heightened, or exceptional, states of mind.

Meidal, Björn, *Från profet till folktribun. Strindberg och Strindbergsfejden 1910–12*, Stockholm: Tidens Förlag, 1982. A study of the dialectic between Strindberg's religion and politics during his later years, and the fierce public debate on political, religious, and social issues that he initiated in 1910.

Meyer, Michael, *Strindberg: a Biography*, London: Secker & Warburg, 1985. Although factually dependable, the most widely disseminated English biography is undermined by its author's lack of sympathy for his subject, which results in various interpretative misreadings and a very partial sense of Strindberg's achievement as a writer.

Olsson, Ulf, *Jag blir galen. Strindberg, vansinnet och vetenskapen*, Stockholm/Stehag: Brutus Östlings Bokförlag Symposion, 2002. An original, Foucauldian study which analyses not only the role of madness in works like *The Father*, but the enduring and politically charged ascription of madness to the author in their critical reception.

Olsson, Ulf, ed., *Strindbergs förvandlingar*, Eslöv: Brutus Östlings Bokförlag Symposion, 1999. Eleven essays on Strindberg as autobiographer, novelist, dramatist, and misogynist.

Reinert, Otto, ed., *Strindberg: a Collection of Critical Essays*, Englewood Cliffs, N.J.: Prentice-Hall Inc., 1971.

Robinson, Michael, *Studies in Strindberg*, Norwich: Norvik Press, 1998. Includes studies of the paintings, autobiographies, and Strindberg's relationship with music, as well as essays on *Creditors* and *The Dance of Death*.

Robinson, Michael, ed., *Strindberg and Genre*, Norwich: Norvik Press, 1991. Twenty essays which confirm the range of Strindberg's work in several genres, often focusing on some of the lesser known works.

Shideler, Ross, *Questioning the Father: from Darwin to Zola, Ibsen, Strindberg, and Hardy*, Stanford, Calif.: Stanford University Press, 1999. Studies the bourgeois male's resistance to the loss of the father's privilege following publication of *The Origin of Species* in *The Son of a Servant* and several of the plays.

Smedmark, Carl Reinhold, ed., *Essays on Strindberg*, Stockholm: Beckmans, 1966. Includes essays on *Miss Julie*, *The Ghost Sonata*, the Chamber Plays and *Among French Peasants*.

Sprinchorn, Evert, *Strindberg as Dramatist*, New Haven and London: Yale University Press, 1982. A valuable study that extends its discussion of Strindberg's dramatic imagination beyond illuminating chapters on *Miss Julie*, *Crimes and Crimes*, *A Dream Play*, the historical dramas and the Chamber Plays to *A Madman's Defence* and other prose works.

Steene, Birgitta, *The Greatest Fire: A Study of August Strindberg*, Carbondale, Ill.: Southern Illinois University Press, 1973. A reliable overview of Strindberg's career as a whole.

August Strindberg: an Introduction to his Major Works, Stockholm: Almqvist & Wiksell, 1982.

Steene, Birgitta, ed., *Strindberg and History*, Stockholm: Almqvist & Wiksell International, 1992. Fifteen essays on Strindberg as a writer of historical fiction and drama focusing primarily on *Charles XII*, *Kristina* and *Gustav III*.

Stockenström, Göran, *Ismael i öknen. Strindberg som mystiker*. Acta Universitatis Upsaliensis: Historia litterarum, Uppsala, 1972. A major study of several important post-Inferno works, based on an examination of the striking combination of mystical and modernist ideas that matured in Strindberg's mind during the Inferno period. Documents the way he absorbs, transforms and exploits the concepts of Swedenborg in many of the later plays and prose works. Includes a substantial English summary.

Svensson, Conny, *Strindberg om världshistorien*, Stockholm: Gidlunds Förlag, 2000. Describes how, during the early years of the twentieth century, Strindberg's preoccupation with history shifted from a national to a global perspective in a study of the short stories on historical themes as well as the late history plays.

Wechsel, Kirsten, ed., in cooperation with Lill-Ann Körber, *Strindberg and His Media*, EKF Wissenschaft, Skandinavistik, vol. I, Leipzig and Berlin: Edition Kirchof & Franke, 2003.

Plays

Bandle, Oskar, Walter Baumgartner and Jürg Glauser, eds., *Strindbergs Dramen im Lichte neuerer Methodendiskussionen*, Beiträge zum IV. Internationalen Strindberg-Symposion in Zürich, Basel: Helbing & Lichtenhahn, 1981. Fifteen conference papers in English and German on eight of the plays.

Bark, Richard, *Strindbergs drömspelsteknik – i drama och teater*, Lund: Studentlitteratur, 1981. Analyses Strindberg's dreamplay technique in *To Damascus I, A Dream Play* and *The Ghost Sonata*, and studies its realization in productions by Max Reinhardt, Olof Molander, Ingmar Bergman and others.

Børge, Vagn. *Strindbergs mystiske Teater*, Copenhagen: Ejnar Munksgaard, 1942. An early attempt to define the nature of Strindberg's post-Inferno dramaturgy, mainly exemplified by *A Dream Play*.

Bulman, Joan, *Strindberg and Shakespeare: Shakespeare's Influence on Strindberg's Historical Drama*, London: Jonathan Cape, 1933. An enduring study which demonstrates how Strindberg rejuvenated nineteenth-century historical drama via the example of Shakespeare.

Carlson, Harry G., *Strindberg and the Poetry of Myth*, Berkeley: University of California Press, 1982. Finds in Strindberg's life-long interest in mythology a novel way of approaching eight of the plays: *Master Olof, The Father, Miss Julie, Creditors, To Damascus I, Easter, A Dream Play* and *The Ghost Sonata*.

Dahlström, Carl Enoch William Leonard, *Strindberg's Dramatic Expressionism*, 2nd edn, with the author's essay 'Origins of Strindberg's Expressionism', New York: Benjamin Blom, 1968. Reprints Dahlström's influential pioneering study of 1930 with its attempt at a rigorous definition of Strindberg's expressionism in *The Father* and *Miss Julie*, as well as the post-Inferno plays.

Delblanc, Sven, *Stormhatten. Tre Strindbergsstudier*, Stockholm: Alba, 1979. Studies of *By the Open Sea, A Dream Play* and the chamber plays.

Ekman, Hans-Göran, *Klädernas magi. En Strindbergstudie*, Värnamo: Gidlunds, 1991. Analyses the importance of costume in Strindberg's plays, both in a straightforward theatrical sense in the eight plays studied and, more significantly, as a deeply personal symbolic and structural device, which sheds light on his personality.

Strindberg and the Five Senses: Studies in Strindberg's Chamber Plays, London: Athlone Press, 2000 (originally published as *Villornas värld. Studier i Strindbergs kammarspel*, 1997).

Falck, August, *Fem år med Strindberg*, Stockholm: Wahlström & Widstrand, 1935. Although not always entirely reliable on factual grounds, this account of Strindberg at the Intimate Theatre by his co-director remains an important source of information, both about the theatre itself and the plays performed there.

Finney, Gail, *Women in Modern Drama: Freud, Feminism, and European Theater at the Turn of the Century*, Ithaca: Cornell University Press, 1989. Includes a revisionary reading of *The Father*.

Johnson, Walter, *Strindberg and the Historical Drama*, Seattle: University of Washington Press, 1963. Discusses all the historical dramas and confirms the enduring importance of several.

Kvam, Kela, *Max Reinhardt og Strindbergs visionære dramatik*, Copenhagen: Akademisk Forlag, 1974. Studies Max Reinhardt's substantial contribution to the performance history of Strindberg's post-Inferno plays (*The Dance of Death, A Dream Play, Thunder in the Air, The Ghost Sonata* and *The Pelican*).

Lamm, Martin, *Strindbergs dramer I-II*, Stockholm: Albert Bonniers Förlag, 1924–26. Lamm's two-volume survey of the plays inaugurated serious Strindberg scholarship. Although its biographical approach has rightly been questioned, it remains a considerable achievement, not least for the way in which Lamm sought to make serious sense of the Inferno crisis and its significance for the plays which succeeded it.

Madsen, Børge Gedsø, *Strindberg's Naturalistic Theatre: its Relation to French Naturalism*, Seattle: University of Washington Press, 1962.

Marker, Frederick J., and Lise-Lone Marker, *Strindberg and Modern Theatre: Post-Inferno Drama on the Stage*, Cambridge: Cambridge University Press, 2002. Primarily on *To Damascus, A Dream Play* and *The Ghost Sonata* Max Reinhardt, Olof Molander and Ingmar Bergman.

Ollén, Gunnar, *Strindbergs dramatik*, Stockholm: Sveriges Radios Förlag, 1982. Documents the genesis of each of Strindberg's plays and their subsequent performance history in Sweden and abroad.

Rokem, Freddie, *Theatrical Space in Ibsen, Chekhov and Strindberg*, Michigan: UMI Research Press, 1986. In Strindberg's case focuses mainly on *Miss Julie, A Dream Play* and *The Ghost Sonata*, and seeks to establish how Strindberg represents the private and the irrational on stage.

Strindberg's Secret Codes, Norwich: Norvik Press, 2004. A collection of linked essays on Strindberg's linguistics as well as his dramaturgy and several of the plays.

Stockenström, Göran, ed., *Strindberg's Dramaturgy*, Minneapolis: University of Minnesota Press, 1988.

Szalczer, Eszter, 'Nature's Dream Play: Modes of Vision and August Strindberg's Re-Definition of the Theatre', *Theatre Journal*, 53:1 (2001), pp. 33–52.

Demonstrates how Strindberg's photography, and his lifelong interest in science and modes of vision, informs not only the naturalistic plays but also his dramatic experiments of the post-Inferno period.

Törnqvist, Egil, *Strindbergian Drama: Themes and Structure*, Stockholm: Almqvist & Wiksell International, 1982. Adopts an illuminating structural approach to the dramaturgy of twelve of the plays in several genres: naturalism, dream play, history play, monodrama and chamber play.

Strindberg's The Ghost Sonata: From Text to Production, Amsterdam: Amsterdam University Press, 2000. Both a textual and a performance study with special attention to Ingmar Bergman's 1973 production, which is documented by a rehearsal diary.

Det talade ordet. Om Strindbergs dramadialog, Stockholm: Carlssons, 2001. Redresses the lack of attention paid in previous studies to Strindberg's dialogue and his use of language in general with reference to a wide range of the plays.

Törnqvist, Egil, and Barry Jacobs, *Strindberg's Miss Julie: a Play and its Transpositions*, Norwich: Norvik Press, 1988. A detailed study of the play and its performance history in all its manifestations on stage, film, radio and television, as well as in translation.

Ward, John, *The Social and Religious Plays of Strindberg*, London: Athlone Press, 1980.

Wilkinson, Lynn R., 'The Politics of the Interior: Strindberg's Chamber Plays', *Scandinavian Studies*, 65:4 (1993), pp. 463–86. Studies the nature of an intimate theatre and the relationship between public and private, and privacy and theatricality, in the chamber plays of 1907.

Wirmark, Margareta, *Den kluvna scenen. Kvinnor i Strindbergs dramatik*, Stockholm: Gidlunds, 1989. Studies thirteen of the plays with prominent roles for women.

Novels and autobiographies

Behschnitt, Wolfgang, *Die Autorfigur. Autobiographischer Aspekt und Konstruktion des Autors im Werk August Strindbergs*. Basel, Schwabe & Co., 1999.

Johannesson, Eric O., *The Novels of August Strindberg: a Study in Theme and Function*, Berkeley: University of California Press, 1968. Remains the best introduction to the prose fiction, including his autobiographical sequence.

Olsson, Ulf, *Levande död. Studier i Strindbergs prosa*, Stockholm/Stenhag: Brutus Österlings Bokförlag Symposion, 1996. Rejecting conventional 'mimetic' and psychobiographical approaches to the prose fiction as no longer pertinent, Olsson deploys recent work in narratology in formulating a new approach which focuses on three basic, interrelated categories: the commodity form, modernity and allegory. Concerned with both the novels and autobiographical fictions; also considers several short stories.

Poulenard, Elie, *August Strindberg, romancier et nouvelliste*, Paris: Presses Universitaires de France, 1962. Studies the novels from *The Red Room* to *The Roofing Feast* together with several collections of short stories but excluding the *Son of a Servant* sequence.

Robinson, Michael, *Strindberg and Autobiography: Writing and Reading a Life*, Norwich: Norvik Press, 1986. Examines Strindberg's theories of writing, compares his autobiographical practice with Freud's psychoanalytical theories of self-production and possession, and considers how he inscribes himself in already existing plots from literature, religion and scientific theory.

Rugg, Linda Haverty, *Picturing Ourselves: Photography and Autobiography*, University of Chicago Press, 1997. Principally concerned with the sequence of photographic self-portraits from 1886 and Strindberg's understanding of photography as a quasi-occult medium.

Smedmark, Carl Reinhold, *Mäster Olof och Röda rummet*, Stockholm: Almqvist & Wiksell, 1952.

Stounbjerg, Per, *Uro og urenhed. Studier i Strindbergs selvbiografiske prosa*, Århus: Aarhus Universitetsforlag, 2005. English summary, pp. 429–38.

Poetry

Bellquist, John Eric, *Strindberg as a Modern Poet: a Critical and Comparative Study*, Berkeley, Los Angeles, London: University of California Press, 1986.

Ollén, Gunnar, *Strindbergs 1900-talslyrik*, Stockholm: A. B. Seelig & Co., 1941.

Spens, James, *'I Musernas bidé'. En essä om Strindbergs 'fula' poesi omkring 1883*, Stockholm: Almqvist & Wiksell International, 2000. Discusses the *Sårfeber* (Wound Fever) sequence in *Dikter på vers och prosa* and the first three *Sleepwalking Nights*.

Letters

Dahlbäck, Kerstin, *Ändå tycks allt vara osagt. August Strindberg som brevskrivare*, Stockholm: Natur och Kultur, 1994. Recognizes Strindberg's mastery in what rivals drama as the most prolific and accomplished genre in his *œuvre*, one that he saw as the model for imaginative writing in general. Dahlbäck analyses several representative letters and correspondences, drawing comparisons with his literary works and demonstrating his seemingly infinite ability to adapt himself verbally to his various addressees.

Painting and Photography

Granath, Olle, *August Strindberg: Painter, Photographer, Writer*, London: Tate Publishing, 2005.

Hedström, Per, ed., *Strindberg: Painter and Photographer*, New Haven and London: Yale University Press; Stockholm, 2001.

Hemmingsson, Per, *August Strindberg som fotograf*, Århus: Kalejdoskop Förlag, 1989. Includes a substantial essay in English on Strindberg's accomplishment as a photographer.

Schmidt, Torsten Måtte, ed., *Strindbergs måleri. En monografi*, Malmö: Allhems Förlag, 1972. Copious illustrations make this volume worth consulting even by readers without Swedish.

Söderström, Göran, *Strindberg och bildkonsten*, Uddevala: Forum, 1972. Effectively a biography which charts Strindberg's career in terms of his painting and his acquaintance with painters.

INDEX

Cambridge Companions to ...

AUTHORS